TRADING OPTION GREEKS

Since 1996, Bloomberg Press has published books for financial professionals on investing, economics, and policy affecting investors. Titles are written by leading practitioners and authorities, and have been translated into more than 20 languages.

The Bloomberg Financial Series provides both core reference knowledge and actionable information for financial professionals. The books are written by experts familiar with the work flows, challenges, and demands of investment professionals who trade the markets, manage money, and analyze investments in their capacity of growing and protecting wealth, hedging risk, and generating revenue.

For a list of available titles, please visit our web site at www.wiley.com/go/bloombergpress.

TRADING OPTION GREEKS

How Time, Volatility, and Other Pricing Factors Drive Profits

Second Edition

Dan Passarelli

BLOOMBERG PRESS
An Imprint of
WILEY

Published by John Wiley & Sons, Inc., Hoboken, New Jersey.
First edition was published in 2008 by Bloomberg Press.
Published simultaneously in Canada.

Long-Term AnticiPation Securities® (LEAPS) is a registered trademark of the Chicago Board Options Exchange.

Standard & Poor's 500® (S&P 500) and Standard & Poor's Depository Receipts™ (SPDRs) are registered trademarks of the McGraw-Hill Companies, Inc.

Power Shares QQQ™ is a registered trademark of Invesco PowerShares Capital Management LLC.

NASDAQ-100 Index® is a registered trademark of The NASDAQ Stock Market, Inc.

For general information on our other products and services or for technical support, please contact our Customer Care Department within the United States at (800) 762-2974, outside the United States at (317) 572-3993 or fax (317) 572-4002.

Wiley also publishes its books in a variety of electronic formats. Some content that appears in print may not be available in electronic books. For more information about Wiley products, visit our web site at *www.wiley.com*.

Library of Congress Cataloging-in-Publication Data:

Passarelli, Dan, 1971-
  Trading option Greeks : how time, volatility, and other pricing factors drive profits / Dan Passarelli. – 2nd ed.
    p. cm. – (Bloomberg financial series)
  Includes index.
  ISBN 978-1-118-13316-3 (cloth); ISBN 978-1-118-22512-7 (ebk);
  ISBN 978-1-118-26322-8 (ebk); ISBN 978-1-118-23861-5 (ebk)
    1. Options (Finance)   2. Stock options.   3. Derivative securities.   I. Title.
  HG6024.A3P36 2012
  332.64′53—dc23

                                                                              2012019462

Printed in the United States of America

SKY10081996_081424

This book is dedicated to Kathleen, Sam, and Isabel. I wouldn't trade them for all the money in the world.

Disclaimer

This book is intended to be educational in nature, both theoretically and practically. It is meant to generally explore the factors that influence option prices so that the reader may gain an understanding of how options work in the real world. This book does not prescribe a specific trading system or method. This book makes no guarantees.

Any strategies discussed, including examples using actual securities and price data, are strictly for illustrative and educational purposes only and are not to be construed as an endorsement, recommendation, or solicitation to buy or sell securities. Examples may or may not be based on factual or historical data.

In order to simplify the computations, examples may not include commissions, fees, margin, interest, taxes, or other transaction costs. Commissions and other costs will impact the outcome of all stock and options transactions and must be considered prior to entering into any transactions. Investors should consult their tax adviser about potential tax consequences. Past performance is not a guarantee of future results.

Options involve risks and are not suitable for everyone. While much of this book focuses on the risks involved in option trading, there are market situations and scenarios that involve unique risks that are not discussed. Prior to buying or selling an option, a person should read *Characteristics and Risks of Standardized Options (ODD)*. Copies of the ODD are available from your broker, by calling 1-888-OPTIONS, or from The Options Clearing Corporation, One North Wacker Drive, Chicago, Illinois 60606.

Contents

PART II: SPREADS

PART III: VOLATILITY

Foreword

The past several years have brought about a resurgence in market volatility and options volume unlike anything that has been seen since the close of the twentieth century. As markets have become more interdependent, interrelated, and international, the U.S. listed option markets have solidified their place as the most liquid and transparent venue for risk management and hedging activities of the world's largest economy. Technology, competition, innovation, and reliability have become the hallmarks of the industry, and our customer base has benefited tremendously from this ongoing evolution.

However, these advances can be properly tapped only when the users of the product continue to expand their knowledge of the options product and its unique features. Education has always been the driver of growth in our business, and it will be the steward of the next generation of options traders. Dan Passarelli's new and updated book *Trading Option Greeks* is a necessity for customers and traders alike to ensure that they possess the knowledge to succeed and attain their objectives in the high-speed, highly technical arena that the options market has become.

The retail trader of the past has given way to a new retail trader of the present—one with an increased level of technology, support, capital treatment, and product selection. The impact of the staggering growth in such products as the CBOE Holdings' VIX options and futures, and the literally dozens of other products tied to it, have made the volatility asset class a new, unique, and permanent pillar of today's option markets.

Dan's updated book continues his mission of supporting, preparing, and reinforcing the trader's understanding of pricing, volatility, market terminology, and strategy, in a way that few other books have been able. Using a perspective forged from years as an options market maker, professional trader, and customer, Dan has once again provided a resource for those who wish to know best how the option markets behave today, and how they are likely to continue to behave in the future. It is important to understand not only what happens in the options space, but also *why* it happens. This book is intended to provide those answers. I wish you all the best in your trading!

William J. Brodsky
Chairman and CEO
Chicago Board Options Exchange

Preface

I've always been fascinated by trading. When I was young, I'd see traders on television, in their brightly colored jackets, shouting on the seemingly chaotic trading floor, and I'd marvel at them. What a wonderful job that must be! These traders seemed to me to be very different from the rest of us. It's all so very esoteric.

It is easy to assume that professional traders have closely kept secrets to their ways of trading—something that secures success in trading for them, but is out of reach for everyone else. In fact, nothing could be further from the truth. If there are any "secrets" of professional traders, this book will expose them.

True enough, in years past there have been some barriers to entry to trading success that did indeed make it difficult for nonprofessionals to succeed. For example, commissions, bid-ask spreads, margin requirements, and information flow all favored the professional trader. Now, these barriers are gone. Competition among brokers and exchanges—as well as the ubiquity of information as propagated on the Internet—has torn down those walls. The only barrier left between the Average Joe and the options pro is that of knowledge. Those who have it will succeed; those who do not will fail.

To be sure, the knowledge held by successful traders is not that of what will happen in the future; it is the knowledge of how to manage the uncertainty. No matter what our instincts tell us, we do not know what will happen in the future with regard to the market. As Socrates put it, "The only true wisdom is in knowing you know nothing." The masters of option trading are masters of managing the risk associated with what they don't know—the risk of uncertainty.

As an instructor, I've talked to many traders who were new to options who told me, "I made a trade based on what I thought was going to happen. I was right, but my position lost money!" Choosing the right strategy makes all the difference when it comes to mastery of risk management and ultimate trading success. Knowing which option strategy is the right strategy for a given situation comes with knowledge and experience.

All option strategies are differentiated by their unique risk characteristics. Some are more sensitive to directional movement of the underlying asset than others; some are more affected by time passing than others. The exact exposure positions have to these market influences determines the success of individual trades and, indeed, the long-term success of the trader who knows how to exploit these risk characteristics. These option-value sensitivities can be controlled when a trader understands the option greeks.

Option greeks are metrics used to measure an option's sensitivity to influences on its price. This book will provide the reader with an understanding of these metrics, to help the reader truly master the risk of uncertainty associated with option trading.

Successful traders strive to create option positions with risk-reward profiles that benefit them the most in a given situation. A trader's objectives will dictate the right strategy for the right situation. Traders can tailor a position to fit a specific forecast with respect to the time horizon; the degree of bullishness, bearishness, neutrality, or volatility in the underlying stock; and the desired amount of leverage. Furthermore, they can exploit opportunities unique to options. They can trade option greeks. This opens the door to many new opportunities.

A New Direction

Traders, both professional and retail, need ways to act on their forecasts without the constraints of convention. "Get long, or do nothing" is no longer a viable business model for people active in the market. "Up is good; down is bad" is burned into traders' minds from the beginning of their market education. This concept has its place in the world of investing, but becoming an active trader in the option market requires thinking in a new direction.

Market makers and other expert option traders look at the market differently from other traders. One fundamental difference is that these traders trade all four directions: up, down, sideways, and volatile.

Trading Strategies

Buying stock is a trading strategy that most people understand. In practical terms, traders who buy stock are generally not concerned with the literal ownership stake in a corporation, just the opportunity to profit if the stock rises. Although it's important for traders to understand that the price of a stock is largely tied to the success or failure of the corporation, it's essential to keep in mind exactly what the objective tends to be for trading a stock: to profit from changes in its price. A bullish position can also be taken in the options market. The most basic example is buying a call.

A bearish position can be taken by trading stock or options, as well. If traders expect the value of a stock they own to fall, they will sell the stock. This eliminates the risk of losses from the stock's falling. If the traders do not own the stock that they think will decline, they can take a more active stance and short it. The short-seller borrows the stock from a party that owns it and then sells the borrowed shares to another party. The goal of selling stock short is to later repurchase the shares at a lower price before returning the stock to its owner. It is simply reversing the order of "buy low/sell high." The risk is that the stock rises and shares have to be bought at a higher price than that at which they were sold. Although shorting stock can lead to profits when the market cooperates, in the options market, there are alternative ways to profit from falling prices. The most basic example is buying a put.

A trader can use options to take a bullish or bearish position, given a directional forecast. Sideways, nontrending stocks and their antithesis, volatile stocks, can be traded as well. In the later market conditions, profit or loss can be independent of whether the stock rises or falls. Opportunity in option trading is not necessarily black and white—not necessarily up and down. Option trading is nonlinear. Consequently, more opportunities can be exploited by trading options than by trading stock.

Option traders must consider the time period in question, the volatility expected during this period, interest rates, and dividends. Along with the stock price, these factors make up the dynamic components of an option's value. These individual factors can be isolated, measured, and exploited. Incremental changes in any of these elements as measured by option greeks provide opportunity for option traders. Because of these other influences, direction is not the only tradable element of a forecast. Time, volatility, interest rates—these can all be traded using option greeks. These factors and more will all be discussed at great length throughout this book.

This Second Edition of *Trading Option Greeks*

This book addresses the complex price behavior of options by discussing option greeks from both a theoretical and a practical standpoint. There is some tactical discussion throughout, although the objective of this book is to provide education to the reader. This book is meant to be less a how-to manual than a how-come tutorial.

This informative guide will give the retail trader a look inside the mind of a professional trader. It will help the professional trader better understand the essential concepts of his craft. Even the novice trader will be able to apply these concepts to basic options strategies. Comprehensive knowledge of the greeks can help traders to avoid common pitfalls and increase profit potential.

Much of this book is broken down into a discussion of individual strategies. Although the nuances of each specific strategy are not relevant, presenting the material this way allows for a discussion of very specific situations in which greeks come into play. Many of the concepts discussed in a section on one option strategy can be applied to other option strategies.

As in the first edition of *Trading Option Greeks*, Chapter 1 discusses basic option concepts and definitions. It was written to be a review of the basics for the intermediate to advanced trader. For newcomers, it's essential to understand these concepts before moving forward.

A detailed explanation of option greeks begins in Chapter 2. Be sure to leave a bookmark in this chapter, as you will flip to it several times while reading the rest of the book and while studying the market thereafter. Chapter 3 introduces volatility. The same bookmark advice can be applied here, as well. Chapters 4 and 5 explore the minds of option traders. What are the risks they look out for? What are the opportunities they seek? These chapters also discuss direction-neutral and direction-indifferent trading. The remaining chapters take the reader from concept to application, discussing the strategies for nonlinear trading and the tactical considerations of a successful options trader.

New material in this edition includes updated examples, with more current price information throughout many of the chapters. More detailed discussions are also included to give the reader a deeper understanding of important topics. For example, Chapter 8 has a more elaborate explanation of the effect of dividends on option prices. Chapter 17 of this edition has new material on strategy selection, position management, and adjusting, not featured in the first edition of the book.

Acknowledgments

A book like *Trading Option Greeks* is truly a collaboration of the efforts of many people. In my years as a trader, I had many teachers in the School of Hard Knocks. I have had the support of friends and family during the trials and tribulations throughout my trading career, as well as during the time spent writing this book, both the first edition and now this second edition. Surely, there are hundreds of people whose influences contributed to the creation of this book, but there are a few in particular to whom I'd like to give special thanks.

I'd like to give a very special thanks to my mentor and friend from the CBOE's Options Institute, Jim Bittman. Without his help this book would not have been written. Thanks to Marty Kearney and Joe Troccolo for looking over the manuscript. Their input was invaluable. Thanks to Debra Peters for her help during my career at the Options Institute. Thanks to Steve Fossett and Bob Kirkland for believing in me. Thanks to the staff at Bloomberg Press, especially Stephen Isaacs and Kevin Commins. Thanks to my friends at the Chicago Board Options Exchange, the Options Industry Council, and the CME group. Thanks to John Kmiecik for his diligent content editing. Thanks to those who contribute to sharing option ideas on my website, markettaker.com. Thanks to my wife, Kathleen, who has been more patient and supportive than anyone could reasonably ask for. And thanks, especially, to my students and those of you reading this book.

TRADING
OPTION GREEKS

PART I

The Basics of Option Greeks

CHAPTER 1

The Basics

To understand how options work, one needs first to understand what an option is. An option is a contract that gives its owner the right to buy or the right to sell a fixed quantity of an underlying security at a specific price within a certain time constraint. There are two types of options: calls and puts. A call gives the owner of the option the right to buy the underlying security. A put gives the owner of the option the right to sell the underlying security. As in any transaction, there are two parties to an option contract—a buyer and a seller.

Contractual Rights and Obligations

The option buyer is the party who owns the right inherent in the contract. The buyer is referred to as having a long position and may also be called the holder, or owner, of the option. The right doesn't last forever. At some point the option will expire. At expiration, the owner may exercise the right or, if the option has no value to the holder, let it expire without exercising it. But he need not hold the option until expiration. Options are transferable—they can be traded intraday in much the same way as stock is traded. Because it's uncertain what the underlying stock price of the option will be at expiration, much of the time this right has value before it expires. The uncertainty of stock prices, after all, is the raison d'être of the option market.

A long position in an option contract, however, is fundamentally different from a long position in a stock. Owning corporate stock affords the shareholder ownership rights, which may include the right to vote in corporate affairs and the right to receive dividends. Owning an option represents strictly the right either to buy the stock or to sell it, depending on whether it's a call or a put. Option holders do not receive dividends that would be paid to the shareholders of the underlying stock, nor do they have voting rights. The corporation has no knowledge of the parties to the option contract. The contract is created by the buyer and seller of the option and made available by being listed on an exchange.

The party to the contract who is referred to as the option seller, also called the option writer, has a short position in the option. Instead of having a right to take a position in the underlying stock, as the buyer does, the seller incurs an obligation to potentially either buy or sell the stock. When a trader who is long an option exercises, a trader with a short position gets *assigned*. Assignment means the trader with the short option position is called on to fulfill the obligation that was established when the contract was sold.

Shorting an option is fundamentally different from shorting a stock. Corporations have a quantifiable number of outstanding shares available for trading, which must be borrowed to create a short position, but establishing a short position in an option does not require borrowing; the contract is simply created. The strategy of shorting stock is implemented statistically far less frequently than simply buying stock, but that is not at all the case with options. For every open long-option contract, there is an open short-option contract—they are equally common.

Opening and Closing

Traders' option orders are either opening or closing transactions. When traders with no position in a particular option buy the option, they buy to open. If, in the future, the traders wish to eliminate the position by selling the option they own, the traders enter a sell to close order—they are closing the position. Likewise, if traders with no position in a particular option want to sell an option, thereby creating a short position, the traders execute a sell-to-open transaction. When the traders cover the short position by buying back the option, the traders enter a buy-to-close order.

Open Interest and Volume

Traders use many types of market data to make trading decisions. Two items that are often studied but sometimes misunderstood are volume and open interest. Volume, as the name implies, is the total number of contracts traded during a time period. Often, volume is stated on a one-day basis, but could be stated per week, month, year, or otherwise. Once a new period (day) begins, volume begins again at zero. Open interest is the number of contracts that have been created and remain outstanding. Open interest is a running total.

When an option is first listed, there are no open contracts. If Trader A opens a long position in a newly listed option by buying a one-lot, or one contract, from Trader B, who by selling is also opening a position, a contract is created. One contract traded, so the volume is one. Since both parties opened a position and one contract was created, the open interest in this particular option is one contract as well. If, later that day, Trader B closes his short position by buying one contract from Trader C, who had no position to start with, the volume is now two contracts for that day, but open interest is still one. Only one contract exists; it was traded twice. If the next day, Trader C buys her contract back from Trader A, that day's volume is one and the open interest is now zero.

The Options Clearing Corporation

Remember when Wimpy would tell Popeye, "I'll gladly pay you Tuesday for a hamburger today." Did Popeye ever get paid for those burgers? In a contract, it's very important for each party to hold up his end of the bargain—especially when there is money at stake. How does a trader know the party on the other side of an option contract will in fact do that? That's where the Options Clearing Corporation (OCC) comes into play.

The OCC ultimately guarantees every options trade. In 2010, that was almost 3.9 billion listed-options contracts. The OCC accomplishes this through many clearing members. Here's how it works: When Trader X buys an option through a broker, the broker submits the trade information to its clearing firm. The trader on the other side of this transaction, Trader Y, who is probably a market maker, submits the trade to his clearing firm. The two clearing firms (one representing Trader X's buy, the other representing Trader Y's sell) each submit the trade information to the OCC, which "matches up" the trade.

If Trader Y buys back the option to close the position, how does that affect Trader X if he wants to exercise it? It doesn't. The OCC, acting as an intermediary, assigns one of its clearing members with a customer that is short the option in question to deliver the stock to Trader X's clearing firm, which in turn delivers the stock to Trader X. The clearing member then assigns one of its customers who is short the option. The clearing member will assign the trader either randomly or first in, first out.

Effectively, the OCC is the ultimate counterparty to both the exercise and the assignment.

Standardized Contracts

Exchange-listed options contracts are standardized, meaning the terms of the contract, or the contract specifications, conform to a customary structure. Standardization makes the terms of the contracts intuitive to the experienced user.

To understand the contract specifications in a typical equity option, consider an example:

Buy 1 IBM December 170 call at 5.00

Quantity

In this example, one contract is being purchased. More could have been purchased, but not less—options cannot be traded in fractional units.

Option Series, Option Class, and Contract Size

All calls or puts of the same class, the same expiration month, and the same strike price are called an *option series*. For example, the IBM December 170 calls are a series. Options series are displayed in an option chain on an online broker's user interface. An option chain is a full or partial list of the options that are listed on an underlying.

Option class means a group of options that represent the same underlying. Here, the option class is denoted by the symbol IBM—the contract represents rights on International Business Machines Corp. (IBM) shares. Buying one contract usually gives the holder the right to buy or to sell 100 shares of the underlying stock. This number is referred to as *contract size*. Though this is usually the case, there are times when the contract size is something other than 100 shares of a stock. This situation may occur after certain types of stock splits, spin-offs, or stock dividends, for example. In the minority of cases in which the one contract represents rights on something besides 100 shares, there may be more than one class of options listed on a stock.

A fairly unusual example was presented by the Ford Motor Company options in the summer of 2000. In June 2000, Ford spun off Visteon Corporation. Then, in August 2000, Ford offered shareholders a choice of converting their shares into (a) new shares of Ford plus $20 cash per share, (b) new Ford stock plus fractional shares with an aggregate value of $20, or (c) new Ford stock plus a combination of more new Ford stock and cash. There were three classes of options listed on Ford after both of these changes: F represented 100 shares of the new Ford stock; XFO represented 100 shares of Ford plus $20 per share ($2,000) plus cash in lieu of $1.24; and FOD represented 100 shares of new Ford, 13 shares of Visteon, and $2,001.24.

Sometimes these changes can get complicated. If there is ever a question as to what the underlying is for an option class, the authority is the OCC. A lot of time, money, and stress can be saved by calling the OCC at 888-OPTIONS and clarifying the matter.

Expiration Month

Options expire on the Saturday following the third Friday of the stated month, which in this case is December. The final trading day for an option is commonly the day before expiration—here, the third Friday of December. There are usually at least four months listed for trading on an option class. There may be a total of six months if Long-Term Equity AnticiPation Securities® or LEAPS® are listed on the class. LEAPS can have one year to about two-and-a-half years until expiration. Some underlyings have one-week options called Weeklys^{SM} listed on them.

Strike Price

The price at which the option holder owns the right to buy or to sell the underlying is called the strike price, or exercise price. In this example, the holder owns the right to buy the stock at $170 per share. There is method to the madness regarding how strike prices are listed. Strike prices are generally listed in $1, $2.50, $5, or $10 increments, depending on the value of the strikes and the liquidity of the options.

The relationship of the strike price to the stock price is important in pricing options. For calls, if the stock price is above the strike price, the call is in-the-money (ITM). If the stock and the strike prices are close, the call is at-the-money (ATM). If the stock price is below the strike price the call is out-of-the-money (OTM). This relationship is just the opposite for puts. If the stock price is below the strike price, the put is in-the-money. If the stock price and the strike price are about the same, the put is at-the-money. And, if the stock price is above the put strike, it is out-of-the-money.

Option Type

There are two types of options: calls and puts. Calls give the holder the right to buy the underlying and the writer the obligation to sell the underlying. Puts give the holder the right to sell the underlying and the writer the obligation to buy the underlying.

Premium

The price of an option is called its premium. The premium of this option is $5. Like stock prices, option premiums are stated in dollars and cents per share. Since the option represents 100 shares of IBM, the buyer of this option will pay $500 when the transaction occurs. Certain types of spreads may be quoted in fractions of a penny.

An option's premium is made up of two parts: intrinsic value and time value. Intrinsic value is the amount by which the option is in-the-money. For example, if IBM stock were trading at 171.30, this 170-strike call would be in-the-money by 1.30. It has 1.30 of intrinsic value. The remaining 3.70 of its $5 premium would be time value.

$$\text{Time value} = \text{Total Option Premium} - \text{Intrinsic Value}$$

Options that are out-of-the-money have no intrinsic value. Their values consist only of time premium. Sometimes options have no time value left. Options that consist of only intrinsic value are trading at what traders call *parity*. Time value is sometimes called *premium over parity*.

Exercise Style

One contract specification that is not specifically shown here is the exercise style. There are two main exercise styles: American and European. American-exercise options can be exercised, and therefore assigned, anytime after the contract is entered into until either the trader closes the position or it expires. European-exercise options can be exercised and assigned only at expiration. Exchange-listed equity options are all American-exercise style. Other kinds of options are commonly European exercise. Whether an option is American or European has nothing to with the country in which it's listed.

ETFs, Indexes, and HOLDRs

So far, we've focused on equity options—options on individual stocks. But investors have other choices for trading securities options. Options on baskets of stocks can be traded, too. This can be accomplished using options on exchange-traded funds (ETFs), index options, or options on holding company depositary receipts (HOLDRs).

ETF Options

Exchange-traded funds are vehicles that represent ownership in a fund or investment trust. This fund is made up of a basket of an underlying index's securities—usually equities. The contract specifications of ETF options are similar to those of equity options. Let's look at an example.

One actively traded optionable ETF is the Standard & Poor's Depositary Receipts (SPDRs or Spiders). Spider shares and options trade under the symbol SPY. Exercising one SPY call gives the exerciser a long position of 100 shares of Spiders at the strike price of the option. Expiration for ETF options typically falls on the same day as for equity options—the Saturday following the third Friday of the month. The last trading day is the Friday before. ETF options are American exercise. Traders of ETFs should be aware of the relationship between the price of the ETF shares and the value of the underlying index. For example, the stated value of the Spiders is about one tenth the stated value of the S&P 500. The PowerShares QQQ ETF, representing the Nasdaq 100, is about one fortieth the stated value of the Nasdaq 100.

Index Options

Trading options on the Spiders ETF is a convenient way to trade the Standard & Poor's (S&P) 500. But it's not the only way. There are other option contracts listed on the S&P 500. The SPX is one of the major ones. The SPX is an index option contract. There are some very important differences between ETF options like SPY and index options like SPX.

The first difference is the underlying. The underlying for ETF options is 100 shares of the ETF. The underlying for index options is the numerical value of the index. So if the S&P 500 is at 1303.50, the underlying for SPX options is 1303.50. When an SPX call option is exercised, instead of getting 100 shares of something, the exerciser gets the ITM cash value of the option times $100. Again, with SPX at 1303.50, if a 1300 call is exercised, the exerciser gets $350—that's 1303.50 minus 1300, times $100. This is called *cash settlement.*

Many index options are European, which means no early exercise. At expiration, any long ITM options in a trader's inventory result in an account credit; any short ITMs result in a debit of the ITM value times $100. The settlement process for determining whether a European-style index option is in-the-money at expiration is a little different, too. Often, these indexes are a.m. settled. A.m.-settled index options will have actual expiration on the conventional Saturday following the third Friday of the month. But the final trading day is the Thursday before the expiration day. The final settlement value of the index is determined by the opening prices of the components of the index on Friday morning.

HOLDR Options

Like ETFs, holding company depositary receipts also represent ownership in a basket of stocks. The main difference is that investors owning HOLDRs retain the ownership rights of the individual stocks in the fund, such as the right to vote shares and the right to receive dividends. Options on HOLDRs, for all intents and purposes, function much like options on ETFs.

Strategies and At-Expiration Diagrams

One of the great strengths of options is that there are so many different ways to use them. There are simple, straightforward strategies like buying a call. And there are complex spreads with creative names like jelly roll, guts, and iron butterfly. A spread is a strategy that involves combining an option with one or more other options or stock. Each component of the spread is referred to as a leg. Each spread has its own unique risk and reward characteristics that make it appropriate for certain market outlooks.

Throughout this book, many different spreads will be discussed in depth. For now, it's important to understand that all spreads are made up of a combination of four basic option positions: buy call, sell call, buy put, and sell put. Understanding complex option strategies requires understanding these basic positions and their common, practical uses. When learning options, it's helpful to see what the option's payout is if it is held until expiration.

Buy Call

Why buy the right to buy the stock when you can simply buy the stock? All option strategies have trade-offs, and the long call is no different. Whether the stock or the call is preferable depends greatly on the trader's forecast and motivations.

Consider a long call example:

Buy 1 INTC June 22.50 call at 0.85.

In this example, a trader is bullish on Intel (INTC). He believes Intel will rise at least 20 percent, from $22.25 per share to around $27 by June expiration, about two months from now. He is concerned, however, about downside risk and wants to limit his exposure. Instead of buying 100 shares of Intel at $22.25—a total investment of $2,225—the trader buys 1 INTC June 22.50 call at 0.85, for a total of $85.

The trader is paying 0.85 for the right to buy 100 shares of Intel at $22.50 per share. If Intel is trading below the strike price of $22.50 at expiration, the call will expire and the total premium of 0.85 will be lost. Why? The trader will not exercise the right to buy the stock at a $22.50 if he can buy it cheaper in the market. Therefore, if Intel is below $22.50 at expiration, this call will expire with no value.

However, if the stock is trading above the strike price at expiration, the call can be exercised, in which case the trader may purchase the stock below its trading price. Here, the call has value to the trader. The higher the stock, the more the call is worth. For the trade to be profitable, at expiration the stock must be trading above the trader's break-even price. The break-even price for a long call is the strike price plus the premium paid—in this example, $23.35 per share. The point here is that if the call is exercised, the effective purchase price of the stock upon exercise is $23.35. The stock is literally bought at the strike price, which is $22.50, but the premium of 0.85 that the trader has paid must be taken into account. Exhibit 1.1 illustrates this example.

Exhibit 1.1 is an at-expiration diagram for the Intel 22.50 call. It shows the profit and loss, or P&(L), of the option if it is held until expiration. The X-axis represents the prices at which INTC could be trading at expiration. The Y-axis represents the associated profit or loss on the position. The at-expiration diagram of any long call position will always have this same hockey-stick shape, regardless of the stock or strike. There is always a limit of loss, represented by the horizontal line, which in this case is drawn at −0.85.

EXHIBIT 1.1 Long Intel call.

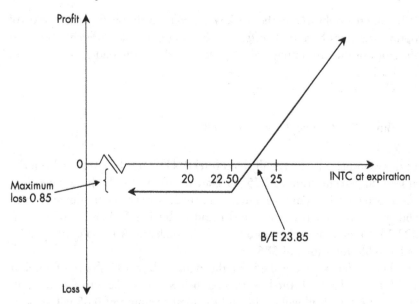

And there is always a line extending upward and to the right, which represents effectively a long stock position stemming from the strike.

The trade-offs between a long stock position and a long call position are shown in Exhibit 1.2.

The thin dotted line represents owning 100 shares of Intel at $22.25. Profits are unlimited, but the risk is substantial—the stock *can* go to zero. Herein lies the trade-off. The long call has unlimited profit potential with limited risk. Whenever an option is purchased, the most that can be lost is the premium paid for the option. But the benefit of reduced risk comes at a cost. If the stock is above the strike at expiration, the call will always underperform the stock by the amount of the premium.

Because of this trade-off, conservative traders will sometimes buy a call rather than the associated stock and sometimes buy the stock rather than the call. Buying a call can be considered more conservative when the volatility of the stock is expected to rise. Traders are willing to risk a comparatively small premium when a large price decline is feared possible. Instead, in an interest-bearing vehicle, they harbor the capital that would otherwise have been used to purchase the stock. The cost of this protection is acceptable to the trader if high-enough price advances are anticipated. In terms of percentage, much

EXHIBIT 1.2 Long Intel call vs. long Intel stock.

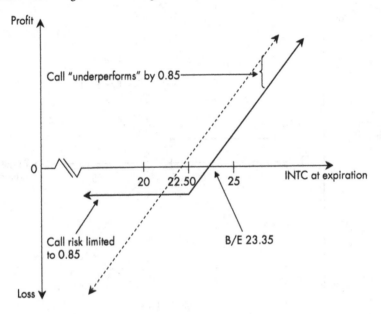

higher returns *and losses* are possible with the long call. If the stock is trading at $27 at expiration, as the trader in this example expected, the trader reaps a 429 percent profit on the $0.85 investment ([$27 − 23.35] / $0.85). If Intel is below the strike price at expiration, the trader loses 100 percent.

This makes call buying an excellent speculative alternative. Those willing to accept bigger risk can further increase returns by purchasing more calls. In this example, around 26 Intel calls—representing the rights on 2,600 shares—can be purchased at 85 cents for the cost of 100 shares at $22.25. This is the kind of leverage that allows for either a lower cash outlay than buying the stock—reducing risk—or the same cash outlay as buying the stock but with much greater exposure—creating risk in pursuit of higher returns.

Sell Call

Selling a call creates the obligation to sell the stock at the strike price. Why is a trader willing to accept this obligation? The answer is option premium. If the position is held until expiration without getting assigned, the entire premium represents a profit for the trader. If assignment occurs, the trader

EXHIBIT 1.3 Naked Target call.

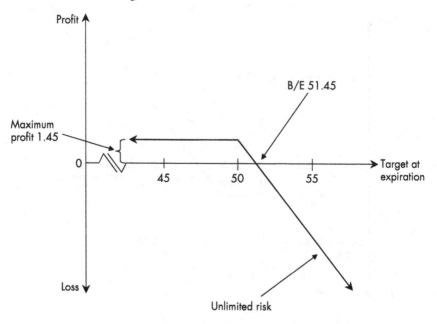

will be obliged to sell stock at the strike price. If the trader does not have a long position in the underlying stock (a naked call), a short stock position will be created. Otherwise, if stock is owned (a covered call), that stock is sold. Whether the trader has a profit or a loss depends on the movement of the stock price and how the short call position was constructed.

Consider a naked call example:

Sell 1 TGT October 50 call at 1.45

In this example, Target Corporation (TGT) is trading at $49.42. A trader, Sam, believes Target will continue to be trading below $50 by October expiration, about two months from now. Sam sells 1 Target two-month 50 call at 1.45, opening a short position in that series. Exhibit 1.3 will help explain the expected payout of this naked call position if it is held until expiration.

If TGT is trading below the exercise price of 50, the call will expire worthless. Sam keeps the 1.45 premium, and the obligation to sell the stock ceases to exist. If Target is trading above the strike price, the call will be in-the-money. The higher the stock is above the strike price, the more intrinsic value the call will have. As a seller, Sam wants the call to have little or no intrinsic value at expiration. If the stock is below the break-even price at expiration, Sam will still have a profit. Here, the break-even price is $51.45—the strike price plus the call premium. Above the break-even, Sam has a loss. Since stock prices can rise to infinity (although, for the record, I have never seen this happen), the naked call position has unlimited risk of loss.

Because a short stock position may be created, a naked call position must be done in a margin account. For retail traders, many brokerage firms require different levels of approval for different types of option strategies. Because the naked call position has unlimited risk, establishing it will generally require the highest level of approval—and a high margin requirement.

Another tactical consideration is what Sam's objective was when he entered the trade. His goal was to profit from the stock's being below $50 during this two-month period—not to short the stock. Because equity options are American exercise and can be exercised/assigned any time from the moment the call is sold until expiration, a short stock position cannot always be avoided. If assigned, the short stock position will extend Sam's period of risk—because stock doesn't expire. Here, he will pay one commission shorting the stock when assignment occurs and one more when he *buys back* the unwanted position. Many traders choose to close the naked call position before expiration rather than risk assignment.

It is important to understand the fundamental difference between buying calls and selling calls. Buying a call option offers limited risk and unlimited reward. Selling a naked call option, however, has limited reward—the call premium—and unlimited risk. This naked call position is not so much bearish as *not bullish*. If Sam thought the stock was going to zero, he would have chosen a different strategy.

Now consider a covered call example:

Buy 100 shares TGT at $49.42
Sell 1 TGT October 50 call at 1.45

Unlimited and *risk* are two words that don't sit well together with many traders. For that reason, traders often prefer to sell calls as part of a spread. But since spreads are strategies that involve multiple components, they have different risk characteristics from an outright option. Perhaps the most commonly used call-selling spread strategy is the covered call (sometimes called a *covered write* or a *buy-write*). While selling a call naked is a way to

EXHIBIT 1.4 Target covered call.

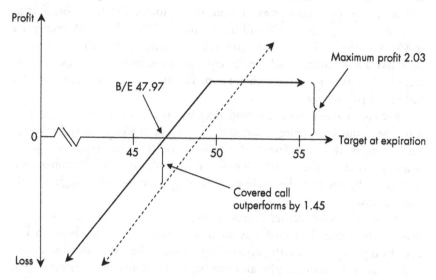

take advantage of a "not bullish" forecast, the covered call achieves a different set of objectives.

After studying Target Corporation, another trader, Isabel, has a neutral to slightly bullish forecast. With Target at $49.42, she believes the stock will be range-bound between $47 and $51.50 over the next two months, ending with October expiration. Isabel buys 100 shares of Target at $49.42 and sells 1 TGT October 50 call at 1.45. The implications for the covered-call strategy are twofold: Isabel must be content to own the stock at current levels, and—since she sold the right to buy the stock at $50, that is, a 50 call, to another party—she must be willing to sell the stock if the price rises to or through $50 per share. Exhibit 1.4 shows how this covered call performs if it is held until the call expires.

The solid kinked line represents the covered call position, and the thin, straight dotted line represents owning the stock outright. At the expiration of the call option, if Target is trading below $50 per share—the strike price—the call expires and Isabel is left with a long position of 100 shares *plus* $1.45 per share of expired-option premium. Below the strike, the buy-write always outperforms simply owning the stock by the amount of the premium. The call premium provides limited downside protection; the stock Isabel owns can decline $1.45 in value to $47.97 before the trade is a loser. In the unlikely event the stock collapses and becomes worthless, this limited downside protection is not so comforting. Ultimately, Isabel has $47.97 per share at risk.

The trade-off comes if Target is above $50 at expiration. Here, assignment will likely occur, in which case the stock will be sold. The call can be assigned before expiration, too, causing the stock to be *called away* early. Because the covered call involves this obligation to sell the sock at the strike price, upside potential is limited. In this case, Isabel's profit potential is $2.03. The stock can rise from $49.42 to $50—a $0.58 profit—plus $1.45 of option premium.

Isabel does not want the stock to decline too much. Below $47.97, the trade is a loser. If the stock rises too much, the stock is sold prematurely and upside opportunity is lost. Limited reward and unlimited risk. (Technically, the risk is not unlimited—the stock can only go to zero. But if the stock drops from $49.42 to zero in a short time, the risk will certainly feel unlimited.) The covered call strategy is for a neutral to moderately bullish outlook.

Sell Put

Selling a put has many similarities to the covered call strategy. We'll discuss the two positions and highlight the likenesses. Chapter 6 will detail the nuts and bolts of why these similarities exist.

Consider an example of selling a put:

Sell 1 BA January 65 put at 1.20

In this example, trader Sam is neutral to moderately bullish on Boeing (BA) between now and January expiration. He is not bullish enough to buy BA at the current market price of $69.77 per share. But if the shares dropped below $65, he'd gladly scoop some up. Sam sells 1 BA January 65 put at 1.20. The at-expiration diagram in Exhibit 1.5 shows the P&(L) of this trade if it is held until expiration.

At the expiration of this option, if Boeing is above $65, the put expires and Sam retains the premium of $1.20. The obligation to buy stock expires with the option. Below the strike, put owners will be inclined to exercise their option to sell the stock at $65. Therefore, those short the put, as Sam is in this example, can expect assignment. The break-even price for the position is $63.80. That is the strike price minus the option premium. If assigned, this is the effective purchase price of the stock. The obligation to buy at $65 is fulfilled, but the $1.20 premium collected makes the purchase effectively $63.80. Here, again, there is limited profit

EXHIBIT 1.5 Boeing short put.

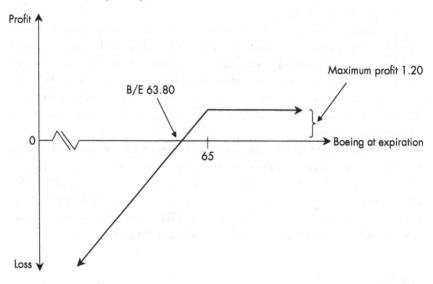

opportunity ($1.20 if the stock is above the strike price) and seemingly unlimited risk (the risk of potential stock ownership at $63.80) if Boeing is below the strike price.

Why would a trader short a put and willingly assume this substantial risk with comparatively limited reward? There are a number of motivations that may warrant the short put strategy. In this example, Sam had the twin goals of profiting from a neutral to moderately bullish outlook on Boeing and buying it if it traded below $65. The short put helps him achieve both objectives.

Much like the covered call, if the stock is above the strike at expiration, this trader reaches his maximum profit potential—in this case 1.20. And if the price of Boeing is below the strike at expiration, Sam has ownership of the stock from assignment. Here, a strike price that is lower than the current stock level is used. The stock needs to decline in order for Sam to get assigned and become long the stock. With this strategy, he was able to establish a target price at which he would buy the stock. Why not use a limit order? If the put is assigned, the effective purchase price is $63.80 even if the stock price is above this price. If the put is not assigned, the premium is kept.

A consideration every trader must make before entering the short put position is how the purchase of the stock will be financed in the event the put is assigned. Traders hoping to acquire the stock will often hold enough cash in their trading account to secure the purchase of the stock. This is called a *cash-secured put.* In this example, Sam would hold $6,380 in his account in addition to the $120 of option premium received. This affords him enough free capital to fund the $6,500 purchase of stock the short put dictates. More speculative traders may be willing to buy the stock on margin, in which case the trader will likely need around 50 percent of the stock's value.

Some traders sell puts without the intent of ever owning the stock. They hope to profit from a low-volatility environment. Just as the short call is a not-bullish stance on the underlying, the short put is a not-bearish play. As long as the underlying is above the strike price at expiration, the option premium is all profit. The trader must actively manage the position for fear of being assigned. Buying the put back to close the position eliminates the risk of assignment.

Buy Put

Buying a put gives the holder the right to sell stock at the strike price. Of course, puts can be a part of a host of different spreads, but this chapter discusses the two most basic and common put-buying strategies: the long put and the protective put. The long put is a way to speculate on a bearish move in the underlying security, and the protective put is a way to protect a long position in the underlying security.

Consider a long put example:

Buy 1 SPY May 139 put at 2.30

In this example, the Spiders have had a good run up to $140.35. Trader Isabel is looking for a 10 percent correction in SPY between now and the end of May, about three months away. She buys 1 SPY May 139 put at 2.30. This put gives her the right to sell 100 shares of SPY at $139 per share. Exhibit 1.6 shows Isabel's P&(L) if the put is held until expiration.

If SPY is above the strike price of 139 at expiration, the put will expire and the entire premium of 2.30 will be lost. If SPY is below the strike price at expiration, the put will have value. It can be exercised, creating a short position in the Spiders at an effective price of $136.70 per share. This price is found by subtracting the premium paid, 2.30, from the strike price, 139. This is the point at which the position breaks even. If SPY is below $136.70 at expiration, Isabel has a profit. Profits will increase on a tick-for-tick basis, with downward movements in SPY down to zero. The long put has limited risk and substantial reward potential.

EXHIBIT 1.6 SPY long put.

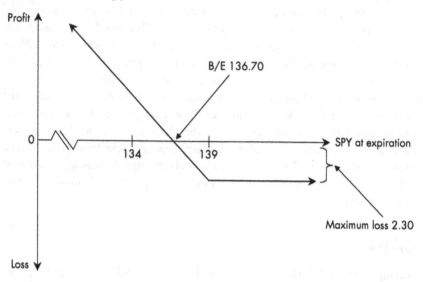

An alternative for Isabel is to short the ETF at the current price of $140.35. But a short position in the underlying may not be as attractive to her as a long put. The margin requirements for short stock are significantly higher than for a long put. Put buyers must post only the premium of the put—that is the most that can be lost, after all.

The margin requirement for short stock reflects unlimited loss potential. Margin requirements aside, risk is a very real consideration for a trader deciding between shorting stock and buying a put. If the trader expects high volatility, he or she may be more inclined to limit upside risk while leveraging downside profit potential by buying a put. In general, traders buy options when they expect volatility to increase and sell them when they expect volatility to decrease. This will be a common theme throughout this book.

Consider a protective put example:

This is an example of a situation in which volatility is expected to increase.

Own 100 shares SPY at 140.35
Buy 1 SPY May139 put at 2.30

Although Isabel bought a put because she was bearish on the Spiders, a different trader, Kathleen, may buy a put for a different reason—she's bullish

EXHIBIT 1.7   SPY protective put.

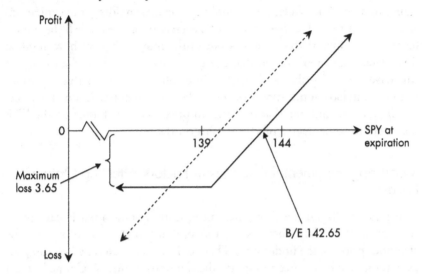

but concerned about increasing volatility. In this example, Kathleen has owned 100 shares of Spiders for some time. SPY is currently at $140.35. She is bullish on the market but has concerns about volatility over the next two or three months. She wants to protect her investment. Kathleen buys 1 SPY May 139 put at 2.30. (If Kathleen bought the shares of SPY and the put at the same time, as a spread, the position would be called a married put.)

Kathleen is buying the right to sell the shares she owns at $139. Effectively, it is an insurance policy on this asset. Exhibit 1.7 shows the risk profile of this new position.

The solid kinked line is the protective put (put and stock), and the thin dotted line is the outright position in SPY alone, without the put. The most Kathleen stands to lose with the protective put is $3.65 per share. SPY can decline from $140.35 to $139, creating a loss of $1.35, plus the $2.30 premium spent on the put. If the stock does not fall and the insuring put hence does not come into play, the cost of the put must be recouped to justify its expense. The break-even point is $142.65.

This position implies that Kathleen is still bullish on the Spiders. When traders believe a stock or ETF is going to decline, they sell the shares. Instead, Kathleen sacrifices 1.6 percent of her investment up front by purchasing the put for $2.30. She defers the sale of SPY until the period of perceived risk ends. Her motivation is not to sell the ETF; it is to hedge volatility.

Once the anticipated volatility is no longer a concern, Kathleen has a choice to make. She can let the option run its course, holding it to expiration, at which point it will either expire or be exercised; or she can sell the option before expiration. If the option is out-of-the-money, it may have residual time value prior to expiration that can be recouped. If it is in-the-money, it will have intrinsic value and maybe time value as well. In this situation, Kathleen can look at this spread as two trades—one that has declined in price, the SPY shares, and one that has risen in price, the put. Losses on the ETF shares are to some degree offset by gains on the put.

Measuring Incremental Changes in Factors Affecting Option Prices

At-expiration diagrams are very helpful in learning how a particular option strategy works. They show what the option's price will ultimately be at various prices of the underlying. There is, however, a caveat when using at-expiration diagrams. According to the Options Industry Council, most options are closed before they reach expiration. Traders not planning to hold an option until it expires need to have a way to develop reasonable expectations as to what the option's price will be given changes that can occur in factors affecting the option's price. The tool option traders use to aid them in this process is option greeks.

CHAPTER 2

Greek Philosophy

My wife, Kathleen, is not an options trader. Au contraire. However, she, like just about everyone, uses them from time to time—though without really thinking about it. She was on eBay the other day bidding on a pair of shoes. The bid was $45 with three days left to go. She was concerned about the price rising too much and missing the chance to buy them at what she thought was a good price. She noticed, though, that someone else was selling the same shoes with a buy-it-now price of $49—a good-enough price in her opinion. Kathleen was effectively afforded a call option. She had the opportunity to buy the shoes at (the strike price of) $49, a right she could exercise until the offer expired.

The biggest difference between the option in the eBay scenario and the sort of options discussed in this book is transferability. Actual options are tradable—they can be bought and sold. And it is the contract itself that has value—there is one more iteration of pricing.

For example, imagine the $49 opportunity was a coupon or certificate that guaranteed the price of $49, which could be passed along from one person to another. And there was the chance that the $49-price guarantee could represent a discount on the price paid for the shoes—maybe a big discount—should the price of the shoes rise in the eBay auction. The certificate guaranteeing the $49 would have value. Anyone planning to buy the shoes would want the safety of knowing they were guaranteed not to pay more than $49 for the shoes. In fact, some people would even consider paying to buy the certificate itself if they thought the price of the shoes might rise significantly.

Price vs. Value: How Traders Use Option-Pricing Models

Like in the common-life example just discussed, the right to buy or sell an underlying security—that is, an option—can have value, too. The specific value of an option is determined by supply and demand. There are several variables in an option contract, however, that can influence a trader's willingness to demand (desire to buy) or supply (desire to sell) an option at a given price. For example, a trader would rather own—that is, there would be higher demand for—an option that has more time until expiration than a shorter-dated option, all else held constant. And a trader would rather own a call with a lower strike than a higher strike, all else kept constant, because it would give the right to buy at a lower price.

Several elements contribute to the value of an option. It took academics many years to figure out exactly what those elements are. Fischer Black and Myron Scholes together pioneered research in this area at the University of Chicago. Ultimately, their work led to a Nobel Prize for Myron Scholes. Fischer Black died before he could be honored.

In 1973, Black and Scholes published a paper called "The Pricing of Options and Corporate Liabilities" in the *Journal of Political Economy*, that introduced the Black-Scholes option-pricing model to the world. The Black-Scholes model values European call options on non-dividend-paying stocks. Here, for the first time, was a widely accepted model illustrating what goes into the pricing of an option. Option prices were no longer wild guesswork. They could now be rationalized. Soon, additional models and alterations to the Black-Scholes model were developed for options on indexes, dividend-paying stocks, bonds, commodities, and other optionable instruments. All the option-pricing models commonly in use today have slightly different means but achieve the same end: the option's theoretical value. For American-exercise equity options, six inputs are entered into any option-pricing model to generate a theoretical value: stock price, strike price, time until expiration, interest rate, dividends, and volatility.

Theoretical value—what a concept! A trader plugs six numbers into a pricing model, and it tells him what the option is worth, right? Well, in practical terms, that's not exactly how it works. An option is worth what the market bears. Economists call this price discovery. The price of an option is determined by the forces of supply and demand working in a free and open market. Herein lies an important concept for option traders: the difference between price and value.

Price can be observed rather easily from any source that offers option quotes (web sites, your broker, quote vendors, and so on). Value is calculated by a pricing model. But, in practice, the theoretical value is really not an output at all. It is already known: the market determines it. The trader rectifies price and value by setting the theoretical value to fall between the bid and the offer of the option by adjusting the inputs to the model. Professional traders often refer to the theoretical value as the fair value of the option.

At this point, please note the absence of the mathematical formula for the Black-Scholes model (or any other pricing model, for that matter). Although the foundation of trading option greeks is mathematical, this book will keep the math to a minimum—which is still quite a bit. The focus of this book is on practical applications, not academic theory. It's about learning to drive the car, not mastering its engineering.

The trader has an equation with six inputs equaling one known output. What good is this equation? An option-pricing model helps a trader understand how market forces affect the value of an option. Five of the six inputs are dynamic; the only constant is the strike price of the option in question. If the price of the option changes, it's because one or more of the five variable inputs has changed. These variables are independent of each other, but they can change in harmony, having either a cumulative or net effect on the option's value. An option trader needs to be concerned with the relationship of these variables (price, time, volatility, interest). This multi-dimensional view of asset pricing is unique to option traders.

Delta

The five figures commonly used by option traders are represented by Greek letters: delta, gamma, theta, vega, rho. The figures are referred to as option greeks. Vega, of course, is not an actual letter of the greek alphabet, but in the options vernacular, it is considered one of the greeks.

The greeks are a derivation of an option-pricing model, and each Greek letter represents a specific sensitivity to influences on the option's value. To understand concepts represented by these five figures, we'll start with delta, which is defined in four ways:

1. The rate of change of an option value relative to a change in the underlying stock price.

2. The derivative of the graph of an option value in relation to the stock price.
3. The equivalent of underlying shares represented by an option position.
4. The estimate of the likelihood of an option expiring in-the-money.[1]

Definition 1: Delta (Δ) is the rate of change of an option's value relative to a change in the price of the underlying security. A trader who is bullish on a particular stock may choose to buy a call instead of buying the underlying security. If the price of the stock rises by $1, the trader would expect to profit on the call—but by how much? To answer that question, the trader must consider the delta of the option.

Delta is stated as a percentage. If an option has a 50 delta, its price will change by 50 percent of the change of the underlying stock price. Delta is generally written as either a whole number, without the percent sign, or as a decimal. So if an option has a 50 percent delta, this will be indicated as 0.50, or 50. For the most part, we'll use the former convention in our discussion.

Call values increase when the underlying stock price increases and vice versa. Because calls have this positive correlation with the underlying, they have positive deltas. Here is a simplified example of the effect of delta on an option:

Stock price $60 ⟶ $61
Call value 3.00 ⟶ 0.50 delta ⟶ 3.50

Consider a $60 stock with a call option that has a 0.50 delta and is trading for 3.00. Considering only the delta, if the stock price increases by $1, the theoretical value of the call will rise by 0.50. That's 50 percent of the stock price change. The new call value will be 3.50. If the stock price decreases by $1, the 0.50 delta will cause the call to decrease in value by 0.50, from 3.00 to 2.50.

Puts have a negative correlation to the underlying. That is, put values decrease when the stock price rises and vice versa. Puts, therefore, have negative deltas. Here is a simplified example of the delta effect on a −0.40-delta put:

Stock price $60 ⟶ $61
Put value 2.25 ⟶ −0.40 delta ⟶ 1.85

As the stock rises from $60 to $61, the delta of −0.40 causes the put value to go from $2.25 to $1.85. The put decreases by 40 percent of the stock price increase. If the stock price instead declined by $1, the put value would increase by $0.40, to $2.65.

Unfortunately, real life is a bit more complicated than the simplified examples of delta used here. In reality, the value of both the call and the put will likely be higher with the stock at $61 than was shown in these examples. We'll expand on this concept later when we tackle the topic of gamma.

Definition 2: Delta can also be described another way. Exhibit 2.1 shows the value of a call option with three months to expiration at a variable stock price. As the stock price rises, the call is worth more; as the stock price declines, the call value moves toward zero. Mathematically, for any given point on the graph, the derivative will show the rate of change of the option price. *The delta is the first derivative of the graph of the option price relative to the stock price.*

Definition 3: In terms of absolute value (meaning that plus and minus signs are ignored), the delta of an option is between 1.00 and 0. Its price can change in tandem with the stock, as with a 1.00 delta; or it cannot change at all as the stock moves, as with a 0 delta; or anything in between. By definition, stock has a 1.00 delta—it *is* the underlying security. A $1 rise in the stock yields a $100 profit on a round lot of 100 shares. A call with a 0.60 delta rises by $0.60 with a $1 increase in the stock. The owner of a call representing rights on 100 shares earns $60 for a $1 increase in the underlying. It's as if the call owner in this example is long 60 shares of the underlying stock. *Delta is the option's equivalent of a position in the underlying shares.*

A trader who buys five 0.43-delta calls has a position that is effectively long 215 shares—that's 5 contracts × 0.43 deltas × 100 shares. In option lingo, the trader is long 215 deltas. Likewise, if the trader were short five 0.43-delta calls, the trader would be short 215 deltas.

EXHIBIT 2.1 Call value compared with stock price.

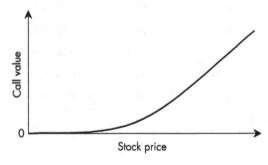

The same principles apply to puts. Being long 10 0.59-delta puts makes the trader short a total of 590 deltas, a position that profits or loses like being short 590 shares of the underlying stock. Conversely, if the trader were short 10 0.59-delta puts, the trader would theoretically make $590 if the stock were to rise $1 and lose $590 if the stock fell by $1—just like being long 590 shares.

Definition 4: The final definition of delta is considered the trader's definition. It's mathematically imprecise but is used nonetheless as a general rule of thumb by option traders. A trader would say the *delta is a statistical approximation of the likelihood of the option expiring in-the-money*. An option with a 0.75 delta would have a 75 percent chance of being in-the-money at expiration under this definition. An option with a 0.20 delta would be thought of having a 20 percent chance of expiring in-the-money.

Dynamic Inputs

Option deltas are not constants. They are calculated from the dynamic inputs of the pricing model—stock price, time to expiration, volatility, and so on. When these variables change, the changes affect the delta. These changes can be mathematically quantified—they are systematic. Understanding these patterns and other quirks as to how delta behaves can help traders use this tool more effectively. Let's discuss a few observations about the characteristics of delta.

First, call and put deltas are closely related. Exhibit 2.2 is a partial option chain of 70-day calls and puts in Rambus Incorporated (RMBS). The stock was trading at $21.30 when this table was created. In Exhibit 2.2, the 20 calls have a 0.66 delta.

EXHIBIT 2.2 RMBS Option chain with deltas.

Call Market	Call Delta	Strike	Put Market	Put Delta
4.80–5.00	0.81	**17.5**	0.90–1.00	−0.19
3.30–3.50	0.66	**20**	1.90–2.00	−0.34
2.35–2.40	0.49	**22.5**	3.20–3.40	−0.51
1.55–1.60	0.34	**25**	5.00–5.10	−0.67
0.70–0.80	0.14	**30**	9.10–9.30	−0.89

RMBS stock price = 21.30
70 days until expiration

Notice the deltas of the put-call pairs in this exhibit. As a general rule, the absolute value of the call delta plus the absolute value of the put delta add up to close to 1.00. The reason for this has to do with a mathematical relationship called put-call parity, which is briefly discussed later in this chapter and described in detail in Chapter 6. But with equity options, the put-call pair doesn't always add up to exactly 1.00.

Sometimes the difference is simply due to rounding. But sometimes there are other reasons. For example, the 30-strike calls and puts in Exhibit 2.2 have deltas of 0.14 and −0.89, respectively. The absolute values of the deltas add up to 1.03. Because of the possibility of early exercise of American options, the put delta is a bit higher than the call delta would imply. When puts have a greater chance of early exercise, they begin to act more like short stock and consequently will have a greater delta. Often, dividend-paying stocks will have higher deltas on some in-the-money calls than the put in the pair would imply. As the ex-dividend date—the date the stock begins trading without the dividend—approaches, an in-the-money call can become more apt to be exercised, because traders will want to own stock to capture the dividend. Here, the call begins to act more like long stock, leading to a higher delta.

Moneyness and Delta

The next observation is the effect of moneyness on the option's delta. Moneyness describes the degree to which the option is in- or out-of-the-money. As a general rule, options that are in-the-money (ITM) have deltas greater than 0.50. Options that are out-of-the-money (OTM) have deltas less than 0.50. Finally, options that are at-the-money (ATM) have deltas that are about 0.50. The more in-the-money the option is, the closer to 1.00 the delta is. The more out-of-the-money, the closer the delta is to 0.

But ATM options are usually not exactly 0.50. For ATMs, both the call and the put deltas are generally systematically a value other than 0.50. Typically, the call has a higher delta than 0.50 and the put has a lower absolute value than 0.50. Incidentally, the call's theoretical value is generally greater than the put's when the options are right at-the-money as well. One reason for this disparity between exactly at-the-money calls and puts is the interest rate. The more time until expiration, the more effect the interest rate will have, and, therefore, the higher the call's theoretical and delta will be relative to the put.

Effect of Time on Delta

In a close contest, the last few minutes of a football game are often the most exciting—not because the players run faster or knock heads harder but because one strategic element of the game becomes more and more important: time. The team that's in the lead wants the game clock to run down with no interruption to solidify its position. The team that's losing uses its precious time-outs strategically. The more playing time left, the less certain defeat is for the losing team.

Although mathematically imprecise, the trader's definition can help us gain insight into how time affects option deltas. The more time left until an option's expiration, the less certain it is whether the option will be ITM or OTM at expiration. The deltas of both the ITM and the OTM options reflect that uncertainty. The more time left in the life of the option, the closer the deltas tend to gravitate to 0.50. A 0.50 delta represents the greatest level of uncertainty—a coin toss. Exhibit 2.3 shows the deltas of a hypothetical equity call with a strike price of 50 at various stock prices with different times until expiration. All other parameters are held constant.

As shown in Exhibit 2.3, the more time until expiration, the closer ITMs and OTMs move to 0.50. At expiration, of course, the option is either a 100 delta or a 0 delta; it's either stock or not.

Effect of Volatility on Delta

The level of volatility affects option deltas as well. We'll discuss volatility in more detail in future chapters, but it's important to address it here as it relates to the concept of delta. Exhibit 2.4 shows how changing the volatility percentage (explained further in Chapter 3), as opposed to the time to expiration, affects option deltas. In this table, the delta of a call with 91 days until expiration is studied.

Notice the effect that volatility has on the deltas of this option with the underlying stock at various prices. In this table, at a low volatility with the call deep in- or out-of-the-money, the delta is very large or very small, respectively. At 10 percent volatility with the stock at $58 a share, the delta is 1.00. At that same volatility level with the stock at $42 a share, the delta is 0.

But at higher volatility levels, the deltas change. With the stock at $58, a 45 percent volatility gives the 50-strike call a 0.79 delta—much smaller than it was at the low volatility level. With the stock at $42, a 45-percent volatility returns a 0.30 delta for the call. Generally speaking, ITM option deltas are smaller given a higher volatility assumption, and OTM option deltas are bigger with a higher volatility.

EXHIBIT 2.3 Estimated delta of 50-strike call—impact of time.

Stock Price	At Expiration	1 Month to Expiration	2 Months to Expiration	3 Months to Expiration	4 Months to Expiration	5 Months to Expiration	6 Months to Expiration	7 Months to Expiration
$42	0	0	0.06	0.11	0.16	0.20	0.23	0.26
$44	0	0.05	0.14	0.20	0.25	0.28	0.31	0.34
$46	0	0.15	0.25	0.31	0.35	0.38	0.40	0.42
$48	0	0.32	0.40	0.43	0.46	0.48	0.49	0.50
$50	0.50	0.53	0.55	0.56	0.57	0.58	0.58	0.59
$52	1.00	0.73	0.67	0.67	0.67	0.66	0.66	0.66
$54	1.00	0.87	0.80	0.77	0.75	0.74	0.73	0.73
$56	1.00	0.95	0.88	0.85	0.82	0.80	0.79	0.78
$58	1.00	0.98	0.94	0.90	0.88	0.86	0.85	0.83

EXHIBIT 2.4 Estimated delta of 50-strike call—impact of volatility.

Stock Price	10% Vol	15% Vol	20% Vol	25% Vol	30% Vol	35% Vol	40% Vol	45% Vol
$42	0	0.02	0.06	0.11	0.16	0.21	0.25	0.30
$44	0.01	0.07	0.14	0.20	0.25	0.29	0.32	0.35
$46	0.08	0.18	0.26	0.31	0.35	0.38	0.40	0.42
$48	0.28	0.36	0.40	0.43	0.45	0.47	0.48	0.50
$50	0.58	0.56	0.56	0.56	0.56	0.56	0.56	0.56
$52	0.84	0.75	0.70	0.67	0.66	0.64	0.64	0.63
$54	0.96	0.88	0.82	0.77	0.74	0.72	0.70	0.69
$56	0.99	0.95	0.89	0.85	0.81	0.78	0.76	0.74
$58	1.00	0.98	0.94	0.90	0.87	0.83	0.81	0.79

Effect of Stock Price on Delta

An option that is $5 in-the-money on a $20 stock will have a higher delta than an option that is $5 in-the-money on a $200 stock. Proportionately, the former is more in-the-money. Comparing two options that are in-the-money by the same percentage yields similar results.

As the stock price changes because the strike price remains stable, the option's delta will change. This phenomenon is measured by the option's gamma.

Gamma

The strike price is the only constant in the pricing model. When the stock price moves relative to this constant, the option in question becomes more in-the-money or out-of-the-money. This means the delta changes. This isolated change is measured by the option's gamma, sometimes called *curvature*.

Gamma (Γ) is the rate of change of an option's delta given a change in the price of the underlying security. Gamma is conventionally stated in terms of deltas per dollar move. The simplified examples above under Definition 1 of delta, used to describe the effect of delta, had one important piece of the puzzle missing: gamma. As the stock price moved higher in those examples, the delta would not remain constant. It would change due to the effect of gamma. The following example shows how the delta would change given a 0.04 gamma attributed to the call option.

Stock Price $60 ───────────→ $61 ───────────→ $62
Call Delta 0.50 ─→ 0.04 gamma ─→ 0.54 ─→ 0.04 gamma ─→ 0.58

The call in this example starts as a 0.50-delta option. When the stock price increases by $1, the delta increases by the amount of the gamma. In this example, delta increases from 0.50 to 0.54, adding 0.04 deltas. As the stock price continues to rise, the delta continues to move higher. At $62, the call's delta is 0.58.

This increase in delta will affect the value of the call. When the stock price first begins to rise from $60, the option value is increasing at a rate of 50 percent—the call's delta at that stock price. But by the time the stock is at $61, the option value is increasing at a rate of 54 percent of the stock price. To estimate the theoretical value of the call at $61, we must first estimate the average change in the delta between $60 and $61. The average delta between $60 and $61 is roughly 0.52. It's difficult to calculate the average delta exactly because gamma is not constant; this is discussed in more detail later in the chapter. A more realistic example of call values in relation to the stock price would be as follows:

Stock Price $60 ───────────→ $61 ───────────→ $62
Call Delta 0.50 ─→ 0.04 gamma ─→ 0.54 ─→ 0.04 gamma ─→ 0.58
Call Value 3.00 ─→ (Avg Δ ≈ 0.52) ─→ 3.52 ─→ (Avg Δ ≈ 0.56) ─→ 4.08

Each $1 increase in the stock shows an increase in the call value about equal to the average delta value between the two stock prices. If the stock were to decline, the delta would get smaller at a decreasing rate.

Stock Price $60 ───────────→ $59 ───────────→ $58
Call Delta 0.50 ─→ 0.04 gamma ─→ 0.46 ─→ 0.04 gamma ─→ 0.42
Call Value 3.00 ─→ (Avg Δ ≈ 0.48) ─→ 2.52 ─→ (Avg Δ ≈ 0.44) ─→ 2.08

As the stock price declines from $60 to $59, the option delta decreases from 0.50 to 0.46. There is an average delta of about 0.48 between the two stock prices. At $59 the new theoretical value of the call is 2.52. The gamma continues to affect the option's delta and thereby its theoretical value as the stock continues its decline to $58 and beyond.

Puts work the same way, but because they have a negative delta, when there is a positive stock-price movement the gamma makes the put delta less negative, moving closer to 0. The following example clarifies this.

Stock Price $60 ──────────────→ $61 ──────────────→ $62

Put Delta − 0.40 ──→ 0.04 gamma ──→ −0.36 ──→ 0.04 gamma ──→ −0.32

Put Value   2.25 ──→ (Avg Δ ≈ −0.38) ──→ 1.87 ──→ (Avg Δ ≈ −0.34) ──→ 1.53

As the stock price rises, this put moves more and more out-of-the-money. Its theoretical value is decreasing by the rate of the changing delta. At $60, the delta is −0.40. As the stock rises to $61, the delta changes to −0.36. The average delta during that move is about −0.38, which is reflected in the change in the value of the put.

If the stock price declines and the put moves more toward being in-the-money, the delta becomes more negative—that is, the put acts more like a short stock position.

Stock Price $60 ──────────────→ $59 ──────────────→ $58

Put Delta −0.40 ──→ 0.04 gamma ──→ −0.44 ──→ 0.04 gamma ──→ −0.48

Put Value   2.25 ──→ (Avg Δ ≈ −0.42) ──→ 2.67 ──→ (Avg Δ ≈ −0.46) ──→ 3.13

Here, the put value rises by the average delta value between each incremental change in the stock price.

These examples illustrate the effect of gamma on an option without discussing the impact on the trader's position. When traders buy options, they acquire positive gamma. Since gamma causes options to gain value at a faster rate and lose value at a slower rate, (positive) gamma helps the option buyer. A trader buying one call or put in these examples would have +0.04 gamma. Buying 10 of these options would give the trader a +0.4 gamma.

When traders sell options, gamma works against them. When options lose value, they move toward zero at a slower rate. When the underlying moves adversely, gamma speeds up losses. Selling options yields a negative gamma position. A trader selling one of the above calls or puts would have −0.04 gamma per option.

The effect of gamma is less significant for small moves in the underlying than it is for bigger moves. On proportionately large moves, the delta can change quite a bit, making a big difference in the position's P&(L).

EXHIBIT 2.5 Call delta compared with stock price.

In Exhibit 2.1, the left side of the diagram showed the call price not increasing at all with advances in the stock—a 0 delta. The right side showed the option advancing in price 1-to-1 with the stock—a 1.00 delta. Between the two extremes, the delta changes. From this diagram another definition for gamma can be inferred: gamma is the second derivative of the graph of the option price relative to the stock price. Put another way, gamma is the first derivative of a graph of the delta relative to the stock price. Exhibit 2.5 illustrates the delta of a call relative to the stock price.

Not only does the delta change, but it changes at a changing rate. Gamma is not constant. Moneyness, time to expiration, and volatility each have an effect on the gamma of an option.

Dynamic Gamma

When options are far in-the-money or out-of-the-money, they are either 1.00 delta or 0 delta. At the extremes, small changes in the stock price will not cause the delta to change much. When an option is at-the-money, it's a different story. Its delta can change very quickly.

- ITM and OTM options have a low gamma.
- ATM options have a relatively high gamma.

Exhibit 2.6 is an example of how moneyness translates into gamma on QQQ calls.

With QQQ at $44, 92 days until expiration, and a constant volatility input of 19 percent, the 36- and 54-strike calls are far enough in- and out-of-the-money, respectively, that if the Qs move a small amount in either direction from the current price of $44, the movement won't change their

EXHIBIT 2.6 Gamma of QQQ calls with QQQ at $44.

QQQ Call Strike	Gamma	QQQ Call Strike	Gamma	QQQ Call Strike	Gamma
36	0.007	43	0.085	50	0.050
37	0.013	44	0.092	51	0.039
38	0.023	45	0.093	52	0.029
39	0.034	46	0.090	53	0.021
40	0.047	47	0.083	54	0.015
41	0.062	48	0.073		
42	0.075	49	0.061		

EXHIBIT 2.7 Option gamma.

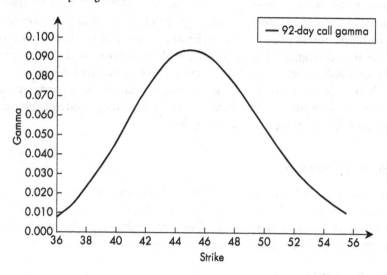

deltas much at all. The chances of their money status changing between now and expiration would not be significantly different statistically given a small stock price change. They have the smallest gammas in the table.

The highest gammas shown here are around the ATM strike prices. (Note that because of factors not yet discussed, the strike that is exactly at-the-money may not have the highest gamma. The highest gamma is likely to occur at a slightly higher strike price.) Exhibit 2.7 shows a graph of the corresponding numbers in Exhibit 2.6.

EXHIBIT 2.8 Gamma as time passes.

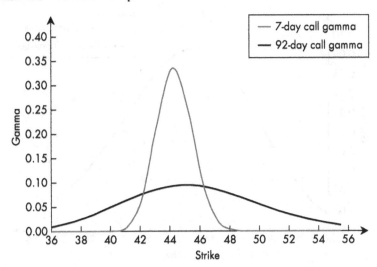

A decrease in the time to expiration solidifies the likelihood of ITMs or OTMs remaining as such. But an ATM option's moneyness at expiration remains to the very end uncertain. As expiration draws nearer, the gamma decreases for ITMs and OTMs and increases for the ATM strikes. Exhibit 2.8 shows the same 92-day QQQ calls plotted against 7-day QQQ calls.

At seven days until expiration, there is less time for price action in the stock to change the expected moneyness at expiration of ITMs or OTMs. ATM options, however, continue to be in play. Here, the ATM gamma is approaching 0.35. But the strikes below 41 and above 48 have 0 gamma.

Similarly-priced securities that tend to experience bigger price swings may have strikes $3 away-from-the-money with seven-day gammas greater than zero. The volatility of the underlying will affect gamma, too. Exhibit 2.9 shows the same 19 percent volatility QQQ calls in contrast with a graph of the gamma if the volatility is doubled.

Raising the volatility assumption flattens the curve, causing ITM and OTM to have higher gamma while lowering the gamma for ATMs.

Short-term ATM options with low volatility have the highest gamma. Lower gamma is found in ATMs when volatility is higher and it is lower for ITMs and OTMs and in longer-dated options.

EXHIBIT 2.9   Gamma as volatility changes.

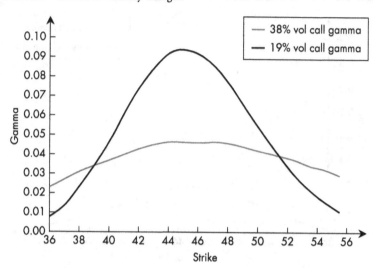

Theta

Option prices can be broken down into two parts: intrinsic value and time value. Intrinsic value is easily measurable. It is simply the ITM part of the premium. Time value, or extrinsic value, is what's left over—the premium paid over parity for the option. All else held constant, the more time left in the life of the option, the more valuable it is—there is more time for the stock to move. And as the useful life of an option decreases, so does its time value.

The decline in the value of an option because of the passage of time is called time decay, or erosion. Incremental measurements of time decay are represented by the Greek letter theta (θ). *Theta is the rate of change in an option's price given a unit change in the time to expiration.* What exactly is the *unit* involved here? That depends.

Some providers of option greeks will display thetas that represent one day's worth of time decay. Some will show thetas representing seven days of decay. In the case of a one-day theta, the figure may be based on a seven-day week or on a week counting only trading days. The most common and, arguably, most useful display of this figure is the one-day theta based on the seven-day week. There are, after all, seven days in a week, each day of which can see an occurrence with the potential to cause a revaluation in the stock price (that is, news can come out on Saturday or Sunday). The one-day theta based on a seven-day week will be used throughout this book.

Taking the Day Out

When the number of days to expiration used in the pricing model declines from, say, 32 days to 31 days, the price of the option decreases by the amount of the theta, all else held constant. But when is the day "taken out"? It is intuitive to think that after the market closes, the model is changed to reflect the passing of one day's time. But, in fact, this change is logically anticipated and may be priced in early.

In the earlier part of the week, option prices can often be observed getting cheaper relative to the stock price sometime in the middle of the day. This is because traders will commonly take the day out of their model during trading hours after the underlying stabilizes following the morning business. On Fridays and sometimes Thursdays, traders will take all or part of the weekend out. Commonly, by Friday afternoon, traders will be using Monday's days to value their options.

When option prices are seen getting cheaper on, say, a Friday, how can one tell whether this is the effect of the market taking the weekend out or a change in some other input, such as volatility? To some degree, it doesn't matter. Remember, the model is used to reflect what the market is doing, not the other way around. In many cases, it's logical to presume that small devaluations in option prices intraday can be attributed to the routine of the market taking the day out.

Friend or Foe?

Theta can be a good thing or a bad thing, depending on the position. Theta hurts long option positions; whereas it helps short option positions. Take an 80-strike call with a theoretical value of 3.16 on a stock at $82 a share. The 32-day 80 call has a theta of 0.03. If a trader owned one of these calls, the trader's position would theoretically lose 0.03, or $0.03, as the time until expiration change from 32 to 31 days. This trader has a negative theta position. A trader short one of these calls would have an overnight theoretical profit of $0.03 attributed to theta. This trader would have a positive theta.

Theta affects put traders as well. Using all the same modeling inputs, the 32-day 80-strike put would have a theta of 0.02. A put holder would theoretically lose $0.02 a day, and a put writer would theoretically make $0.02. Long options carry with them negative theta; short options carry positive theta.

A higher theta for the call than for the put of the same strike price is common when an interest rate greater than zero is used in the pricing model. As will be discussed in greater detail in the section on rho, interest causes the time value of the call to be higher than that of the corresponding put. At expiration, there is no time value left in either option. Because the call begins with more time value, its premium must decline at a faster rate than that of the put. Most modeling software will attribute the disparate rates of decline in value all to theta, whereas some modeling interfaces will make clear the distinction between the effect of time decay and the effect of interest on the put-call pair.

The Effect of Moneyness and Stock Price on Theta

Theta is not a constant. As variables influencing option values change, theta can change, too. One such variable is the option's moneyness. Exhibit 2.10 shows theoretical values (theos), time values, and thetas for 3-month options on Adobe (ADBE). In this example, Adobe is trading at $31.30 a share with three months until expiration. The more ITM a call or a put gets, the higher its theoretical value. But when studying an option's time decay, one needs to be concerned only with the option's time value, because intrinsic value is not subject to time decay.

The ATM options shown here have higher time value than ITM or OTM options. Hence, they have more time premium to lose in the same three-month period. ATM options have the highest rate of decay, which is reflected in higher thetas. As the stock price changes, the theta value will change to reflect its change in moneyness.

EXHIBIT 2.10 Adobe theos and thetas (Adobe at $31.30).

Call Theo.	Call Time Value	Call Theta	Strike	Put Theo.	Put Time Value	Put Theta
11.55	0.25	0.004	20	0.01	0.01	0.004
9.15	0.35	0.008	22.5	0.07	0.07	0.003
6.8	0.5	0.011	25	0.2	0.2	0.006
4.7	0.9	0.017	27.5	0.59	0.59	0.011
2.9	1.6	0.019	30	1.28	1.28	0.014
1.54	1.54	0.018	32.5	2.42	1.22	0.013
0.7	0.7	0.015	35	4.1	0.4	0.009
0.27	0.27	0.008	37.5	6.26	0.06	0.003
0.09	0.09	0.005	40	8.7	0	0

If this were a higher-priced stock, say, 10 times the stock price used in this example, with all other inputs held constant, the option values, and therefore the thetas, would be higher. If this were a stock trading at $313, the 325-strike call would have a theoretical value of 16.39 and a one-day theta of 0.189, given inputs used otherwise identical to those in the Adobe example.

The Effects of Volatility and Time on Theta

Stock price is not the only factor that affects theta values. Volatility and time to expiration come into play here as well. The volatility input to the pricing model has a direct relationship to option values. The higher the volatility, the higher the value of the option. Higher-valued options decay at a faster rate than lower-valued options—they have to; their time values will both be zero at expiration. All else held constant, the higher the volatility assumption, the higher the theta.

The days to expiration have a direct relationship to option values as well. As the number of days to expiration decreases, the rate at which an option decays may change, depending on the relationship of the stock price to the strike price. ATM options tend to decay at a nonlinear rate—that is, they lose value faster as expiration approaches—whereas the time values of ITM and OTM options decay at a steadier rate.

Consider a hypothetical stock trading at $70 a share. Exhibit 2.11 shows how the theoretical values of the 75-strike call and the 70-strike call decline with the passage of time, holding all other parameters constant.

EXHIBIT 2.11 Rate of decay: ATM vs. OTM.

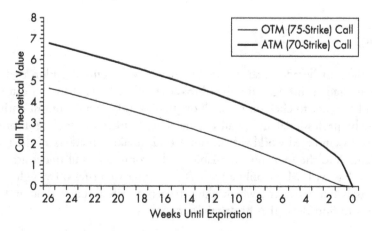

EXHIBIT 2.12 Theta as expiration approaches.

Days to Exp.	ATM Theta
10	0.075
9	0.079
8	0.084
7	0.089
6	0.096
5	0.106
4	0.118
3	0.137
2	0.171
1	0.443

The OTM 75-strike call has a fairly steady rate of time decay over this 26-week period. The ATM 70-strike call, however, begins to lose its value at an increasing rate as expiration draws nearer. The acceleration of premium erosion continues until the option expires. Exhibit 2.12 shows the thetas for this ATM call during the last 10 days before expiration.

Incidentally, in this example, when there is one day to expiration, the theoretical value of this call is about 0.44. The final day before expiration ultimately sees the entire time premium erode.

Vega

Over the past decade or so, computers have revolutionized option trading. Options traded through an online broker are filled faster than you can say, "Oops! I meant to click on puts." Now trading is facilitated almost entirely online by professional and retail traders alike. Market and trading information is disseminated worldwide in subseconds, making markets all the more efficient. And the tools now available to the common retail trader are very powerful as well. Many online brokers and other web sites offer high-powered tools like screeners, which allow traders to sift through thousands of options to find those that fit certain parameters.

Using a screener to find ATM calls on same-priced stocks—say, stocks trading at $40 a share—can yield a result worth talking about here. One $40 stock can have a 40-strike call trading at around 0.50, while a different $40 stock can have a 40 call with the same time to expiration trading at more like 2.00. Why? The model doesn't know the name of the company, what industry it's in, or what its price-to-earnings ratio is. It is a mathematical equation with six inputs. If five of the inputs—the stock price, strike price, time to expiration, interest rate, and dividends—are identical for two different options but they're trading at different prices, the difference must be the sixth variable, which is volatility.

Implied Volatility (IV) and Vega

The volatility component of option values is called implied volatility (IV). (For more on implied volatility and how it relates to vega, see Chapter 3.) IV is a percentage, although in practice the percent sign is often omitted. This is the value entered into a pricing model, in conjunction with the other variables, that returns the option's theoretical value. The higher the volatility input, the higher the theoretical value, holding all other variables constant. The IV level can change and often does—sometimes dramatically. When IV rises or falls, option prices rise and fall in line with it. But by how much?

The relationship between changes in IV and changes in an option's value is measured by the option's vega. *Vega is the rate of change of an option's theoretical value relative to a change in implied volatility.* Specifically, if the IV rises or declines by one percentage point, the theoretical value of the option rises or declines by the amount of the option's vega, respectively. For example, if a call with a theoretical value of 1.82 has a vega of 0.06 and IV rises one percentage point from, say, 17 percent to 18 percent, the new theoretical value of the call will be 1.88—it would rise by 0.06, the amount of the vega. If, conversely, the IV declines 1 percentage point, from 17 percent to 16 percent, the call value will drop to 1.76—that is, it would decline by the vega.

A put with the same expiration month and the same strike on the same underlying will have the same vega value as its corresponding call. In this example, raising or lowering IV by one percentage point would cause the corresponding put value to rise or decline by $0.06, just like the call.

An increase in IV and the consequent increase in option value helps the P&(L) of long option positions and hurts short option positions. Buying a call or a put establishes a long vega position. For short options, the opposite is true. Rising IV adversely affects P&(L), whereas falling IV helps. Shorting a call or put establishes a short vega position.

The Effect of Moneyness on Vega

Like the other greeks, vega is a snapshot that is a function of multiple facets of determinants influencing option value. The stock price's relationship to the strike price is a major determining factor of an option's vega. IV affects only the time value portion of an option. Because ATM options have the greatest amount of time value, they will naturally have higher vegas. ITM and OTM options have lower vega values than those of the ATM options.

Exhibit 2.13 shows an example of 186-day options on AT&T Inc. (T), their time value, and the corresponding vegas.

Note that the 30-strike calls and puts have the highest time values. This strike boasts the highest vega value, at 0.085. The lower the time premium, the lower the vega—therefore, the less incremental IV changes affect the option. Since higher-priced stocks have higher time premium (in absolute terms, not necessarily in percentage terms) they will have higher vega. Incidentally, if this were a $300 stock instead of a $30 stock, the 186-day ATMs would have a 0.850 vega, if all other model inputs remain the same.

The Effect of Implied Volatility on Vega

The distribution of vega values among the strike prices shown in Exhibit 2.13 holds for a specific IV level. The vegas in Exhibit 2.13 were calculated using a 20 percent IV. If a different IV were used in the calculation, the

EXHIBIT 2.13 AT&T theos and vegas (T at $30, 186 days to Expry, 20% IV).

Call Theo.	Call Time Value	Strike	Put Theo.	Put Time Value	Vega
7.64	0.14	**22.5**	0.03	0.03	**0.009**
5.3	0.3	**25**	0.17	0.17	**0.033**
3.28	0.78	**27.5**	0.64	0.64	**0.066**
1.78	1.78	**30**	1.63	1.63	**0.085**
0.85	0.85	**32.5**	3.18	0.68	**0.077**
0.35	0.35	**35**	5.17	0.17	**0.053**
0.13	0.13	**37.5**	7.5	0	**0.02**

relationship of the vegas to one another might change. Exhibit 2.14 shows what the vegas would be at different IV levels.

Note in Exhibit 2.14 that at all three IV levels, the ATM strike maintains a similar vega value. But the vegas of the ITM and OTM options can be significantly different. Lower IV inputs tend to cause ITM and OTM vegas to decline. Higher IV inputs tend to cause vegas to increase for ITMs and OTMs.

The Effect of Time on Vega

As time passes, there is less time premium in the option that can be affected by changes in IV. Consequently, vega gets smaller as expiration approaches. Exhibit 2.15 shows the decreasing vega of a 50-strike call on a $50 stock with a 25 percent IV as time to expiration decreases. Notice that as the value of this ATM option decreases at its nonlinear rate of decay, the vega decreases in a similar fashion.

EXHIBIT 2.14 Vega and IV.

Strike	Vega at 15 IV	Vega at 20 IV	Vega at 25 IV
22.5	0.002	0.009	0.019
25	0.017	0.033	0.045
27.5	0.056	0.066	0.071
30	0.085	0.085	0.085
32.5	0.069	0.077	0.081
35	0.035	0.053	0.065
37.5	0.012	0.02	0.045

EXHIBIT 2.15 The effect of time on vega.

Weeks Until Expiration	Vega of ATM Call	Weeks Until Expiration	Vega of ATM Call	Weeks Until Expiration	Vega of ATM Call
1	0.028	5	0.061	9	0.082
2	0.039	6	0.067	10	0.086
3	0.048	7	0.073	11	0.091
4	0.055	8	0.077	12	0.094

Rho

One of my early jobs in the options business was clerking on the floor of the Chicago Board of Trade in what was called the bond room. On one of my first days on the job, the trader I worked for asked me what his position was in a certain strike. I told him he was long 200 calls and long 300 puts. "I'm long 500 puts?" he asked. "No," I corrected, "you're long 200 calls and 300 puts." At this point, he looked at me like I was from another planet and said, "That's 500. A put is a call; a call is a put." That lesson was the beginning of my journey into truly understanding options.

Put-Call Parity

Put and call values are mathematically bound together by an equation referred to as put-call parity. In its basic form, put-call parity states:

$$c + PV(x) = p + s$$

where

c   = call value,
PV(x) = present value of the strike price,
p   = put value, and
s   = stock price.

The put-call parity assumes that options are not exercised before expiration (that is, that they are European style). This version of the put-call parity is for European options on non-dividend-paying stocks. Put-call parity can be modified to reflect the values of options on stocks that pay dividends. In practice, equity-option traders look at the equation in a slightly different way:

$$Stock = Call + Strike - Put - Interest^2 + Dividend$$

Traders serious about learning to trade options must know put-call parity backward and forward. Why? First, by algebraically rearranging this equation, it can be inferred that synthetically equivalent positions can be established by simply adding stock to an option. Again, a put is a call; a call is a put.

$$Call = Stock + Put + Interest - Dividend - Strike$$

and

$$\text{Put} = \text{Call} + \text{Strike} - \text{Interest} + \text{Dividend} - \text{Stock}$$

For example, a long call is synthetically equal to a long stock position plus a long put on the same strike, once interest and dividends are figured in. A synthetic long stock position is created by buying a call and selling a put of the same month and strike. Understanding synthetic relationships is intrinsic to understanding options. A more comprehensive discussion of synthetic relationships and tactical considerations for creating synthetic positions is offered in Chapter 6.

Put-call parity also aids in valuing options. If put-call parity shows a difference in the value of the call versus the value of the put with the same strike, there may be an arbitrage opportunity. That translates as "riskless profit." Buying the call and selling it synthetically (short put and short stock) could allow a profit to be locked in if the prices are disparate. Arbitrageurs tend to hold synthetic put and call prices pretty close together. Generally, only professional traders can capture these types of profit opportunities, by trading big enough positions to make very small profits (a penny or less per contract sometimes) matter. Retail traders may be able to take advantage of a disparity in put and call values to some extent, however, by buying or selling the synthetic as a substitute for the actual option if the position can be established at a better price synthetically.

Another reason that a working knowledge of put-call parity is essential is that it helps attain a better understanding of how changes in the interest rate affect option values. The greek rho measures this change. Rho is the rate of change in an option's value relative to a change in the interest rate.

Although some modeling programs may display this number differently, most display a rho for the call and a rho for the put, both illustrating the sensitivity to a one-percentage-point change in the interest rate. When the interest rate rises by one percentage point, the value of the call increases by the amount of its rho and the put decreases by the amount of its rho. Likewise, when the interest rate decrease by one percentage point, the value of the call decreases by its rho and the put increases by its rho. For example, a call with a rho of 0.12 will increase \$0.12 in value if the interest rate used in the model is increased by one percentage point. Of course, interest rates usually don't rise or fall one percentage point in one day. More commonly, rates will have incremental changes of 25 basis points. That means a call with a 0.12 rho will theoretically gain \$0.03 given an increase of 0.25 percentage points.

Mathematically, this change in option value as a product of a change in the interest rate makes sense when looking at the formula for put-call parity.

$$\uparrow \textbf{Call} = \text{Stock} + \text{Put} + \uparrow \textbf{Interest} - \text{Dividend} - \text{Strike}$$

and

$$\downarrow \textbf{Put} = \text{Call} + \text{Strike} - \uparrow \textbf{Interest} + \text{Dividend} - \text{Stock}$$

But the change makes sense intuitively, too, when a call is considered as a cheaper substitute for owning the stock. For example, compare a $100 stock with a three-month 60-strike call on that same stock. Being so far ITM, there would likely be no time value in the call. If the call can be purchased at parity, which alternative would be a superior investment, the call for $40 or the stock for $100? Certainly, the call would be. It costs less than half as much as the stock but has the same reward potential; and the $60 not spent on the stock can be invested in an interest-bearing account. This interest advantage adds value to the call. Raising the interest rate increases this value, and lowering it decreases the interest component of the value of the call.

A similar concept holds for puts. Professional traders often get a short-stock rebate on proceeds from a short-stock sale. This is simply interest earned on the capital received when the stock is shorted. Is it better to pay interest on the price of a put for a position that gives short exposure or to receive interest on the credit from shorting the stock? There is an interest disadvantage to owning the put. Therefore, a rise in interest rates devalues puts.

This interest effect becomes evident when comparing ATM call and put prices. For example, with interest at 5 percent, three-month options on an $80 stock that pays a $0.25 dividend before option expiration might look something like this:

$$\text{Stock} = 80$$

$$\text{Three-month 80-strike call} = 3.75$$

$$\text{Three-month 80-strike put} = 3.00$$

The ATM call is higher in theoretical value than the ATM put by $0.75. That amount can be justified using put-call parity:

$$Stock = Call + Strike - Put - Interest + Dividend$$
$$80 = 3.75 + 80 - 3.00 - 1 + 0.25$$

(Here, simple interest of $1 is calculated as $80 \times 0.05 \times [90 / 360] = 1$.)

Changes in market conditions are kept in line by the put-call parity. For example, if the price of the call rises because of an increase in IV, the price of the put will rise in step. If the interest rate rises by a quarter of a percentage point, from 5 percent to 5.25 percent, the interest calculated for three months on the 80-strike will increase from $1 to $1.05, causing the difference between the call and put price to widen. Another variable that affects the amount of interest and therefore option prices is the time until expiration.

The Effect of Time on Rho

The more time until expiration, the greater the effect interest rate changes will have on options. In the previous example, a 25-basis-point change in the interest rate on the 80-strike based on a three-month period caused a change of 0.05 to the interest component of put-call parity. That is, $80 \times 0.0025 \times (90/360) = 0.05$. If a longer period were used in the example—say, one year—the effect would be more profound; it will be $0.20: $80 \times 0.0025 \times (360/360) = 0.20$. This concept is evident when the rhos of options with different times to expiration are studied.

Exhibit 2.16 shows the rhos of ATM Procter & Gamble Co. (PG) calls with various expiration months. The 750-day Long-Term Equity AnticiPation

EXHIBIT 2.16   The effect of time on rho (Procter & Gamble @ $64.34)

	Rho of 22-Day Procter & Gamble ATM Call	Rho of 113-Day Procter & Gamble ATM Call	Rho of 386-Day Procter & Gamble ATM LEAPS Call	Rho of 750-Day Procter & Gamble ATM LEAPS Call
Procter & Gamble 65 Call	0.015	0.106	0.414	0.858

Securities (LEAPS) have a rho of 0.858. As the number of days until expiration decreases, rho decreases. The 22-day calls have a rho of only 0.015. Rho is usually a fairly insignificant factor in the value of short-term options, but it can come into play much more with long-term option strategies involving LEAPS.

Why the Numbers Don't Don't Always Add Up

There will be many times when studying the rho of options in an option chain will reveal seemingly counterintuitive results. To be sure, the numbers don't always add up to what appears logical. One reason for this is rounding. Another is that traders are more likely to use simple interest in calculating value, whereas the model uses compound interest. Hard-to-borrow stocks and stocks involved in mergers and acquisitions may have put-call parities that don't work out right. But another, more common and more significant fly in the ointment is early exercise.

Since the interest input in put-call parity is a function of the strike price, it is reasonable to expect that the higher the strike price, the greater the effect of interest on option prices will be. For European options, this is true to a large extent, in terms of aggregate impact of interest on the call and put pair. Strikes below the price where the stock is trading have a higher rho associated with the call relative to the put, whereas strikes above the stock price have a higher rho associated with the put relative to the call. Essentially, the more in-the-money an option is, the higher its rho. But with European options, observing the aggregate of the absolute values of the call and put rhos would show a higher combined rho the higher the strike.

With American options, the put can be exercised early. A trader will exercise a put before expiration if the alternative—being short stock and receiving a short stock rebate—is a wiser choice based on the price of the put. Professional traders may own stock as a hedge against a put. They may exercise deep ITM puts (1.00-delta puts) to avoid paying interest on capital charges related to the stock. The potential for early exercise is factored into models that price American options. Here, when puts get deeper in-the-money—that is, more apt to be exercised—the rho decreases. When the strike price is very high relative to the stock price—meaning the put is very deep ITM—and there is little or no time value left to the call or the put, the aggregate put-call rho can be zero. Rho is discussed in greater detail in Chapter 7.

THE GREEKS DEFINED

Delta (Δ) is:

1. The rate of change in an option's value relative to a change in the underlying asset price.
2. The derivative of the graph of an option's value in relation to the underlying asset price.
3. The equivalent of underlying asset represented by an option position.
4. The estimate of the likelihood of an option's expiring in-the-money.

Gamma (Γ) is the rate of change in an option's delta given a change in the price of the underlying asset.

Theta (θ) is the rate of change in an option's value given a unit change in the time to expiration.

Vega is the rate of change in an option's value relative to a change in implied volatility.

Rho (ρ) is the rate of change in an option's value relative to a change in the interest rate.

Where to Find Option Greeks

There are many sources from which to obtain greeks. The Internet is an excellent resource. Googling "option greeks" will display links to over four million web pages, many of which have real-time greeks or an option calculator. An option calculator is a simple interface that accepts the input of the six variables to the model and yields a theoretical value and the greeks for a single option.

Some web sites devoted to option education, such as MarketTaker.com/option_modeling, have free calculators that can be used for modeling positions and using the greeks.

In practice, many of the option-trading platforms commonly in use have sophisticated analytics that involve greeks. Most options-friendly online brokers provide trading platforms that enable traders to conduct comprehensive manipulations of the greeks. For example, traders can look at the greeks for their positions up or down one, two, or three standard deviations. Or they can see what happens to their position greeks if IV or time changes. With many trading platforms, position greeks are updated in real time with changes in the stock price—an invaluable feature for active traders.

Caveats with Regard to Online Greeks

Often, online greeks are one click away, requiring little effort on the part of the trader. Having greeks calculated automatically online is a quick and convenient way to eyeball greeks for an option. But there is one major problem with online greeks: reliability.

For active option traders, greeks are essential. There is no point in using these figures if their accuracy cannot be assured. Experienced traders can often spot these inaccuracies a proverbial mile away.

When looking at greeks from an online source that does not require you to enter parameters into a model (as would be the case with professional option-trading platforms), special attention needs to be paid to the relationship of the option's theoretical values to the bid and offer. One must be cautious if the theoretical value of the option lies outside the bid-ask spread. This scenario can exist for brief periods of time, but arbitrageurs tend to prevent this from occurring routinely. If several options in a chain all have theoretical values below the bid or above the offer, there is probably a problem with one or more of the inputs used in the model. Remember, an option-pricing model is just that: a model. It reflects what is occurring in the market. It doesn't tell where an option should be trading.

The complex changes that occur intraday in the market—taking the day or weekend out, changes in stock price, volatility, and the interest rate—are not always kept current. The user of the model must keep close watch. It's not reasonable to expect the computer to do the thinking for you. Automatically calculated greeks can be used as a starting point. But before using these figures in the decision-making process, the trader may have to override the parameters that were used in the online calculation to make the theos line up with market prices. Professional traders will ignore online greeks altogether. They will use the greeks that are products of the inputs they entered in their trading software. It comes down to this: if you want something done right, do it yourself.

Thinking Greek

The challenge of trading option greeks is to adapt to thinking in terms of delta, gamma, theta, vega, and rho. One should develop a feel for how greeks react to changing market conditions. Greeks need to be monitored as closely as and in some cases more closely than the option's price itself. This greek philosophy forms the foundation of option trading for active traders. It offers a logical way to monitor positions and provides a medium in and of itself to trade.

Notes

1. Please note that definition 4 is not necessarily mathematically accurate. This "trader's definition" is included in the text because many option traders use delta as a quick rule of thumb for estimating probability without regard to the mathematical shortcomings of doing so.
2. Note that the interest input in the equation is the interest, in dollars and cents, on the strike. Technically, this would be calculated as compounded interest, but in practice many traders use simple interest as a quick and convenient way to do the calculation.

CHAPTER 3

Understanding Volatility

Most option strategies involve trading volatility in one way or another. It's easy to think of trading in terms of direction. But trading volatility? Volatility is an abstract concept; it's a different animal than the linear trading paradigm used by most conventional market players. As an option trader, it is essential to understand and master volatility.

Many traders trade without a solid understanding of volatility and its effect on option prices. These traders are often unhappily surprised when volatility moves against them. They mistake the adverse option price movements that result from volatility for getting ripped off by the market makers or some other market voodoo. Or worse, they surrender to the fact that they simply don't understand why sometimes these unexpected price movements occur in options. They accept that that's just the way it is.

Part of what gets in the way of a ready understanding of volatility is context. The term *volatility* can have a few different meanings in the options business. There are three different uses of the word *volatility* that an option trader must be concerned with: historical volatility, implied volatility, and expected volatility.

Historical Volatility

Imagine there are two stocks: Stock A and Stock B. Both are trading at around $100 a share. Over the past month, a typical end-of-day net change in the price of Stock A has been up or down $5 to $7. During that same period, a typical daily move in Stock B has been something more like up or down $1 or $2. Stock A has tended to move more than Stock B as a percentage of its price, without regard to direction. Therefore, Stock A is more volatile—in the common usage of the word—than Stock B. In the options vernacular, Stock A has a higher historical volatility than Stock B. Historical volatility (HV) is the annualized standard deviation of daily returns. Also called *realized volatility, statistical volatility,* or *stock volatility,* HV is a measure of how volatile the price movement of a security has been during a certain period of time. But exactly how much higher is Stock A's HV than Stock B's?

In order to objectively compare the volatilities of two stocks, historical volatility must be quantified. HV relates this volatility information in an objective numerical form. The volatility of a stock is expressed in terms of standard deviation.

Standard Deviation

Although knowing the mathematical formula behind standard deviation is not entirely necessary, understanding the concept is essential. Standard deviation, sometimes represented by the Greek letter sigma (), is a mathematical calculation that measures the dispersion of data from a mean value. In this case, the mean is the average stock price over a certain period of time. The farther from the mean the dispersion of occurrences (data) was during the period, the greater the standard deviation.

Occurrences, in this context, are usually the closing prices of the stock. Some utilizers of volatility data may use other inputs (a weighted average of high, low, and closing prices, for example) in calculating standard deviation. Close-to-close price data are the most commonly used.

The number of occurrences, a function of the time period, used in calculating standard deviation may vary. Many online purveyors of this data use the closing prices from the last 30 consecutive trading days to calculate HV. Weekends and holidays are not factored into the equation since there is no trading, and therefore no volatility, when the market isn't open. After each day, the oldest price is taken out of the calculation and replaced by the most recent closing price. Using a shorter or longer period can yield different results and can be useful in studying a stock's volatility.

Knowing the number of days used in the calculation is crucial to understanding what the output represents. For example, if the last 5 trading days were extremely volatile, but the 25 days prior to that were comparatively calm, the 5-day standard deviation would be higher than the 30-day standard deviation.

Standard deviation is stated as a percentage move in the price of the asset. If a $100 stock has a standard deviation of 15 percent, a one-standard-deviation move in the stock would be either $85 or $115—a 15 percent move in either direction. Standard deviation is used for comparison purposes. A stock with a standard deviation of 15 percent has experienced bigger moves—has been more volatile—during the relevant time period than a stock with a standard deviation of 6 percent.

When the frequency of occurrences are graphed, the result is known as a distribution curve. There are many different shapes that a distribution curve can take, depending on the nature of the data being observed. In general, option-pricing models assume that stock prices adhere to a lognormal distribution.

The shape of the distribution curve for stock prices has long been the topic of discussion among traders and academics alike. Regardless of what the true shape of the curve is, the concept of standard deviation applies just the same. For the purpose of illustrating standard deviation, a normal distribution is used here.

When the graph of data adheres to a normal distribution, the result is a symmetrical bell-shaped curve. Standard deviation can be shown on the bell curve to either side of the mean. Exhibit 3.1 represents a typical bell curve with standard deviation.

Large moves in a security are typically less frequent than small ones. Events that cause big changes in the price of a stock, like a company's being acquired by another or discovering its chief financial officer cooking the books, are not a daily occurrence. Comparatively smaller price fluctuations that reflect less extreme changes in the value of the corporation are more typically seen day to day. Statistically, the most probable outcome for a price change is found around the midpoint of the curve. What constitutes

EXHIBIT 3.1 Standard deviation.

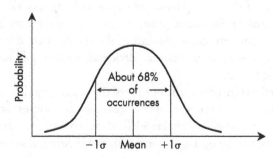

a large move or a small move, however, is unique to each individual security. For example, a two percent move in an index like the Standard & Poor's (S&P) 500 may be considered a big one-day move, while a two percent move in a particularly active tech stock may be a daily occurrence. Standard deviation offers a statistical explanation of what constitutes a typical move.

In Exhibit 3.1, the lines to either side of the mean represent one standard deviation. About 68 percent of all occurrences will take place between up one standard deviation and down one standard deviation. Two- and three-standard-deviation values could be shown on the curve as well. About 95 percent of data occur between up and down two standard deviations and about 99.7 percent between up and down three standard deviations. One standard deviation is the relevant figure in determining historical volatility.

Standard Deviation and Historical Volatility

When standard deviation is used in the context of historical volatility, it is annualized to state what the one-year volatility would be. Historical volatility is the annualized standard deviation of daily returns. This means that if a stock is trading at $100 a share and its historical volatility is 10 percent, then about 68 percent of the occurrences (closing prices) are expected to fall between $90 and $110 during a one-year period (based on recent past performance).

Simply put, historical volatility shows how volatile a stock has been based on price movements that have occurred in the past. Although option traders may study HV to make informed decisions as to the value of options traded on a stock, it is not a direct function of option prices. For this, we must look to implied volatility.

Implied Volatility

Volatility is one of the six inputs of an option-pricing model. Some of the other inputs—strike price, stock price, the number of days until expiration, and the current interest rate—are easily observable. Past dividend policy allows an educated guess as to what the dividend input should be. But where can volatility be found?

As discussed in Chapter 2, the output of the pricing model—the option's theoretical value—in practice is not necessarily an output at all. When option traders use the pricing model, they commonly substitute the actual price at which the option is trading for the theoretical value. A value in the middle of the bid-ask spread is often used. The pricing model can be considered to be a complex algebra equation in which any variable can be solved for. If the theoretical value is known—which it is—it along with the five known inputs can be combined to solve for the unknown volatility.

Implied volatility (IV) is the volatility input in a pricing model that, in conjunction with the other inputs, returns the theoretical value of an option matching the market price.

For a specific stock price, a given implied volatility will yield a unique option value. Take a stock trading at $44.22 that has the 60-day 45-strike call at a theoretical value of $1.10 with an 18 percent implied volatility level. If the stock price remains constant, but IV rises to 19 percent, the value of the call will rise by its vega, which in this case is about 0.07. The new value of the call will be $1.17. Raising IV another point, to 20 percent, raises the theoretical value by another $0.07, to $1.24. The question is: What would cause implied volatility to change?

Supply and Demand: Not Just a Good Idea, It's the Law!

Options are an excellent vehicle for speculation. However, the existence of the options market is better justified by the primary economic purpose of options: as a risk management tool. Hedgers use options to protect their assets from adverse price movements, and when the perception of risk increases, so does demand for this protection. In this context, risk means volatility—the potential for larger moves to the upside and downside. The relative prices of options are driven higher by increased demand for protective options when the market anticipates greater volatility. And option prices are driven lower by greater supply—that is, selling of options—when the market expects lower volatility. Like those of all assets, option prices are subject to the law of supply and demand.

When volatility is expected to rise, demand for options is not limited to hedgers. Speculative traders would arguably be more inclined to buy a call than to buy the stock if they are bullish but expect future volatility to be high. Calls require a lower cash outlay. If the stock moves adversely, there is less capital at risk, but still similar profit potential.

When volatility is expected to be low, hedging investors are less inclined to pay for protection. They are more likely to sell back the options they may have bought previously to recoup some of the expense. Options are a decaying asset. Investors are more likely to write calls against stagnant stocks to generate income in anticipated low-volatility environments. Speculative traders will implement option-selling strategies, such as short strangles or iron condors, in an attempt to capitalize on stocks they believe won't move much. The rising supply of options puts downward pressure on option prices.

Many traders sum up IV in two words: *fear* and *greed*. When option prices rise and fall, not because of changes in the stock price, time to expiration, interest rates, or dividends, but because of pure supply and demand, it is implied volatility that is the varying factor. There are many contributing factors to traders' willingness to demand or supply options. Anticipation of events such as earnings reports, Federal Reserve announcements, or the release of other news particular to an individual stock can cause anxiety, or fear, in traders and consequently increase demand for options that causes IV to rise. IV can fall when there is complacency in the market or when the anticipated news has been announced and anxiety wanes. "Buy the rumor, sell the news" is often reflected in option implied volatility. When there is little fear of market movement, traders use options to squeeze out more profits—greed.

Arbitrageurs, such as market makers who trade delta neutral—a strategy that will be discussed further in Chapters 12 and 13—must be relentlessly conscious of implied volatility. When immediate directional risk is eliminated from a position, IV becomes the traded commodity. Arbitrageurs who focus their efforts on trading volatility (colloquially called *vol traders*) tend to think about bids and offers in terms of IV. In the mind of a vol trader, option prices are translated into volatility levels. A trader may look at a particular option and say it is 30 bid at 31 offer. These values do not represent the prices of the options but rather the corresponding implied volatilities. The meaning behind the trader's remark is that the market is willing to buy implied volatility at 30 percent and sell it at 31 percent. The actual prices of the options themselves are much less relevant to this type of trader.

Should HV and IV Be the Same?

Most option positions have exposure to volatility in two ways. First, the profitability of the position is usually somewhat dependent on movement (or lack of movement) of the underlying security. This is exposure to HV. Second, profitability can be affected by changes in supply and demand for the options. This is exposure to IV. In general, a long option position benefits when volatility—both historical and implied—increases. A short option position benefits when volatility—historical and implied—decreases. That said, buying options is buying volatility and selling options is selling volatility.

The Relationship of HV and IV

It's intuitive that there should exist a direct relationship between the HV and IV. Empirically, this is often the case. Supply and demand for options, based on the market's expectations for a security's volatility, determines IV.

It is easy to see why IV and HV often act in tandem. But, although HV and IV are related, they are not identical. There are times when IV and HV move in opposite directions. This is not so illogical, if one considers the key difference between the two: HV is calculated from past stock price movements; it is what has happened. IV is ultimately derived from the market's expectation for future volatility.

If a stock typically has an HV of 30 percent and nothing is expected to change, it can be reasonable to expect that in the future the stock will continue to trade at a 30 percent HV. By that logic, assuming that nothing is expected to change, IV should be fairly close to HV. Market conditions do change, however. These changes are often regular and predictable. Earnings reports are released once a quarter in many stocks, Federal Open Market Committee meetings happen regularly, and dates of other special announcements are often disclosed to the public in advance. Although the outcome of these events cannot be predicted, when they will occur often can be. It is around these widely anticipated events that HV-IV divergences often occur.

HV-IV Divergence

An HV-IV divergence occurs when HV declines and IV rises or vice versa. The classic example is often observed before a company's quarterly earnings announcement, especially when there is lack of consensus among analysts' estimates. This scenario often causes HV to remain constant or decline while IV rises. The reason? When there is a great deal of uncertainty as to what the quarterly earnings will be, investors are reluctant to buy *or* sell the stock until the number is released. When this happens, the stock price movement (volatility) consolidates, causing the calculated HV to decline. IV, however, can rise as traders scramble to buy up options—bidding up their prices. When the news is out, the feared (or hoped for) move in the stock takes place (or doesn't), and HV and IV tend to converge again.

Expected Volatility

Whether trading options or stocks, simple or complex strategies, traders must consider volatility. For basic buy-and-hold investors, taking a potential investment's volatility into account is innate behavior. Do I buy conservative (nonvolatile) stocks or more aggressive (volatile) stocks? Taking into account volatility, based not just on a gut feeling but on hard numbers, can lead to better, more objective trading decisions.

Expected Stock Volatility

Option traders must have an even greater focus on volatility, as it plays a much bigger role in their profitability—or lack thereof. Because options can create highly leveraged positions, small moves can yield big profits or losses. Option traders must monitor the likelihood of movement in the underlying closely. Estimating what historical volatility (standard deviation) will be in the future can help traders quantify the probability of movement beyond a certain price point. This leads to better decisions about whether to enter a trade, when to adjust a position, and when to exit.

There is no way of knowing for certain what the future holds. But option data provide traders with tools to develop expectations for future stock volatility. IV is sometimes interpreted as the market's estimate of the future volatility of the underlying security. That makes it a ready-made estimation tool, but there are two caveats to bear in mind when using IV to estimate future stock volatility.

The first is that the market can be wrong. The market can wrongly price stocks. This mispricing can lead to a correction (up or down) in the prices of those stocks, which can lead to additional volatility, which may not be priced in to the options. Although there are traders and academics believe that the option market is fairly efficient in pricing volatility, there is a room for error. There is the possibility that the option market can be wrong.

Another caveat is that volatility is an annualized figure—the annualized standard deviation. Unless the IV of a LEAPS option that has exactly one year until expiration is substituted for the expected volatility of the underlying stock over exactly one year, IV is an incongruent estimation for the future stock volatility. In practice, the IV of an option must be adjusted to represent the period of time desired.

There is a common technique for deannualizing IV used by professional traders and retail traders alike.[1] The first step in this process to deannualize IV is to turn it into a one-day figure as opposed to one-year figure. This is accomplished by dividing IV by the square root of the number of trading days in a year. The number many traders use to approximate the number of trading days per year is 256, because its square root is a round number: 16. The formula is

$$\frac{IV}{\sqrt{256}} = 1\text{-day expected } \sigma$$

For example, a \$100 stock that has an at-the-money (ATM) call trading at a 32 percent volatility implies that there is about a 68 percent chance that the underlying stock will be between \$68 and \$132 in one year's time— that's \$100 ± (\$100 × 0.32). The estimation for the market's expectation for the volatility of the stock for one day in terms of standard deviation as a percentage of the price of the underlying is computed as follows:

$$\frac{0.32}{\sqrt{256}} = \frac{0.32}{16} = 0.02 \text{ or } 2\%$$

In one day's time, based on an IV of 32 percent, there is a 68 percent chance of the stock's being within 2 percent of the stock price—that's between \$98 and \$102.

There may be times when it is helpful for traders to have a volatility estimation for a period of time longer than one day—a week or a month, for example. This can be accomplished by multiplying the one-day volatility by the square root of the number of trading days in the relevant period. The equation is as follows:

$$\frac{IV}{\sqrt{256}} \times \sqrt{\text{Number of trading days in period}}$$

If the period in question is one month and there are 22 business days remaining in that month, the same \$100 stock with the ATM call trading at a 32 percent implied volatility would have a one-month volatility of 9.38 percent.

$$\left(\frac{0.32}{\sqrt{256}}\right) \times \sqrt{22} = 0.0938 \text{ or } 9.38\%$$

Based on this calculation for one month, it can be estimated that there is a 68 percent chance of the stock's closing between \$90.62 and \$109.38 based on an IV of 32 percent.

Expected Implied Volatility

Although there is a great deal of science that can be applied to calculating expected actual volatility, developing expectations for implied volatility is more of an art. This element of an option's price provides more risk and more opportunity. There are many traders who make their living distilling direction out of their positions and trading implied volatility. To be successful, a trader must forecast IV.

Conceptually, trading IV is much like trading anything else. A trader who thinks a stock is going to rise will buy the stock. A trader who thinks IV is going to rise will buy options. Directional stock traders, however, have many more analysis tools available to them than do vol traders. Stock traders have both technical analysis (TA) and fundamental analysis at their disposal.

Technical Analysis

There are scores, perhaps hundreds, of technical tools for analyzing stocks, but there are not many that are available for analyzing IV. Technical analysis is the study of market data, such as past prices or volume, which is manipulated in such a way that it better illustrates market activity. TA studies are usually represented graphically on a chart.

Developing TA tools for IV is more of a challenge than it is for stocks. One reason is that there is simply a lot more data to manage—for each stock, there may be hundreds of options listed on it. The only practical way of analyzing options from a TA standpoint is to use implied volatility. IV is more useful than raw historical option prices themselves. Information for both IV and HV is available in the form of volatility charts, or vol charts. (Vol charts are discussed in detail in Chapter 14.) Volatility charts are essential for analyzing options because they give more complete information.

To get a clear picture of what is going on with the price of an option (the goal of technical analysis for any asset), just observing the option price does not supply enough information for a trader to work with. It's incomplete. For example, if a call rises in value, why did it rise? What greek contributed to its value increase? Was it delta because the underlying stock rose? Or was it vega because volatility rose? How did time decay factor in? Using a volatility chart in conjunction with a conventional stock chart (and being aware of time decay) tells the whole, complete, story.

Another reason historical option prices are not used in TA is the option bid-ask spread. For most stocks, the difference between the bid and the ask is equal to a very small percentage of the stock's price. Because options are highly leveraged instruments, their bid-ask width can equal a much higher percentage of the price.

If a trader uses the last trade to graph an option's price, it could look as if a very large percentage move has occurred when in fact it has not. For example, if the option trades a small contract size on the bid (0.80), then on the offer (0.90) it would appear that the option rose 12.5 percent in value. This large percentage move is nothing more than market noise. Using volatility data based off the midpoint-of-the-market theoretical value eliminates such noise.

Fundamental Analysis

Fundamental analysis can have an important role in developing expectations for IV. Fundamental analysis is the study of economic factors that affect the value of an asset in order to determine what it is worth. With stocks, fundamental analysis may include studying income statements, balance sheets, and earnings reports. When the asset being studied is IV, there are fewer hard facts available. This is where the art of analyzing volatility comes into play.

Essentially, the goal is to understand the psychology of the market in relation to supply and demand for options. Where is the fear? Where is the complacency? When are news events anticipated? How important are they? Ultimately, the question becomes: what is the potential for movement in the underlying? The greater the chance of stock movement, the more likely it is that IV will rise. When unexpected news is announced, IV can rise quickly. The determination of the fundamental relevance of surprise announcements must be made quickly.

Unfortunately, these questions are subjective in nature. They require the trader to apply intuition and experience on a case-by-case basis. But there are a few observations to be made that can help a trader make better-educated decisions about IV.

Reversion to the Mean

The IVs of the options on many stocks and indexes tend to trade in a range unique to those option classes. This is referred to as the mean—or average—volatility level. Some securities will have smaller mean IV ranges than others. The range being observed should be established for a period long enough to confirm that it is a typical IV for the security, not just a temporary anomaly. Traders should study IV over the most recent 6-month period. When IV has changed significantly during that period, a 12-month study may be necessary. Deviations from this range, either above or below the established mean range, will occur from time to time. When following a breakout from the established range, it is common for IV to revert back to its normal range. This is commonly called *reversion to the mean* among volatility watchers.

The challenge is recognizing when things change and when they stay the same. If the fundamentals of the stock change in such a way as to give the options market reason to believe the stock will now be more or less volatile on an ongoing basis than it typically has been in the recent past, the IV may not revert to the mean. Instead, a new mean volatility level may be established.

When considering the likelihood of whether IV will revert to recent levels after it has deviated or find a new range, the time horizon and changes in the marketplace must be taken into account. For example, between 1998 and 2003 the mean volatility level of the SPX was around 20 percent to 30 percent. By the latter half of 2006, the mean IV was in the range of 10 percent to 13 percent. The difference was that between 1998 and 2003 was the buildup of "the tech bubble," as it was called by the financial media. Market volatility ultimately leveled off in 2003.

In a later era, between the fall of 2010 and late summer of 2011 SPX implied volatility settled in to trade mostly between 12 and 20 percent. But in August 2011, as the European debt crisis heated up, a new, more volatile range between 24 and 40 percent reigned for some time.

No trader can accurately predict future IV any more than one can predict the future price of a stock. However, with IV there are often recurring patterns that traders can observe, like the ebb and flow of IV often associated with earnings or other regularly scheduled events. But be aware that the IV's rising before the last 15 earnings reports doesn't mean it will this time.

CBOE Volatility Index®

Often traders look to the implied volatility of the market as a whole for guidance on the IV of individual stocks. Traders use the Chicago Board Options Exchange (CBOE) Volatility Index®, or VIX®, as an indicator of overall market volatility.

When people talk about the market, they are talking about a broad-based index covering many stocks on many diverse industries. Usually, they are referring to the S&P 500. Just as the IV of a stock may offer insight about investors' feelings about that stock's future volatility, the volatility of options on the S&P 500—SPX options—may tell something about the expected volatility of the market as a whole.

VIX is an index published by the Chicago Board Options Exchange that measures the IV of a hypothetical 30-day option on the SPX. A 30-day option on the SPX only truly exists once a month—30 days before expiration. CBOE computes a hypothetical 30-day option by means of a weighted average of the two nearest-term months.

When the S&P 500 rises or falls, it is common to see individual stocks rise and fall in sympathy with the index. Most stocks have some degree of market risk. When there is a perception of higher risk in the market as a whole, there can consequently be a perception of higher risk in individual stocks. The rise or fall of the IV of SPX can translate into the IV of individual stocks rising or falling.

Implied Volatility and Direction

Who's afraid of falling stock prices? Logically, declining stocks cause concern for investors in general. There is confirmation of that statement in the options market. Just look at IV. With most stocks and indexes, there is an inverse relationship between IV and the underlying price. Exhibit 3.2 shows the SPX plotted against its 30-day IV, or the VIX.

EXHIBIT 3.2 SPX vs. 30-day IV (VIX).

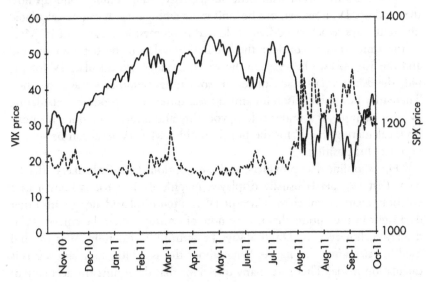

The heavier line is the SPX, and the lighter line is the VIX. Note that as the price of SPX rises, the VIX tends to decline and vice versa. When the market declines, the demand for options tends to increase. Investors hedge by buying puts. Traders speculate on momentum by buying puts and speculate on a turnaround by buying calls. When the market moves higher, investors tend to sell their protection back and write covered calls or cash-secured puts. Option speculators initiate option-selling strategies. There is less fear when the market is rallying.

This inverse relationship of IV to the price of the underlying is not unique to the SPX; it applies to most individual stocks as well. When a stock moves lower, the market usually bids up IV, and when the stock rises, the market tends to offer IV creating downward pressure.

Calculating Volatility Data

Accurate data are essential for calculating volatility. Many of the volatility data that are readily available are useful, but unfortunately, some are not. HV is a value that is easily calculated from publicly accessible past closing prices of a stock. It's rather straightforward. Traders can access HV from many sources. Retail traders often have access to HV from their brokerage firm. Trading firms or clearinghouses often provide professional traders with HV data. There are some excellent online resources for HV as well.

HV is a calculation with little subjectivity—the numbers add up how they add up. IV, however, can be a bit more ambiguous. It can be calculated different ways to achieve different desired outcomes; it is user-centric. Most of the time, traders consider the theoretical value to be between the bid and the ask prices. On occasion, however, a trader will calculate IV for the bid, the ask, the last trade price, or, sometimes, another value altogether. There may be a valid reason for any of these different methods for calculating IV. For example, if a trader is long volatility and aspires to reduce his position, calculating the IV for the bid shows him what IV level can be sold to liquidate his position.

Firms, online data providers, and most options-friendly brokers offer IV data. Past IV data is usually displayed graphically in what is known as a volatility chart or vol chart. Current IV is often displayed along with other data right in the option chain. One note of caution: when the current IV is displayed, however, it should always be scrutinized carefully. Was the bid used in calculating this figure? What about the ask? How long ago was this calculation made? There are many questions that determine the accuracy of a current IV, and rarely are there any answers to support the number. Traders should trust only IV data they knowingly generated themselves using a pricing model.

Volatility Skew

There are many platforms (software or Web-based) that enable traders to solve for volatility values of multiple options within the same option class. Values of options of the same class are interrelated. Many of the model parameters are shared among the different series within the same class. But IV can be different for different options within the same class. This is referred to as the *volatility skew*. There are two types of volatility skew: term structure of volatility and vertical skew.

Term Structure of Volatility

Term structure of volatility—also called *monthly skew* or *horizontal skew*—is the relationship among the IVs of options in the same class with the same strike but with different expiration months. IV, again, is often interpreted as the market's estimate of future volatility. It is reasonable to assume that the market will expect some months to be more volatile than others. Because of this, different expiration cycles can trade at different IVs. For example, if a company involved in a major product-liability lawsuit is expecting a verdict on the case to be announced in two months, the one-month IV may be low, as the stock is not expected to move much until the suit is resolved. The two-month volatility may be much higher, however, reflecting the expectations of a big move in the stock up or down, depending on the outcome.

The term *structure of volatility* also varies with the normal ebb and flow of volatility within the business cycle. In periods of declining volatility, it is common for the month with the least amount of time until expiration, also known as the front month, to trade at a lower volatility than the back months, or months with more time until expiration. Conversely, when volatility is rising, the front month tends to have a higher IV than the back months.

Exhibit 3.3 shows historical option prices and their corresponding IVs for 32.5-strike calls on General Motors (GM) during a period of low volatility.

In this example, no major news is expected to be released on GM, and overall market volatility is relatively low. The February 32.5 call has the lowest IV, at 32 percent. Each consecutive month has a higher IV than

EXHIBIT 3.3 GM term structure of volatility.

Series	Bid-Ask	Theo	IV
Feb 32.5 Call	0.75–0.85	0.80	32.0%
Mar 32.5 Call	1.25–1.35	1.30	32.7%
Jun 32.5 Call	2.45–2.55	2.50	34.1%
Sep 32.5 Call	3.30–3.50	3.40	34.6%

GM at $31.96

EXHIBIT 3.4 GM vegas.

Series	Theo	IV	Vega
Feb 32.5 Call	0.80	32.0%	0.031
Mar 32.5 Call	1.30	32.7%	0.046
Jun 32.5 Call	2.50	34.1%	0.076
Sep 32.5 Call	3.40	34.6%	0.098

GM at 31.96
Days to expiration: February 21, March 51, June 142, September 240

the previous month. A graduated increasing or decreasing IV for each consecutive expiration cycle is typical of the term structure of volatility.

Under normal circumstances, the front month is the most sensitive to changes in IV. There are two reasons for this. First, front-month options are typically the most actively traded. There is more buying and selling pressure. Their IV is subject to more activity. Second, vegas are smaller for options with fewer days until expiration. This means that for the same monetary change in an option's value, the IV needs to move more for short-term options.

Exhibit 3.4 shows the same GM options and their corresponding vegas. If the value of the September 32.5 calls increases by $0.10, IV must rise by 1 percentage point. If the February 32.5 calls increase by $0.10, IV must rise 3 percentage points. As expiration approaches, the vega gets even smaller. With seven days until expiration, the vega would be about 0.014. This means IV would have to change about 7 points to change the call value $0.10.

Vertical Skew

The second type of skew found in option IV is vertical skew, or strike skew. Vertical skew is the disparity in IV among the strike prices within the same

EXHIBIT 3.5 Citigroup vertical skew.

Strike	Call Theo	Put Theo	IV
31	4.80	1.70	49.6
32	4.19	2.02	47.6
33	3.55	2.36	45.8
34	2.94	2.76	44.2
35	2.40	3.22	42.6
36	1.93	3.75	41.2
37	1.53	4.33	40.1
38	1.17	4.96	39.0

Citigroup at $34.160, 84 days to expiration

month for an option class. The options on most stocks and indexes experience vertical skew. As a general rule, the IV of downside options—calls and puts with strike prices lower than the at-the-money (ATM) strike—trade at higher IVs than the ATM IV. The IV of upside options—calls and puts with strike prices higher than the ATM strike—typically trade at lower IVs than the ATM IV.

The downside is often simply referred to as puts and the upside as calls. The rationale for this lingo is that OTM options (puts on the downside and calls on the upside) are usually more actively traded than the ITM options. By put-call parity, a put can be synthetically created from a call, and a call can be synthetically created from a put simply by adding the appropriate long or short stock position.

Exhibit 3.5 shows the vertical skew for 86-day options on Citigroup Inc. (C) on a typical day, with IVs rounded to the nearest tenth.

Notice the IV of the puts (downside options) is higher than that of the calls (upside options), with the 31 strike's volatility more than 10 points higher than that of the 38 strike. Also, the difference in IV per unit change in the strike price is higher for the downside options than it is for the upside ones. The difference between the IV of the 31 strike is 2 full points higher than the 32 strike, which is 1.8 points higher than the 33 strike. But the 36 strike's IV is only 1.1 points higher than the 37 strike, which is also just 1.1 points higher than the 38 strike.

This incremental difference in the IV per strike is often referred to as the slope. The puts of most underlyings tend to have a greater slope to their skew than the calls. Many models allow values to be entered for the upside slope and the downside slope that mathematically increase or decrease IVs of each strike incrementally. Some traders believe the slope should be a straight line, while others believe it should be an exponentially sloped line.

If the IVs were graphed, the shape of the skew would vary among asset classes. This is sometimes referred to as the volatility smile or sneer, depending on the shape of the IV skew. Although Exhibit 3.5 is a typical paradigm for the slope for stock options, bond options and other commodity options would have differently shaped skews. For example, grain options commonly have calls with higher IVs than the put IVs.

Volatility skew is dependent on supply and demand. Greater demand for downside protection may cause the overall IV to rise, but it can cause the IV of puts to rise more relative to the calls or vice versa. There are many traders who make their living trading volatility skew.

Note

1. This technique provides only an estimation of future volatility.

CHAPTER 4

Option-Specific Risk and Opportunity

New endeavors can be intimidating. The first day at a new job or new school is a challenge. Option trading is no different. When traders first venture into the world of options, they tend to start with what they know—trading direction. Buying stocks is at the heart of the comfort zone for many traders. Buying a call as a substitute for buying a stock is a logical progression. And for the most part, call buying is a pretty straightforward way to take a bullish position in a stock. But it's not *just* a bullish position. The greeks come into play with the long call, providing both risk and opportunity.

Long ATM Call

Kim is a trader who is bullish on the Walt Disney Company (DIS) over the short term. The time horizon of her forecast is three weeks. Instead of buying 100 shares of Disney at $35.10 per share, Kim decides to buy one Disney March 35 call at $1.10. In this example, March options have 44 days until expiration. How can Kim profit from this position? How can she lose?

Exhibit 4.1 shows the profit and loss (P&(L)) for the call at different time periods. The top line is when the trade is executed; the middle, dotted line is after three weeks have passed; and the bottom, darker line is at expiration. Kim wants Disney to rise in price, which is evident by looking at the graph for any of the three time horizons. She would anticipate a loss if the stock price declines. These expectations are related to the position's delta, but that is not the only risk exposure Kim has. As indicated by the three different lines in Exhibit 4.1, the call loses value over time. This is

73

EXHIBIT 4.1   P&(L) of Disney 35 call.

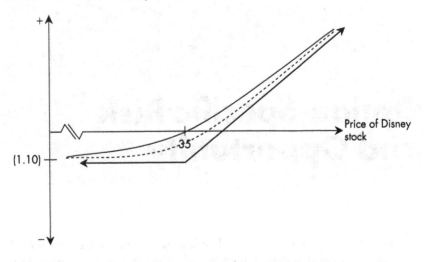

EXHIBIT 4.2   Greeks for 35 Disney call.

Delta	0.57
Gamma	0.166
Theta	−0.013
Vega	0.048
Rho	0.023

called *theta risk*. She has other risk exposure as well. Exhibit 4.2 lists the greeks for the DIS March 35 call.

Kim's immediate directional exposure is quantified by the delta, which is 0.57. Delta is immediate directional exposure because it's subject to change by the amount of the gamma. The positive gamma of this position helps Kim by increasing the delta as Disney rises and decreasing it as it falls. Kim, however, has time working against her—theta. At this point, she theoretically loses $0.013 per day. Since her call is close to being at-the-money, she would anticipate her theta becoming more negative as expiration approaches if Disney's share price remains unchanged. She also has positive vega exposure. A one-percentage-point increase in implied volatility (IV) earns Kim just under $0.05. A one-point decrease costs her about $0.05. With so few days until expiration, the 35-strike call has very little rho

EXHIBIT 4.3   Disney 35 call price—time matrix—value.

Stock Price	44 Days	41 Days	38 Days	35 Days	32 Days	29 Days	26 Days	23 Days	20 Days
40	5.24	5.22	5.20	5.18	5.17	5.15	5.13	5.12	5.10
39	4.26	4.24	4.22	4.20	4.18	4.16	4.14	4.12	4.10
38	3.32	3.29	3.27	3.24	3.22	3.19	3.16	3.14	3.12
37	2.44	2.41	2.38	2.34	2.31	2.27	2.24	2.21	2.17
36	1.66	1.63	1.59	1.55	1.51	1.47	1.42	1.38	1.33
35	1.04	1.00	0.96	0.91	0.87	0.82	0.78	0.73	0.67
34	0.57	0.53	0.50	0.46	0.43	0.39	0.35	0.31	0.26
33	0.27	0.25	0.22	0.19	0.17	0.15	0.12	0.10	0.07
32	0.11	0.09	0.08	0.06	0.05	0.04	0.03	0.02	0.01
31	0.03	0.03	0.02	0.02	0.01	0.01	0.01	0.00	0.00

exposure. A full one-percentage-point change in the interest rate changes her call's value by only $0.023.

Delta

Some of Kim's risks warrant more concern than others. With this position, delta is of the greatest concern, followed by theta. Kim expects the call to rise in value and accepts the risk of decline. Delta exposure was her main rationale for establishing the position. She expects to hold it for about three weeks. Kim is willing to accept the trade-off of delta exposure for theta, which will cost her three weeks of erosion of option premium. If the anticipated delta move happens sooner than expected, Kim will have less decay. Exhibit 4.3 shows the value of her 35 call at various stock prices over time. The left column is the price of Disney. The top row is the number of days until expiration.

The effect of delta is evident as the stock rises or falls. When the position is established (44 days until expiration), the change in the option price if the stock were to move from $35 to $36 is 0.62 (1.66 − 1.04). Between stock prices of $36 and $37, the option gains 0.78 (2.44 −1.66). If the stock were to decline in value from $35 to $34, the option loses 0.47 (1.04 − 0.57). The option gains value at a faster rate as the stock rises and loses value at a slower rate as the stock falls. This is the effect of gamma.

EXHIBIT 4.4 Disney call price–time matrix–delta.

Stock Price	44 Days	41 Days	38 Days	35 Days	32 Days	29 Days	26 Days	23 Days	20 Days
40	0.985	0.988	0.990	0.992	0.994	0.996	0.997	0.998	0.999
39	0.962	0.966	0.971	0.976	0.979	0.984	0.988	0.991	0.995
38	0.917	0.923	0.928	0.935	0.942	0.951	0.958	0.966	0.975
37	0.834	0.840	0.848	0.856	0.866	0.874	0.884	0.896	0.911
36	0.712	0.715	0.719	0.724	0.729	0.735	0.743	0.753	0.764
35	0.551	0.549	0.547	0.545	0.543	0.541	0.539	0.537	0.534
34	0.377	0.369	0.361	0.352	0.342	0.331	0.318	0.303	0.285
33	0.222	0.211	0.198	0.186	0.174	0.160	0.144	0.125	0.107
32	0.109	0.099	0.089	0.077	0.067	0.058	0.046	0.036	0.026
31	0.041	0.036	0.031	0.024	0.019	0.015	0.010	0.007	0.004

Gamma

With this type of position, gamma is an important but secondary consideration. Gamma is most helpful to Kim in developing expectations of what the delta will be as the stock price rises or falls. Exhibit 4.4 shows the delta at various stock prices over time.

Kim pays attention to gamma only to gauge her delta. Why is this important to her? In this trade, Kim is focused on direction. Knowing how much her call will rise or fall in step with the stock is her main concern. Notice that her delta tends to get bigger as the stock rises and smaller as the stock falls. As time passes, the delta gravitates toward 1.00 or 0, depending on whether the call is in-the-money (ITM) or out-of-the-money (OTM).

Theta

Option buying is a veritable race against the clock. With each passing day, the option loses theoretical value. Refer back to Exhibit 4.3. When three weeks pass and the time to expiration decreases from 44 days to 23, what happens to the call value? If the stock price stays around its original level, theta will be responsible for a loss of about 30 percent of the premium. If Disney is at $35 with 23 days to expiration, the call will be worth $0.73. With a big enough move in either direction, however, theta matters much less.

With 23 days to expiration and Disney at $39, there is only 0.12 of time value—the premium paid over parity for the option. At that point, it is almost all delta exposure. Similarly, if the Disney stock price falls after three weeks to $33, the call will have only 0.10 of time value. Time decay is the least of Kim's concerns if the stock makes a big move.

Vega

After delta and theta, vega is the next most influential contributor to Kim's profit or peril. With Disney at $35.10, the 1.10 premium for the 35-strike call represents $1 of time value—all of which is vulnerable to changes in IV. The option's 1.10 value returns an IV of about 19 percent, given the following inputs:

- Stock: $35.10
- Strike: 35
- Days to expiration: 44
- Interest: 5.25 percent
- No dividend paid during this period

Consequently, the vega is 0.048. What does the 0.048 vega tell Kim? Given the preceding inputs, for each point the IV rises or falls, the option's value gains or loses about $0.05.

Some of the inputs, however, will change. Kim anticipates that Disney will rise in price. She may be right or wrong. Either way, it is unlikely that the stock will remain exactly at $35.10 to option expiration. The only certainty is that time will pass.

Both price and time will change Kim's vega exposure. Exhibit 4.5 shows the changing vega of the 35 call as time and the underlying price change.

When comparing Exhibit 4.5 to Exhibit 4.3, it's easy to see that as the time value of the option declines, so does Kim's exposure to vega. As time passes, vega gets smaller. And as the call becomes more in- or out-of-the-money, vega gets smaller. Since she plans to hold the position for around three weeks, she is not concerned about small fluctuations in IV in the interim.

If indeed the rise in price that Kim anticipates comes to pass, vega becomes even less of a concern. With 23 days to expiration and DIS at $37, the call value is 2.21. The vega is $0.018. If IV decreases as the stock price rises—a common occurrence—the adverse effect of vega will be minimal. Even if IV declines by 5 points, to a historically low IV for DIS, the call loses less than $0.10. That's less than 5 percent of the new value of the option.

EXHIBIT 4.5 Disney 35 call price—time matrix—vega.

Stock Price	44 Days	41 Days	38 Days	35 Days	32 Days	29 Days	26 Days	23 Days	20 Days
40	0.006	0.005	0.003	0.002	0.002	0.001	0.001	0.001	0.000
39	0.010	0.010	0.009	0.007	0.005	0.004	0.003	0.002	0.001
38	0.021	0.018	0.016	0.015	0.014	0.011	0.008	0.007	0.005
37	0.032	0.031	0.030	0.028	0.024	0.020	0.019	0.018	0.014
36	0.042	0.039	0.037	0.036	0.034	0.033	0.031	0.029	0.027
35	0.048	0.047	0.045	0.043	0.041	0.039	0.037	0.035	0.033
34	0.043	0.041	0.040	0.038	0.036	0.035	0.033	0.031	0.029
33	0.036	0.034	0.031	0.027	0.023	0.022	0.020	0.018	0.013
32	0.020	0.019	0.018	0.015	0.012	0.010	0.009	0.006	0.005
31	0.010	0.008	0.007	0.006	0.004	0.003	0.002	0.001	0.001

If dividend policy changes or the interest rate changes, the value of Kim's call will be affected as well. Dividends are often fairly predictable. However, a large unexpected dividend payment can have a significant adverse impact on the value of the call. For example, if a surprise $3 dividend were announced, owning the stock would become greatly preferable to owning the call. This preference would be reflected in the call premium. This is a scenario that an experienced trader like Kim will realize is a possibility, although not a probability. Although she knows it can happen, she will not plan for such an event unless she believes it is likely to happen. Possible reasons for such a belief could be rumors or the company's historically paying an irregular dividend.

Rho

For all intents and purposes, rho is of no concern to Kim. In recent years, interest rate changes have not been a major issue for option traders. In the Alan Greenspan years of Federal Reserve leadership, changes in the interest rate were usually announced at the regularly scheduled Federal Open Market Committee (FOMC) meetings, with but a few exceptions. Ben Bernanke, likewise, changed interest rates fairly predictably, when he made any rate changes at all. In these more stable periods, if there is no FOMC meeting scheduled during the life of the call, it's unlikely that rates will change.

Even if they do, the rho with 44 days to expiration is only 0.023. This means that if rates change by a whole percentage point—which is four times the most common incremental change—the call value will change by a little more than $0.02. In this case, this is an acceptable risk. With 23 days to expiration, the ATM 35 call has a rho of only 0.011.

Tweaking Greeks

With this position, some risks are of greater concern than others. Kim may want more exposure to some greeks and less to others. What if she is concerned that her forecasted price increase will take longer than three weeks? She may want less exposure to theta. What if she is particularly concerned about a decline in IV? She may want to decrease her vega. Conversely, she may believe IV will rise and therefore want to increase her vega.

Kim has many ways at her disposal to customize her greeks. All of her alternatives come with trade-offs. She can buy more calls, increasing her greek positions in exact proportion. She can buy or sell stock or options against her call, creating a spread. The simplest way to alter her exposure to option greeks is to choose a different call to buy. Instead of buying the ATM call, Kim can buy a call with a different relationship to the current stock price.

Long OTM Call

Kim can reduce her exposure to theta and vega by buying an OTM call. The trade-off here is that she also reduces her immediate delta exposure. Depending on how much Kim believes Disney will rally, this may or may not be a viable trade-off. Imagine that instead of buying one Disney March 35 call, Kim buys one Disney March 37.50 call, for 0.20.

There are a few observations to be made about this alternative position. First, the net premium, and therefore overall risk, is much lower, 0.20 instead of 1.10. From an expiration standpoint, the breakeven at expiration is $37.70 (the strike price plus the call premium). Since Kim plans on exiting the position after about three weeks, the exact break-even point at the expiration of the contract is irrelevant. But the concept is the same: the stock needs to rise significantly. Exhibit 4.6 shows how Kim's concerns translate into greeks.

This table compares the ATM call with the OTM call. Kim can reduce her theta to half that of the ATM call position by purchasing an OTM. This is certainly a favorable difference. Her vega is lower with the 37.50 call, too. This may or may not be a favorable difference. That depends on Kim's opinion of IV.

EXHIBIT 4.6   Greeks for Disney 35 and 37.50 calls.

	35 Call	37.50 Call
Delta	0.57	0.185
Gamma	0.166	0.119
Theta	−0.013	−0.007
Vega	0.048	0.032
Rho	0.023	0.007

On the surface, the disparity in delta appears to be a highly unfavorable trade-off. The delta of the 37.50 call is less than one third of the delta of the 35 call, and the whole motive for entering into this trade is to trade direction! Although this strategy is very delta oriented, its core is more focused on gamma and theta.

The gamma of the 37.50 call is about 72 percent that of the 35 call. But the theta of the 37.50 call is about half that of the 35 call. Kim is improving her gamma/theta relationship by buying the OTM, but with the call being so far out-of-the-money and so inexpensive, the theta needs to be taken with a grain of salt. It is ultimately gamma that will make or break this delta play.

The price of the option is 0.20—a rather low premium. In order for the call to gain in value, delta has to go to work with help from gamma. At this point, the delta is small, only 0.185. If Kim's forecast is correct and there is a big move upward, gamma will cause the delta to increase, and therefore also the premium to increase exponentially. The call's sensitivity to gamma, however, is dynamic.

Exhibit 4.7 shows how the gamma of the 37.50 call changes as the stock price moves over time. At any point in time, gamma is highest when the call is ATM. However, so is theta. Kim wants to reap as much benefit from gamma as possible while minimizing her exposure to theta. Ideally, she wants Disney to rally through the strike price—through the high gamma and back to the low theta. After three weeks pass, with 23 days until expiration, if Disney is at $37 a share, the gamma almost doubles, to 0.237. When the call is ATM, the delta increases at its fastest rate. As Disney rises above the strike, the gamma figures in the table begin to decline.

Gamma helps as the stock price declines, too. Exhibit 4.8 shows the effect of time and gamma on the delta of the 37.50 call.

The effect of gamma is readily observable, as the delta at any point in time is always higher at higher stock prices and lower at lower stock prices.

EXHIBIT 4.7 Disney 37.50 call price—time matrix—gamma.

Stock Price	44 Days	41 Days	38 Days	35 Days	32 Days	29 Days	26 Days	23 Days	20 Days
40	0.081	0.081	0.080	0.079	0.077	0.075	0.072	0.068	0.061
39	0.124	0.127	0.130	0.133	0.135	0.138	0.141	0.143	0.145
38	0.161	0.167	0.173	0.180	0.188	0.196	0.207	0.219	0.233
37	0.175	0.181	0.188	0.195	0.204	0.213	0.224	0.237	0.253
36	0.157	0.161	0.164	0.167	0.170	0.173	0.176	0.178	0.180
35	0.114	0.113	0.111	0.108	0.105	0.102	0.096	0.088	0.079
34	0.065	0.062	0.058	0.053	0.047	0.042	0.035	0.028	0.020
33	0.029	0.025	0.022	0.018	0.015	0.011	0.008	0.005	0.003
32	0.010	0.007	0.006	0.004	0.003	0.002	0.001	0.001	0.000
31	0.002	0.002	0.001	0.001	0.000	0.000	0.000	0.000	0.000

EXHIBIT 4.8 Disney 37.50 call price—time matrix—delta.

Stock Price	44 Days	41 Days	38 Days	35 Days	32 Days	29 Days	26 Days	23 Days	20 Days
40	0.881	0.887	0.894	0.902	0.911	0.920	0.929	0.939	0.951
39	0.779	0.785	0.791	0.798	0.805	0.813	0.823	0.835	0.850
38	0.635	0.637	0.638	0.640	0.642	0.645	0.648	0.652	0.658
37	0.466	0.461	0.456	0.450	0.444	0.436	0.428	0.419	0.408
36	0.298	0.287	0.277	0.266	0.254	0.240	0.224	0.206	0.184
35	0.162	0.151	0.139	0.126	0.114	0.102	0.088	0.071	0.058
34	0.071	0.064	0.056	0.047	0.039	0.032	0.024	0.017	0.011
33	0.025	0.021	0.017	0.013	0.009	0.006	0.004	0.003	0.001
32	0.007	0.005	0.004	0.003	0.002	0.001	0.000	0.000	0.000
31	0.001	0.001	0.001	0.000	0.000	0.000	0.000	0.000	0.000

Kim benefits greatly when the delta grows from its initial level of 0.185 to above 0.50—above the point of being at-the-money. If the stock moves lower, gamma helps take away the pain of the price decline by decreasing the delta.

While delta, gamma, and theta occupy Kim's thoughts, it is ultimately dollars and cents that matter. She needs to translate her study of the greeks into cold, hard cash. Exhibit 4.9 shows the theoretical values of the 37.50 call.

The sooner the price rise occurs, the better. It means less time for theta to eat away profits. If Kim must hold the position for the entire three weeks, she needs a good pop in the stock to make it worth her while. At a $37 share price, the call is worth about 0.50, assuming all other market influences remain constant. That's about a 150 percent profit. At $38, Exhibit 4.9 reveals the call value to be 1.04. That's a 420 percent profit.

On one hand, it's hard for a trader like Kim not to get excited about the prospect of making 420 percent on an 8 percent move in a stock. On the other hand, Kim has to put things in perspective. When the position is established, the call has a 0.185 delta. By the trader's definition of delta, that means the call is estimated to have about an 18.5 percent chance of expiring in-the-money. More than four out of five times, this position will be trading below the strike at expiration.

Although Kim is not likely to hold the position until expiration, this observation tells her something: she's starting in the hole. She is more likely to lose than to win. She needs to be compensated well for her risk on the winners to make up for the more prevalent losers.

Buying OTM calls can be considered more speculative than buying ITM or ATM calls. Unlike what the at-expiration diagrams would lead

EXHIBIT 4.9 Disney 37.50 call price—time matrix—value.

Stock Price	44 Days	41 Days	38 Days	35 Days	32 Days	29 Days	26 Days	23 Days	20 Days
40	2.89	2.86	2.83	2.80	2.76	2.73	2.70	2.67	2.64
39	2.06	2.02	1.98	1.94	1.90	1.86	1.82	1.78	1.74
38	1.35	1.31	1.27	1.22	1.18	1.13	1.09	1.04	0.98
37	0.80	0.76	0.72	0.68	0.64	0.59	0.55	0.50	0.45
36	0.41	0.38	0.35	0.32	0.29	0.25	0.22	0.19	0.15
35	0.19	0.16	0.14	0.12	0.10	0.09	0.07	0.05	0.04
34	0.07	0.06	0.05	0.04	0.03	0.02	0.01	0.01	0.01
33	0.02	0.02	0.01	0.01	0.01	0.00	0.00	0.00	0.00
32	0.00	0.00	0.00	0.00	0.00	0.00	0.00	0.00	0.00
31	0.00	0.00	0.00	0.00	0.00	0.00	0.00	0.00	0.00

one to believe, OTM calls are not simply about direction. There's a bit more to it. They are really about gamma, time, and the magnitude of the stock's move (volatility). Long OTM calls require a big move in the right direction for gamma to do its job.

Long ITM Call

Kim also has the alternative to buy an ITM call. Instead of the 35 or 37.50 call, she can buy the 32.50. The 32.50 call shares some of the advantages the 37.50 call has over the 35 call, but its overall greek characteristics make it a very different trade from the two previous alternatives. Exhibit 4.10 shows a comparison of the greeks of the three different calls.

Like the 37.50 call, the 32.50 has a lower gamma, theta, and vega than the ATM 35-strike call. Because the call is ITM, it has a higher delta: 0.862. In this example, Kim can buy the 32.50 call for 3. That's 0.40 over parity $(3 - [35.10 - 32.50] = 0.40)$. There is not much time value, but more than the 37.50 call has. Thus, theta is of some concern. Ultimately, the ITMs have 0.40 of time value to lose compared with the 0.20 of the OTM calls. Vega is also of some concern, but not as much as in the other alternatives because the vega of the 32.50 is lower than the 35s or the 37.50s. Gamma doesn't help much as the stock rallies—it will get smaller as the stock price rises. Gamma will, however, slow losses somewhat if the stock declines by decreasing delta at an increasing rate.

In this case, the greek of greatest consequence is delta—it is a more purely directional play than the other alternatives discussed. Exhibit 4.11 shows the matrix of the delta of the 32.50 call.

Because the call starts in-the-money and has a relatively low gamma, the delta remains high even if Disney declines significantly. Gamma doesn't really kick in until the stock retreats enough to bring the call closer to being

EXHIBIT 4.10 Greeks for Disney 32.50, 35, and 37.50 calls.

	32.50 Call	35 Call	37.50 Call
Delta	0.862	0.570	0.185
Gamma	0.079	0.166	0.119
Theta	−0.010	−0.013	−0.007
Vega	0.026	0.048	0.032
Rho	0.033	0.023	0.007

EXHIBIT 4.11 Disney 32.50 call price—time matrix—delta.

Stock Price	44 Days	41 Days	38 Days	35 Days	32 Days	29 Days	26 Days	23 Days	20 Days
40	0.998	0.998	0.999	0.999	0.999	1.000	1.000	1.000	1.000
39	0.993	0.995	0.996	0.997	0.998	0.999	0.999	1.000	1.000
38	0.983	0.986	0.989	0.991	0.993	0.995	0.997	0.998	0.999
37	0.962	0.967	0.971	0.976	0.980	0.984	0.988	0.992	0.995
36	0.924	0.929	0.935	0.942	0.950	0.956	0.963	0.972	0.978
35	0.857	0.865	0.871	0.878	0.887	0.896	0.908	0.919	0.931
34	0.756	0.761	0.767	0.774	0.782	0.791	0.800	0.811	0.824
33	0.623	0.624	0.625	0.627	0.629	0.631	0.635	0.639	0.644
32	0.469	0.464	0.459	0.454	0.448	0.442	0.434	0.426	0.416
31	0.314	0.305	0.295	0.283	0.271	0.258	0.244	0.228	0.208

at-the-money. At that point, the position will have suffered a big loss, and the higher gamma is of little comfort.

Kim's motivation for selecting the ITM call above the ATM and OTM calls would be increased delta exposure. The 0.86 delta makes direction the most important concern right out of the gate. Exhibit 4.12 shows the theoretical values of the 32.50 call.

Small directional moves contribute to significant leveraged gains or losses. From share price $35 to $36, the call gains 0.90—from 2.91 to 3.81—about a 30 percent gain. However, from $35 to $34, the call loses 0.80, or 27 percent. With only 0.40 of time value, the nondirectional greeks (theta, gamma, and vega) are a secondary consideration.

If this were a deeper ITM call, the delta would start out even higher, closer to 1.00, and the other relevant greeks would be closer to zero. The deeper ITM a call, the more it acts like the stock and the less its option characteristics (greeks) come into play.

Long ATM Put

The beauty of the free market is that two people can study all the available information on the same stock and come up with completely different outlooks. First of all, this provides for entertaining television on the

EXHIBIT 4.12   Disney 32.50 call price–time matrix–value.

Stock Price	44 Days	41 Days	38 Days	35 Days	32 Days	29 Days	26 Days	23 Days	20 Days
40	7.71	7.69	7.68	7.66	7.65	7.64	7.62	7.61	7.59
39	6.71	6.70	6.68	6.67	6.65	6.64	6.62	6.61	6.59
38	5.72	5.71	5.69	5.67	5.66	5.64	5.62	5.61	5.59
37	4.75	4.73	4.71	4.69	4.67	4.65	4.63	4.61	4.60
36	3.81	3.78	3.75	3.73	3.70	3.68	3.65	3.63	3.61
35	2.91	2.88	2.85	2.82	2.78	2.75	2.71	2.68	2.65
34	2.11	2.07	2.03	1.99	1.94	1.90	1.86	1.81	1.77
33	1.41	1.37	1.33	1.28	1.24	1.19	1.14	1.09	1.03
32	0.87	0.83	0.79	0.74	0.70	0.65	0.60	0.55	0.50
31	0.48	0.44	0.41	0.37	0.33	0.30	0.26	0.23	0.19

business-news channels when the network juxtaposes an outspoken bullish analyst with an equally unreserved bearish analyst. But differing opinions also make for a robust marketplace. Differing opinions are the oil that greases the machine that is price discovery. From a market standpoint, it's what makes the world go round.

It is possible that there is another trader, Mick, in the market studying Disney, who arrives at the conclusion that the stock is overpriced. Mick believes the stock will decline in price over the next three weeks. He decides to buy one Disney March 35 put at 0.80. In this example, March has 44 days to expiration.

Mick initiates this long put position to gain downside exposure, but along with his bearish position comes option-specific risk and opportunity. Mick is buying the same month and strike option as Kim did in the first example of this chapter: the March 35 strike. Despite the different directional bias, Mick's position and Kim's position share many similarities. Exhibit 4.13 offers a comparison of the greeks of the Disney March 35 call and the Disney March 35 put.

The first comparison to note is the contrasting deltas. The put delta is negative, in contrast to the call delta. The absolute value of the put delta is close to 1.00 minus the call delta. The put is just slightly OTM, so its delta is just under 0.50, while that of the call is just over 0.50. The

EXHIBIT 4.13 Greeks for Disney 35 call and 35 put.

	Call	Put
Delta	0.57	−0.444
Gamma	0.166	0.174
Theta	−0.013	−0.009
Vega	0.048	0.048
Rho	0.023	−0.015

EXHIBIT 4.14 Disney 35 put price−time matrix−delta.

Stock Price	44 Days	41 Days	38 Days	35 Days	32 Days	29 Days	26 Days	23 Days	20 Days
40	−0.015	−0.012	−0.010	−0.008	−0.006	−0.004	−0.003	−0.002	−0.001
39	−0.038	−0.034	−0.029	−0.025	−0.021	−0.016	−0.012	−0.009	−0.005
38	−0.084	−0.078	−0.072	−0.066	−0.058	−0.050	−0.042	−0.034	−0.025
37	−0.169	−0.162	−0.155	−0.146	−0.136	−0.128	−0.117	−0.105	−0.090
36	−0.295	−0.291	−0.287	−0.282	−0.276	−0.269	−0.261	−0.251	−0.239
35	−0.462	−0.463	−0.465	−0.466	−0.467	−0.469	−0.470	−0.472	−0.474
34	−0.648	−0.654	−0.662	−0.670	−0.679	−0.689	−0.702	−0.716	−0.733
33	−0.819	−0.830	−0.842	−0.853	−0.865	−0.878	−0.893	−0.911	−0.928
32	−0.956	−0.966	−0.976	−0.985	−0.991	−0.997	−1.00	−1.00	−1.00
31	−1.00	−1.00	−1.00	−1.00	−1.00	−1.00	−1.00	−1.00	−1.00

disparate, yet related deltas represent the main difference between these two trades.

The difference between the gamma of the 35 put and that of the corresponding call is fairly negligible: 0.174 versus 0.166, respectively. The gamma of this ATM put will enter into the equation in much the same way as the gamma of the ATM call. The put's negative delta will become more negative as the stock declines, drawing closer to −1.00. It will get less negative as the stock price rises, drawing closer to zero. Gamma is important here, because it helps the delta. Delta, however, still remains the most important greek. Exhibit 4.14 illustrates how the 35 put delta changes as time and price change.

EXHIBIT 4.15 Disney 35 put price–time matrix–value.

Stock Price	44 Days	41 Days	38 Days	35 Days	32 Days	29 Days	26 Days	23 Days	20 Days
40	0.01	0.01	0.01	0.01	0.00	0.00	0.00	0.00	0.00
39	0.04	0.03	0.03	0.02	0.02	0.01	0.01	0.01	0.00
38	0.10	0.09	0.08	0.07	0.05	0.04	0.03	0.03	0.02
37	0.23	0.21	0.19	0.17	0.15	0.13	0.11	0.09	0.07
36	0.45	0.43	0.40	0.38	0.35	0.32	0.29	0.26	0.23
35	0.83	0.81	0.78	0.75	0.72	0.69	0.66	0.62	0.58
34	1.38	1.36	1.34	1.32	1.29	1.27	1.24	1.21	1.18
33	2.12	2.11	2.09	2.08	2.07	2.06	2.04	2.03	2.02
32	3.01	3.01	3.00	3.00	3.00	3.00	3.00	3.00	3.00
31	4.00	4.00	4.00	4.00	4.00	4.00	4.00	4.00	4.00

Since this put is ATM, it starts out with a big enough delta to offer the directional exposure Mick desires. The delta can change, but gamma ensures that it always changes in Mick's favor. Exhibit 4.15 shows how the value of the 35 put changes with the stock price.

Over time, a decline of only 10 percent in the stock yields high percentage returns. This is due to the leveraged directional nature of this trade—delta.

While the other greeks are not of primary concern, they must be monitored. At the onset, the 0.80 premium is all time value and, therefore subject to the influences of time decay and volatility. This is where trading greeks comes into play.

Conventional trading wisdom says, "Cut your losses early, and let your profits run." When trading a stock, that advice is intellectually easy to understand, although psychologically difficult to follow. Buyers of options, especially ATM options, must follow this advice from the standpoint of theta. Options are decaying assets. The time premium will be zero at expiration. ATMs decay at an increasing nonlinear rate. Exiting a long position before getting too close to expiration can cut losses caused by an increasing theta. When to cut those losses, however, will differ from trade to trade, situation to situation, and person to person.

When buying options, accepting some loss of premium due to time decay should be part of the trader's plan. It comes with the territory. In this example,

EXHIBIT 4.16 Disney 35 put—thetas and theoretical values.

Days	44	37	30	23	16	9	2
θ	−0.009	−0.009	−0.011	−0.013	−0.015	−0.021	−0.049
Theo	0.80	0.73	0.66	0.57	0.48	0.35	0.15

Mick is willing to accept about three weeks of erosion. Mick needs to think about what his put will be worth, not just if the underlying rises or falls but also if it doesn't move at all. At the time the position is established, the theta is 0.009, just under a penny. If Disney share price is unchanged when three weeks pass, his theta will be higher. Exhibit 4.16 shows how thetas and theoretical values change over time if DIS stock remains at $35.10.

Mick needs to be concerned not only about what the theta is now but what it will be when he plans on exiting the position. His plan is to exit the trade in about three weeks, at which point the put theta will be −0.013. If he amortizes his theta over this three-week period, he theoretically loses an average of about 0.01 a day during this time if nothing else changes. The average daily theta is calculated here by subtracting the value of the put at 23 days to expiration from its value when the trade was established to find the loss of premium attributed to time decay, then dividing by the number of days until expiration.

> Difference of premium ÷ Change in days to expiration
> = Average daily theta

Since the theta doesn't change much over the first three weeks, Mick can eyeball the theta rather easily. As expiration approaches and theta begins to grow more quickly, he'll need to do the math.

At nine days to expiration, the theoretical value of Mick's put is about 0.35, assuming all other variables are held constant. By that time, he will have lost 0.45 (0.80 − 0.35) due to erosion over the 35-day period he held the position if the stock hasn't moved. Mick's average daily theta during that period is about 0.0129 (0.45 ÷ 35). The more time he holds the trade, the greater a concern is theta. Mick must weigh his assessment of the likelihood of the option's gaining value from delta against the risk of erosion. If he holds the trade for 35 days, he must make 0.0129 on average per day from delta to offset theta losses. If the forecast is not realized within the expected time frame or if the forecast changes, Mick needs to act fast to curtail average daily theta losses.

Finding the Right Risk

Mick could lower the theta of his position by selecting a put with a greater number of days to expiration. This alternative has its own set of trade-offs: lower gamma and higher vega than the 44-day put. He could also select an ITM put or an OTM put. Like Kim's call alternatives, the OTM put would have less exposure to time decay, lower vega, lower gamma, and a lower delta. It would have a lower premium, too. It would require a bigger price decline than the ATM put and would be more speculative.

The ITM put would also have lower theta, vega, and gamma, but it would have a higher delta. It would take on more of the functionality of a short stock position in much the same way that Kim's ITM call alternative did for a long stock position. In its very essence, however, an option trade, ITM or otherwise, is still fundamentally different than a stock trade.

Stock has a 1.00 delta. The delta of a stock never changes, so it has zero gamma. Stock is not subject to time decay and has no volatility component to its pricing. Even though ITM options have deltas that approach 1.00 and other greeks that are relatively low, they have two important differences from an equity. The first is that the greeks of options are dynamic. The second is the built-in leverage feature of options.

The relationship of an option's strike price to the stock price can change constantly. Options that are ITM now may be OTM tomorrow and vice versa. Greeks that are not in play at the moment may be later. Even if there is no time value in the option now because it is so far away-from-the-money, there is the potential for time premium to become a component of the option's price if the stock moves closer to the strike price. Gamma, theta, and vega always have the potential to come into play.

Since options are leveraged by nature, small moves in the stock can provide big profits or big losses. Options can also curtail big losses if used for hedging. Long option positions can reap triple-digit percentage gains quickly with a favorable move in the underlying. Even though 100 percent of the premium can be lost just as easily, one option contract will have far less nominal exposure than a similar position in the stock.

It's All About Volatility

What are Kim and Mick really trading? Volatility. The motivation for buying an option as opposed to buying or shorting the stock is volatility. To some degree, these options have exposure to both flavors of volatility—implied volatility and historical volatility (HV). The positions in each of the examples have positive vega. Their values are influenced, in part, by IV. Over time, IV begins to lose its significance if the option is no longer close to being at-the-money.

The main objective of each of these trades is to profit from the volatility of the stock's price movement, called future stock volatility or future realized volatility. The strategies discussed in this chapter are contingent on volatility being one directional. The bigger the move in the trader's forecasted direction the better. Volatility in the form of an adverse directional move results in a decline in premium. The gamma in these long option positions makes volatility in the right direction more beneficial and volatility in the wrong direction less costly.

This phenomenon is hardly unique to the long call and the long put. Although some basic strategies, such as the ones studied in this chapter, depend on a particular direction, many don't. Except for interest rate strategies and perhaps some arbitrage strategies, all option trades are volatility trades in one way or another. In general, option strategies can be divided into two groups: volatility-buying strategies and volatility-selling strategies. The following is a breakdown of common option strategies into categories of volatility-buying strategies and volatility-selling strategies:

Volatility-Selling Strategies	Volatility-Buying Strategies
Short Call, Short Put, Covered Call, Covered Put, Bull Call Spread, Bear Call Spread, Bull Put Spread, Bear Put Spread, Short Straddle, Short Strangle, Guts, Ratio Call Spread, Calendar, Butterfly, Iron Butterfly, Broken-Wing Butterfly, Condor, Iron Condor, Diagonals, Double Diagonals, Risk Reversals/Collars.	Long Call, Long Put, Bull Call Spread, Bear Call Spread, Bull Put Spread, Bear Put Spread, Long Straddle, Long Strangle, Guts, Back Spread, Calendar, Butterfly, Iron Butterfly, Broken-Wing Butterfly, Condor, Iron Condor, Diagonals, Double Diagonals, Risk Reversals/Collars.

Long option strategies appear in the volatility-buying group because they have positive gamma and positive vega. Short option strategies appear in the volatility-selling group because of negative gamma and vega. There are some strategies that appear in both groups—for example, the butterfly/condor family, which is typically associated with income generation. These particular volatility strategies are commonly instituted as volatility-selling strategies. However, depending on whether the position is bought or sold and where the stock price is in relation to the strike prices, the position could fall into either group. Some strategies, like the vertical spread family—bull and bear call and put spreads—and risk reversal/collar spreads naturally fall into either category, depending on where the stock is in relation to the strikes. The calendar spread family is unique in that it can have characteristics of each group at the same time.

Direction Neutral, Direction Biased, and Direction Indifferent

As typically traded, volatility-selling option strategies are direction neutral. This means that the position has the greatest results if the underlying price remains in a range—that is, neutral. Although some option-selling strategies—for example, a naked put—may have a positive or negative delta in the short term, profit potential is decidedly limited. This means that if traders are expecting a big move, they are typically better off with option-buying strategies.

Option-buying strategies can be either direction biased or direction indifferent. Direction-biased strategies have been shown throughout this chapter. They are delta trades. Direction-indifferent strategies are those that benefit from increased volatility in the underlying but where the direction of the move is irrelevant to the profitability of the trade. Movement in either direction creates a winner.

Are You a Buyer or a Seller?

The question is: which is better, selling volatility or buying volatility? I have attended option seminars with instructors (many of whom I regard with great respect) teaching that volatility-selling strategies, or income-generating strategies, are superior to buying options. I also know option gurus that tout the superiority of buying options. The answer to the question of which is better is simple: it's all a matter of personal preference.

When I began trading on the floor of Chicago Board Options Exchange (CBOE) in the 1990s, I quickly became aware of a dichotomy among my market-making peers. Those making markets on the floor of the exchange at that time were divided into two groups: teenie buyers and teenie sellers.

Teenie Buyers

Before options traded in decimals (dollars and cents) like they do today, the lowest price increment in which an option could be traded was one sixteenth of a dollar—a *teenie*. Teenie buyers were market makers who would buy back OTM options at one sixteenth to eliminate short positions. They would sometimes even initiate long OTM option positions at a teenie, too. The focus of the teenie-buyer school of thought was the fact that long options have unlimited reward, while short options have unlimited risk. An option purchased so far OTM that it was offered at one sixteenth is unlikely to end up profitable, but it's an inexpensive lottery ticket. At worst, the trader can only lose a teenie. Teenie buyers felt being short OTM options that could be closed by paying a sixteenth was an unreasonable risk.

Teenie Sellers

Teenie sellers, however, focused on the fact that options offered at one sixteenth were far enough OTM that they were very likely to expire worthless. This appears to be free money, unless the unexpected occurs, in which case potential losses can be unlimited. Teenie sellers would routinely save themselves $6.25 (one sixteenth of a dollar per contract representing 100 shares) by selling their long OTMs at a teenie to close the position. They sometimes would even initiate short OTM contracts at one sixteenth.

These long-option or short-option biases hold for other types of strategies as well. Volatility-selling positions, such as the iron condor, can be constructed to have limited risk. The paradigm for these strategies is they tend to produce winners more often than not. But when the position loses, the trader loses more than he would stand to profit if the trade worked out favorably.

Herein lies the issue of preference. Long-option traders would rather trade Babe Ruth—style. For years, Babe Ruth was the record holder for the most home runs. At the same time, he was also the record holder for the most strikeouts. The born fighters that are option buyers accept the fact that they will have more strikeouts, possibly many more strikeouts, than winning trades. But the strategy dictates that the profit on one winner more than makes up for the string of small losers.

Short-option traders, conversely, like to have everything cool and copacetic. They like the warm and fuzzy feeling they get from the fact that month after month they tend to generate winners. The occasional loser that nullifies a few months of profits is all part of the game.

Options and the Fair Game

There may be a statistical advantage to buying stock as opposed to shorting stock, because the market has historically had a positive annualized return over the long run. A statistical advantage to being either an option buyer or an option seller, however, should not exist in the long run, because the option market prices IV. Assuming an overall efficient market for pricing volatility into options, there should be no statistical advantage to systematically buying or selling options.[1]

Consider a game consisting of one six-sided die. Each time a one, two, or three is rolled, the house pays the player $1. Each time a four, five, or six is rolled, the house pays zero. What is the most a player would be willing to pay to play this game? If the player paid nothing, the house would be at a tremendous disadvantage, paying $1 50 percent of the time and nothing the other 50 percent of the time. This would not be a fair game from the house's perspective, as it would collect no money. If the player paid $1, the player would get his dollar back when one, two, or three came up. Otherwise, he would lose his dollar. This is not a fair game from the player's perspective.

The chances of winning this game are 3 out of 6, or 50–50. If this game were played thousands of times, one would expect to receive $1 half the time and receive nothing the other half of the time. The average return per roll one would expect to receive would be $0.50, that's ($1 × 50 percent + $0 × 50 percent). This becomes a fair game with an entrance fee of $0.50.

Now imagine a similar game in which a six-sided die is rolled. This time if a one is rolled, the house pays $1. If any other number is rolled, the house pays nothing. What is a fair price to play this game? The same logic and the same math apply. There is a 16.6 percent chance of a one coming up and the player receiving $1. And there is a 16.6 percent chance of each of the other five numbers being rolled and the player receiving nothing. Mathematically, this translates to: $1 × 16.6 percent + 5($0 × 16.6 percent). Fair value for a chance to play this game is about $0.1667 per roll.

The fair game concept applies to option prices as well. The price of the game, or in this case the price of the option, is determined by the market in the form of IV. The odds are based on the market's expectations of future volatility. If buying options offered a superior payout based on the odds of success, the market would put upward pressure on prices until this arbitrage opportunity ceased to exist. It's the same for selling volatility. If selling were a fundamentally better strategy, the market would depress option prices until selling options no longer produced a way to beat the odds. The options market will always equalize imbalances.

Note

1. This is not to say that unique individual opportunities do not exist for overpriced or underpriced options, only that options are not overpriced or underpriced in general. Thus, neither an option-selling nor option-buying methodology should provide an advantage.

CHAPTER 5

An Introduction to Volatility-Selling Strategies

Along with death and taxes, there is one other fact of life we can all count on: the time value of all options ultimately going to zero. What an alluring concept! In a business where expected profits can be thwarted by an unexpected turn of events, this is one certainty traders can count on. Like all certainties in the financial world, there is a way to profit from this fact, but it's not as easy as it sounds. Alas, the potential for profit only exists when there is risk of loss.

In order to profit from eroding option premiums, traders must implement option-selling strategies, also known as volatility-selling strategies. These strategies have their own set of inherent risks. Selling volatility means having negative vega—the risk of implied volatility rising. It also means having negative gamma—the risk of the underlying being too volatile. This is the nature of selling volatility. The option-selling trader does not want the underlying stock to move—that is, the trader wants the stock to be less volatile. That is the risk.

Profit Potential

Profit for the volatility seller is realized in a roundabout sort of way. The reward for low volatility is achieved through time decay. These strategies have positive theta. Just as the volatility-buying strategies covered in Chapter 4 had time working against them, volatility-selling strategies have

95

time working in their favor. The trader is effectively paid to assume the risk of movement.

Gamma-Theta Relationship

There exists a trade-off between gamma and theta. Long options have positive gamma and negative theta. Short options have negative gamma and positive theta. Positions with greater gamma, whether positive or negative, tend to have greater theta values, negative or positive. Likewise, lower absolute values for gamma tend to go hand in hand with lower absolute values for theta. The gamma-theta relationship is the most important consideration with many types of strategies. Gamma-theta is often the measurement with the greatest influence on the bottom line.

Greeks and Income Generation

With volatility-selling strategies (sometimes called income-generating strategies), greeks are often overlooked. Traders simply dismiss greeks as unimportant to this kind of trade. There is some logic behind this reasoning. Time decay provides the profit opportunity. In order to let all of time premium erode, the position must be held until expiration. Interim changes in implied volatility are irrelevant if the position is held to term. The gamma-theta loses some significance if the position is held until expiration, too. The position has either passed the break-even point on the at-expiration diagram, or it has not. Incremental daily time decay—related gains are not the ultimate goal. The trader is looking for all the time premium, not portions of it.

So why do greeks matter to volatility sellers? Greeks allow traders to be flexible. Consider short-term-momentum stock traders. The traders buy a stock because they believe it will rise over the next month. After one week, if unexpected bearish news is announced causing the stock to break through its support lines, the traders have a decision to make. Short-term speculative traders very often choose to cut their losses and exit the position early rather than risk a larger loss hoping for a recovery.

Volatility-selling option traders are often faced with the same dilemma. If the underlying stays in line with the traders' forecast, there is little to worry about. But if the environment changes, the traders have to react. Knowing the greeks for a position can help traders make better decisions if they plan to close the position before expiration.

Naked Call

A naked call is when a trader shorts a call without having stock or other options to cover or protect it. Since the call is uncovered, it is one of the riskier trades a trader can make. Recall the at-expiration diagram for the naked call from Chapter 1, Exhibit 1.3: Naked TGT Call. Theoretically, there is limited reward and unlimited risk. Yet there are times when experienced traders will justify making such a trade. When a stock has been trading in a range and is expected to continue doing so, traders may wait until it is near the top of the channel, where there is resistance, and then short a call.

For example, a trader, Brendan, has been studying a chart of Johnson & Johnson (JNJ). Brendan notices that for a few months the stock has trading been in a channel between $60 and $65. As he observes Johnson & Johnson beginning to approach the resistance level of $65 again, he considers selling a call to speculate on the stock not rising above $65. Before selling the call, Brendan consults other technical analysis tools, like ADX/DMI, to confirm that there is no trend present. ADX/DMI is used by some traders as a filter to determine the strength of a trend and whether the stock is overbought or oversold. In this case, the indicator shows no strong trend present. Brendan then performs due diligence. He studies the news. He looks for anything specific that could cause the stock to rally. Is the stock a takeover target? Brendan finds nothing. He then does earnings research to find out when they will be announced, which is not for almost two more months.

Next, Brendan pulls up an option chain on his computer. He finds that with the stock trading around $64 per share, the market for the November 65 call (expiring in four weeks) is 0.66 bid at 0.68 offer. Brendan considers when Johnson & Johnson's earnings report falls. Although recent earnings have seldom been a major concern for Johnson & Johnson, he certainly wants to sell an option expiring before the next earnings report. The November fits the mold. Brendan sells ten of the November 65 calls at the bid price of 0.66.

Brendan has a rather straightforward goal. He hopes to see Johnson & Johnson shares remain below $65 between now and expiration. If he is right, he stands to make $660. If he is wrong? Exhibit 5.1 shows how Brendan's calls hold up if they are held until expiration.

Considering the risk/reward of this trade, Brendan is rightfully concerned about a big upward move. If the stock begins to rally, he must be prepared to act fast. Brendan must have an idea in advance of what his pain

EXHIBIT 5.1 Naked Johnson & Johnson call at expiration.

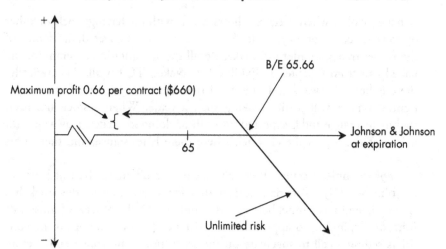

EXHIBIT 5.2 Greeks for short Johnson & Johnson 65 call (per contract).

Delta	−0.34
Gamma	−0.15
Theta	0.02
Vega	−0.07

threshold is. In other words, at what price will he buy back his calls and take a loss if Johnson & Johnson moves adversely?

He decides he will buy all 10 of his calls back at 1.10 per contract if the trade goes against him. (1.10 is an arbitrary price used for illustrative purposes. The actual price will vary, based on the situation and the risk tolerance of the trader. More on when to take profits and losses is discussed in future chapters.) He may choose to enter a good-till-canceled (GTC) stop-loss order to buy back his calls. Or he may choose to monitor the stock and enter the order when he sees the calls offered at 1.10—a mental stop order. What Brendan needs to know is: How far can the stock price advance before the calls are at 1.10?

Brendan needs to examine the greeks of this trade to help answer this question. Exhibit 5.2 shows the hypothetical greeks for the position in this example.

The short call has a negative delta. It also has negative gamma and vega, but it has positive time decay (theta). As Johnson & Johnson ticks higher, the delta increases the nominal value of the call. Although this is not a directional trade per se, delta is a crucial element. It will have a big impact on Brendan's expectations as to how high the stock can rise before he must take his loss.

First, Brendan considers how much the option price can move before he covers. The market now is 0.66 bid at 0.68 offer. To buy back his calls at 1.10, they must be offered at 1.10. The difference between the offer now and the offer price at which Brendan will cover is 0.42 (that's 1.10 − 0.68). Brendan can use delta to convert the change in the ask prices into a stock price change. To do so, Brendan divides the change in the option price by the delta.

$$\text{Change in option price} \div \Delta = \text{Change in stock price}$$
$$-0.42 \div -0.34 = 1.24$$

The −0.34 delta indicates that if JNJ rises $1.24, the calls should be offered at 1.10.

Brendan takes note that the bid-ask spreads are typically 0.01 to 0.03 wide in near-term Johnson & Johnson options trading under 1.00. This is not necessarily the case in other option classes. Less liquid names have wider spreads. If the spreads were wider, Brendan would have more slippage. Slippage is the difference between the assumed trade price and the actual price of the fill as a product of the bid-ask spread. It's the difference between theory and reality. If the bid-ask spread had a typical width of, say, 0.70, the market would be something more like 0.40 bid at 1.10 offer. In this case, if the stock moved even a few cents higher, Brendan could not buy his calls back at his targeted exit price of 1.10. The tighter markets provide lower transaction costs in the form of lower slippage. Therefore, there is more leeway if the stock moves adversely when there are tighter bid-ask option spreads.

But just looking at delta only tells a part of the story. In reality, the delta does not remain constant during the price rise in Johnson & Johnson but instead becomes more negative. Initially, the delta is −0.34 and the gamma is −0.15. After a rise in the stock price, the delta will be more negative by the amount of the gamma. To account for the entire effect of direction, Brendan needs to take both delta and gamma into account. He needs to estimate the average delta based on gamma during the stock price move. The formula for the change in stock price is

$$\text{Change in option value} \div [\Delta + (\Gamma/2)] = \text{Change in stock price}$$
$$-0.42 \div [-0.34 + (0.15/2)] = 1.01$$

Taking into account the effect of gamma as well as delta, Johnson & Johnson needs to rise only $1.01, in order for Brendan's calls to be offered at his stop-loss price of 1.10.

While having a predefined price point to cover in the event the underlying rises is important, sometimes traders need to think on their feet. If material news is announced that changes the fundamental outlook for the stock, Brendan will have to adjust his plan. If the news leads Brendan to become bullish on the stock, he should exit the trade at once, taking a small loss now instead of the bigger loss he would expect later. If the trader is uncertain as to whether to hold or close the position, the Would I Do It Now? rule is a useful rule of thumb.

Would I Do It Now? Rule

To follow this rule, ask yourself, "If I did not already have this position, would I do it now? Would I establish the position at the current market prices, given the current market scenario?" If the answer is no, then the solution is simple: Exit the trade.

For example, if after one week material news is released and Johnson & Johnson is trading higher, at $64.50 per share, and the November 65 call is trading at 0.75, Brendan must ask himself, based on the price of the stock and all known information, "If I were not already short the calls, would I short them now at the current price of 0.75, with the stock trading at $64.50?"

Brendan's opinion of the stock is paramount in this decision. If, for example, based on the news that was announced he is now bullish, he would likely not want to sell the calls at 0.75—he only gets $0.09 more in option premium and the stock is 0.50 closer to the strike. If, however, he is not bullish, there is more to consider.

Theta can be of great use in decision making in this situation. As the number of days until expiration decreases and the stock approaches $65 (making the option more at-the-money), Brendan's theta grows more positive. Exhibit 5.3 shows the theta of this trade as the underlying rises over time.

EXHIBIT 5.3 Theta of Johnson & Johnson.

	28 days	21 days	14 days	7 days	3 days	2 days	1 day
64.00	+0.017	+0.020	+0.024	+0.030	+0.034	+0.031	+0.019
64.50	+0.018	+0.021	+0.026	+0.036	+0.052	+0.060	+0.069
65.00	+0.018	+0.022	+0.027	+0.039	+0.060	+0.074	+0.110

When the position is first established, positive theta comforts Brendan by showing that with each passing day he gets a little closer to his goal—to have the 65 calls expire out-of-the-money (OTM) and reap a profit of the entire 66-cent premium. Theta becomes truly useful if the position begins to move against him. As Johnson & Johnson rises, the trade gets more precarious. His negative delta increases. His negative gamma increases. His goal becomes more out of reach. In conjunction with delta and gamma, theta helps Brendan decide whether the risk is worth the reward.

In the new scenario, with the stock at $64.50, Brendan would collect $18 a day (1.80 × 10 contracts). Is the risk of loss in the short run worth earning $18 a day? With Johnson & Johnson at $64.50, would Brendan now short 10 calls at 0.75 to collect $18 a day, knowing that each day may bring a continued move higher in the stock? The answer to this question depends on Brendan's assessment of the risk of the underlying continuing its ascent. As time passes, if the stock remains closer to the strike, the daily theta rises, providing more reward. Brendan must consider that as theta—the reward—rises, so does gamma: a risk factor.

A small but noteworthy risk is that implied volatility could rise. The negative vega of this position would, then, adversely affect the profitability of this trade. It will make Brendan's 1.10 cover-point approach faster because it makes the option more expensive. Vega is likely to be of less consequence because it would ultimately take the stock's rising though the strike price for the trade to be a loser at expiration.

Short Naked Puts

Another trader, Stacie, has also been studying Johnson & Johnson. Stacie believes Johnson & Johnson is on its way to test the $65 resistance level yet again. She believes it may even break through $65 this time, based on strong fundamentals. Stacie decides to sell naked puts. A naked put is a short put that is not sold in conjunction with stock or another option.

EXHIBIT 5.4   Naked Johnson & Johnson put at expiration.

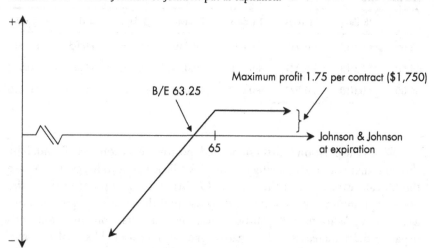

EXHIBIT 5.5   Greeks for short Johnson & Johnson 65 put (per contract).

Delta	0.65
Gamma	−0.15
Theta	0.02
Vega	−0.07

With the stock around $64, the market for the November 65 put is 1.75 bid at 1.80. Stacie likes the fact that the 65 puts are slightly in-the-money (ITM) and thus have a higher delta. If her price rise comes sooner than expected, the high delta may allow her to take a profit early. Stacie sells 10 puts at 1.75.

In the best-case scenario, Stacie retains the entire 1.75. For that to happen, she will need to hold this position until expiration and the stock will have to rise to be trading above the 65 strike. Logically, Stacie will want to do an at-expiration analysis. Exhibit 5.4 shows Stacie's naked put trade if she holds it until expiration.

While harvesting the entire premium as a profit sounds attractive, if Stacie can take the bulk of her profit early, she'll be happy to close the position and eliminate her risk—nobody ever went broke taking a profit. Furthermore, she realizes that her outlook may be wrong: Johnson & Johnson may decline. She may have to close the position early—maybe for a profit, maybe for a loss. Stacie also needs to study her greeks. Exhibit 5.5 shows the greeks for this trade.

The first item to note is the delta. This position has a directional bias. This bias can work for or against her. With a positive 0.65 delta per contract, this position has a directional sensitivity equivalent to being long around 650 shares of the stock. That's the delta × 100 shares × 10 contracts.

$$0.65 \times 100 \times 10 = 650$$

Stacie's trade is not just a bullish version of Brendan's. Partly because of the size of the delta, it's different—specific directional bias aside. First, she will handle her trade differently if it is profitable.

For example, if over the next week or so Johnson & Johnson rises $1, positive delta and negative gamma will have a net favorable effect on Stacie's profitability. Theta is small in comparison and won't have too much of an effect. Delta/gamma will account for a decrease in the put's theoretical value of about $0.73. That's the estimated average delta times the stock move, or [0.65 + (−0.15/2)] × 1.00.

Stacie's actual profit would likely be less than 0.73 because of the bid-ask spread. Stacie must account for the fact that the bid-ask is 0.05 wide (1.75−1.80). Because Stacie would buy to close this position, she should consider the 0.73 price change relative to the 1.80 offer, not the 1.75 trade price—that is, she factors in a nickel of slippage. Thus, she calculates, that the puts will be offered at 1.07 (that's 1.80 − 0.73) when the stock is at $65. That is a gain of $0.68.

In this scenario, Stacie should consider the Would I Do It Now? rule to guide her decision as to whether to take her profit early or hold the position until expiration. Is she happy being short ten 65 puts at 1.07 with Johnson & Johnson at $65? The premium is lower now. The anticipated move has already occurred, and she still has 28 days left in the option that could allow for the move to reverse itself. If she didn't have the trade on now, would she sell ten 65 puts at 1.07 with Johnson & Johnson at $65? Based on her original intention, unless she believes strongly now that a breakout through $65 with follow-through momentum is about to take place, she will likely take the money and run.

Stacie also must handle this trade differently from Brendan in the event that the trade is a loser. Her trade has a higher delta. An adverse move in the underlying would affect Stacie's trade more than it would Brendan's. If Johnson & Johnson declines, she must be conscious in advance of where she will cover.

Stacie considers both how much she is willing to lose and what potential stock-price action will cause her to change her forecast. She consults a stock chart of Johnson & Johnson. In this example, we'll assume there is some resistance developing around $64 in the short term. If this resistance level holds, the trade becomes less attractive. The at-expiration breakeven is $63.25, so the trade can still be a winner if Johnson & Johnson retreats. But Stacie is looking for the stock to approach $65. She will no longer like the risk/reward of this trade if it looks like that price rise won't occur. She makes the decision that if Johnson & Johnson bounces off the $64 level over the next couple weeks, she will exit the position for fear that her outlook is wrong. If Johnson & Johnson drifts above $64, however, she will ride the trade out.

In this example, Stacie is willing to lose 1.00 per contract. Without taking into account theta or vega, that 1.00 loss in the option should occur at a stock price of about $63.28. Theta is somewhat relevant here. It helps Stacie's potential for profit as time passes. As time passes and as the stock rises, so will theta, helping her even more. If the stock moves lower (against her) theta helps ease the pain somewhat, but the further in-the-money the put, the lower the theta.

Vega can be important here for two reasons: first, because of how implied volatility tends to change with market direction, and second, because it can be read as an indication of the market's expectations.

The Double Whammy

With the stock around $64, there is a negative vega of about seven cents. As the stock moves lower, away from the strike, the vega gets a bit smaller. However, the market conditions that would lead to a decline in the price of Johnson & Johnson would likely cause implied volatility (IV) to rise. If the stock drops, Stacie would have two things working against her—delta and vega—a double whammy. Stacie needs to watch her vega. Exhibit 5.6 shows the vega of Stacie's put as it changes with time and direction.

If after one week passes Johnson & Johnson gaps lower to, say, $63.00 a share, the vega will be 0.043 per contract. If IV subsequently rises 5 points as

EXHIBIT 5.6 Johnson & Johnson 65 put vega.

Johnson & Johnson Price	62.50	63.00	63.50	64.00	64.50	65.00	65.50
28-Day 65-Put Vega	0.046	0.053	0.060	0.066	0.070	0.072	0.071
21-Day 65-Put Vega	0.035	0.043	0.050	0.056	0.060	0.062	0.061
14-Day 65-Put Vega	0.022	0.029	0.037	0.044	0.049	0.051	0.050

a result of the stock falling, vega will make Stacie's puts theoretically worth 21.5 cents more per contract. She will lose $215 on vega (that's 0.043 vega × 5 volatility points × 10 contracts) plus the adverse delta/gamma move.

A gap opening will cause her to miss the opportunity to stop herself out at her target price entirely. Even if the stock drifts lower, her targeted stop-loss price will likely come sooner than expected, as the option price will likely increase both by delta/gamma and vega resulting from rising volatility. This can cause her to have to cover sooner, which leaves less room for error. With this trade, increases in IV due to market direction can make it feel as if the delta is greater than it actually is as the market declines. Conversely, IV softening makes it feel as if the delta is smaller than it is as the market rises.

The second reason IV has importance for this trade (as for most other strategies) is that it can give some indication of how much the market thinks the stock can move. If IV is higher than normal, the market perceives there to be more risk than usual of future volatility. The question remains: Is the higher premium worth the risk?

The answer to this question is subjective. Part of the answer is based on Stacie's assessment of future volatility. Is the market right? The other part is based on Stacie's risk tolerance. Is she willing to endure the greater price swings associated with the potentially higher volatility? This can mean getting whipsawed, which is exiting a position after reaching a stop-loss point only to see the market reverse itself. The would-be profitable trade is closed for a loss. Higher volatility can also mean a higher likelihood of getting assigned and acquiring an unwanted long stock position.

Cash-Secured Puts

There are some situations where higher implied volatility may be a beneficial trade-off. What if Stacie's motivation for shorting puts was different? What if she would like to own the stock, just not at the current market price? Stacie can sell ten 65 puts at 1.75 and deposit $63,250 in her trading account to secure the purchase of 1,000 shares of Johnson & Johnson if she gets assigned. The $63,250 is the $65 per share she will pay for the stock if she gets assigned, minus the 1.75 premium she received for the put × $100 × 10 contracts. Because the cash required to potentially purchase the stock is secured by cash sitting ready in the account, this is called a cash-secured put.

Her effective purchase price if assigned is $63.25—the same as her breakeven at expiration. The idea with this trade is that if Johnson & Johnson is anywhere under $65 per share at expiration, she will buy the stock effectively at $63.25. If assigned, the time premium of the put allows her to buy the stock at a discount compared with where it is priced when the trade is established, $64. The higher the time premium—or the higher the implied volatility—the bigger the discount.

This discount, however, is contingent on the stock not moving too much. If it is above $65 at expiration she won't get assigned and therefore can only profit a maximum of 1.75 per contract. If the stock is below $63.25 at expiration, the time premium no longer represents a discount, in fact, the trade becomes a loser. In a way, Stacie is still selling volatility.

Covered Call

The problem with selling a naked call is that it has unlimited exposure to upside risk. Because of this, many traders simply avoid trading naked calls. A more common, and some would argue safer, method of selling calls is to sell them covered.

A covered call is when calls are sold and stock is purchased on a share-for-share basis to cover the unlimited upside risk of the call. For each call that is sold, 100 shares of the underlying security are bought. Because of the addition of stock to this strategy, covered calls are traded with a different motivation than naked calls.

There are clearly many similarities between these two strategies. The main goal for both is to harvest the premium of the call. The theta for the call is the same with or without the stock component. The gamma and vega for the two strategies are the same as well. The only difference is the stock. When stock is added to an option position, the net delta of the position is the only thing affected. Stock has a delta of one, and all its other greeks are zero.

The pivotal point for both positions is the strike price. That's the point the trader wants the stock to be above or below at expiration. With the naked call, the maximum payout is reaped if the stock is below the strike at expiration, and there is unlimited risk above the strike. With the covered call, the maximum payout is reaped if the stock is above the strike at expiration. If the stock is below the strike at expiration, the risk is substantial—the stock can potentially go to zero.

Putting It on

There are a few important considerations with the covered call, both when putting on, or entering, the position and when taking off, or exiting, the trade. The risk/reward implications of implied volatility are important in

EXHIBIT 5.7   Harley-Davidson calls.

	Bid-Ask	Delta	Theta
March 70 Calls	0.85–0.95	0.412	0.032
March 75 Calls	0–0.10	0.049	0.008
April 70 Calls	2.20–2.30	0.483	0.026
April 75 Calls	0.60–0.70	0.204	0.017
May 70 Calls	2.80–2.95	0.503	0.022
May 75 Calls	0.95–1.00	0.249	0.015

February 23 Harley-Davidson at $69

the trade-planning process. Do I want to get paid more to assume more potential risk? More speculative traders like the higher premiums. More conservative (investment-oriented) covered-call sellers like the low implied risk of low-IV calls. Ultimately, a main focus of a covered call is the option premium. How fast can it go to zero without the movement hurting me? To determine this, the trader must study both theta and delta.

The first step in the process is determining which month and strike call to sell. In this example, Harley-Davidson Motor Company (HOG) is trading at about $69 per share. A trader, Bill, is neutral to slightly bullish on Harley-Davidson over the next three months. Exhibit 5.7 shows a selection of available call options for Harley-Davidson with corresponding deltas and thetas.

In this example, the May 70 calls have 85 days until expiration and are 2.80 bid. If Harley-Davidson remained at $69 until May expiration, the 2.80 premium would represent a 4 percent profit over this 85-day period (2.80 ÷ 69). That's an annualized return of about 17 percent ([0.04 / 85)] × 365).

Bill considers his alternatives. He can sell the April (57-day) 70 calls at 2.20 or the March (22-day) 70 calls at 0.85. Since there is a different number of days until expiration, Bill needs to compare the trades on an apples-to-apples basis. For this, he will look at theta and implied volatility.

Presumably, the March call has a theta advantage over the longer-term choices. The March 70 has a theta of 0.032, while the April 70's theta is 0.026 and the May 70's is 0.022. Based on his assessment of theta, Bill would have the inclination to sell the March. If he wants exposure for 90 days, when the March 70 call expires, he can roll into the April 70 call and then the May 70 call (more on this in subsequent chapters). This way Bill can continue to capitalize on the nonlinear rate of decay through May.

Next, Bill studies the IV term structure for the Harley-Davidson ATMs and finds the March has about a 19.2 percent IV, the April has a 23.3 percent IV, and the May has a 23 percent IV. March is the cheapest option by IV standards. This is not necessarily a favorable quality for a short candidate. Bill must weigh his assessment of all relevant information and then decide which trade is best. With this type of a strategy, the benefits of the higher theta can outweigh the disadvantages of selling the lower IV. In this case, Bill may actually like selling the lower IV. He may infer that the market believes Harley-Davidson will be less volatile during this period.

So far, Bill has been focusing his efforts on the 70 strike calls. If he trades the March 70 covered call, he will have a net delta of 0.588 per contract. That's the negative 0.412 delta from shorting the call plus the 1.00 delta of the stock. His indifference point if the trade is held until expiration is $70.85. The indifference point is the point at which Bill would be indifferent as to whether he held only the stock or the covered call. This is figured by adding the strike price of $70 to the 0.85 premium. This is the effective sale price of the stock if the call is assigned. If Bill wants more potential for upside profit, he could sell a higher strike. He would have to sell the April or May 75, since the March 75s are a zero bid. This would give him a higher indifference point, and the upside profits would materialize quickly if HOG moved higher, since the covered-call deltas would be higher with the 75 calls. The April 75 covered-call net delta is 0.796 per contract (the stock delta of 1.00 minus the 0.204 delta of the call). The May 75 covered-call delta is 0.751.

But Bill is neutral to only slightly bullish. In this case, he'd rather have the higher premium—high theta is more desirable than high delta in this situation. Bill buys 1,000 shares of Harley-Davidson at $69 and sells 10 Harley-Davidson March 70 calls at 0.85.

Bill also needs to plan his exit. To exit, he must study two things: an at-expiration diagram and his greeks. Exhibit 5.8 shows the P&(L) at expiration of the Harley-Davidson March 70 covered call. Exhibit 5.9 shows the greeks.

Taking It Off

If the trade works out perfectly for Bill, 22 days from now Harley-Davidson will be trading right at $70. He'd profit on both delta and theta. If the trade isn't exactly perfect, but still good, Harley-Davidson will be anywhere above $68.15 in 22 days. It's the prospect that the trade may not be so good at March expiration that occupies Bill's thoughts, but a trader has to hope for the best and plan for the worst.

EXHIBIT 5.8 Harley-Davidson covered call.

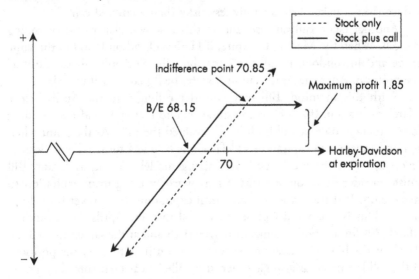

EXHIBIT 5.9 Greeks for Harley-Davidson covered call (per contract).

Delta	0.591
Gamma	−0.121
Theta	0.032
Vega	−0.066

If it starts to trend, Bill needs to react. The consequences to the stock's trending to the upside are not quite so dire, although he might be somewhat frustrated with any lost opportunity above the indifference point. It's the downside risk that Bill will more vehemently guard against.

First, the same IV/vega considerations exist as they did in the previous examples. In the event the trade is closed early, IV/vega may help or hinder profitability. A rise in implied volatility will likely accompany a decline in the stock price. This can bring Bill to his stop-loss sooner. Delta versus theta however, is the major consideration. He will plan his exit price in advance and cover when the planned exit price is reached.

There are more moving parts with the covered call than a naked option. If Bill wants to close the position early, he can leg out, meaning close only one leg of the trade (the call or the stock) at a time. If he legs out of the trade, he's likely to close the call first. The motivation for exiting a trade early is to reduce risk. A naked call is hardly less risky than a covered call.

Another tactic Bill can use, and in this case will plan to use, is rolling the call. When the March 70s expire, if Harley-Davidson is still in the same range and his outlook is still the same, he will sell April calls to continue the position. After the April options expire, he'll plan to sell the Mays.

With this in mind, Bill may consider rolling into the Aprils before March expiration. If it is close to expiration and Harley-Davidson is trading lower, theta and delta will both have devalued the calls. At the point when options are close to expiration and far enough OTM to be offered close to zero, say 0.05, the greeks and the pricing model become irrelevant. Bill must consider in absolute terms if it is worth waiting until expiration to make 0.05. If there is a lot of time until expiration, the answer is likely to be no. This is when Bill will be apt to roll into the Aprils. He'll buy the March 70s for a nickel, a dime, or maybe 0.15 and at the same time sell the Aprils at the bid. This assumes he wants to continue to carry the position. If the roll is entered as a single order, it is called a calendar spread or a time spread.

Covered Put

The last position in the family of basic volatility-selling strategies is the covered put, sometimes referred to as selling puts and stock. In a covered put, a trader sells both puts and stock on a one-to-one basis. The term *covered put* is a bit of a misnomer, as the strategy changes from limited risk to unlimited risk when short stock is added to the short put. A naked put can produce only losses until the stock goes to zero—still a substantial loss. Adding short stock means that above the strike gains on the put are limited, while losses on the stock are unlimited. The covered put functions very much like a naked call. In fact, they are synthetically equal. This concept will be addressed further in the next chapter.

Let's looks at another trader, Libby. Libby is an active trader who trades several positions at once. Libby believes the overall market is in a range and will continue as such over the next few weeks. She currently holds a short stock position of 1,000 shares in Harley-Davidson. She is becoming more neutral on the stock and would consider buying in her short if the market dipped. She may consider entering into a covered-put position. There is one caveat: Libby is leaving for a cruise in two weeks and does not want to carry any positions while she is away. She decides she will sell the covered put and actively manage the trade until her vacation. Libby will sell 10

EXHIBIT 5.10   Greeks for Harley-Davidson covered put (per contract).

Delta	−0.419
Gamma	−0.106
Theta	0.031
Vega	−0.066

EXHIBIT 5.11   HOG 70 put values at 8 days to expiry.

Harley-Davidson	67.50	67.75	68.00	68.25	68.50	68.75	69.00	69.25	69.50	69.75	70.00
Theo.	2.55	2.33	2.12	1.91	1.71	1.53	1.35	1.18	1.03	0.90	0.76

Harley-Davidson March (22-day) 70 puts at 1.85 against her short 1,000 shares of Harley-Davidson, which is trading at $69 per share.

She knows that her maximum profit if the stock declines and assignment occurs will be $850. That's 0.85 × $100 × 10 contracts. Win or lose, she will close the position in two weeks when there are only eight days until expiration. To trade this covered put she needs to watch her greeks.

Exhibit 5.10 shows the greeks for the Harley-Davidson 70-strike covered put.

Libby is really focusing on theta. It is currently about $0.03 per day but will increase if the put stays close-to-the-money. In two weeks, the time premium will have decayed significantly. A move downward will help, too, as the −0.419 delta indicates. Exhibit 5.11 displays an array of theoretical values of the put at eight days until expiration as the stock price changes.

As long as Harley-Davidson stays below the strike price, Libby can look at her put from a premium-over-parity standpoint. Below the strike, the intrinsic value of the put doesn't matter too much, because losses on intrinsic value are offset by gains on the stock. For Libby, all that really matters is the time value. She sold the puts at 0.85 over parity. If Harley-Davidson is trading at $68 with eight days to go, she can buy her puts back for 0.12 over parity. That's a 73-cent profit, or $730 on her 10 contracts. This doesn't account for any changes in the time value that may occur as a result of vega, but vega will be small with Harley-Davidson at $68 and eight days to go. At this point, she would likely close down the whole position—buying the puts and buying the stock—to take a profit on a position that worked out just about exactly as planned.

Her risk, though, is to the upside. A big rally in the stock can cause big losses. From a theoretical standpoint, losses are potentially unlimited with this type of trade. If the stock is above the strike, she needs to have a mental stop order in mind and execute the closing order with discipline.

Curious Similarities

These basic volatility-selling strategies are fairly simple in nature. If the trader believes a stock will not rise above a certain price, the most straightforward way to trade the forecast is to sell a call. Likewise, if the trader believes the stock will not go below a certain price he can sell a put. The covered call and covered put are also ways to generate income on long or short stock positions that have these same price thresholds. In fact, the covered call and covered put have some curious similarities to the naked put and naked call. The similarities between the two pairs of positions are no coincidence. The following chapter sheds light on these similarities.

CHAPTER 6

Put-Call Parity and Synthetics

In order to understand more complex spread strategies involving two or more options, it is essential to understand the arbitrage relationship of the put-call pair. Puts and calls of the same month and strike on the same underlying have prices that are defined in a mathematical relationship. They also have distinctly related vegas, gammas, thetas, and deltas. This chapter will show how the metrics of these options are interrelated. It will also explore synthetics and the idea that by adding stock to a position, a trader may trade with indifference either a call or a put to the same effect.

Put-Call Parity Essentials

Before the creation of the Black-Scholes model, option pricing was hardly an exact science. Traders had only a few mathematical tools available to compare the relative prices of options. One such tool, put-call parity, stems from the fact that puts and calls on the same class sharing the same month and strike can have the same functionality when stock is introduced.

For example, traders wanting to own a stock with limited risk can buy a married put: long stock and a long put on a share-for-share basis. The traders have infinite profit potential, and the risk of the position is limited below the strike price of the option. Conceptually, long calls have the same risk/reward profile—unlimited profit potential and limited risk below the strike. Exhibit 6.1 is an overview of the at-expiration diagrams of a married put and a long call.

EXHIBIT 6.1 Long call vs. long stock + long put (married put).

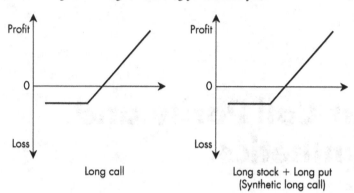

Married puts and long calls sharing the same month and strike on the same security have at-expiration diagrams with the same shape. They have the same volatility value and should trade around the same implied volatility (IV). Strategically, these two positions provide the same service to a trader, but depending on margin requirements, the married put may require more capital to establish, because the trader must buy not just the option but also the stock.

The stock component of the married put could be purchased on margin. Buying stock on margin is borrowing capital to finance a stock purchase. This means the trader has to pay interest on these borrowed funds. Even if the stock is purchased without borrowing, there is opportunity cost associated with the cash used to pay for the stock. The capital is tied up. If the trader wants to use funds to buy another asset, he will have to borrow money, which will incur an interest obligation. Furthermore, if the trader doesn't invest capital in the stock, the capital will rest in an interest-bearing account. The trader forgoes that interest when he buys a stock. However the trader finances the purchase, there is an interest cost associated with the transaction.

Both of these positions, the long call and the married put, give a trader exposure to stock price advances above the strike price. The important difference between the two trades is the value of the stock below the strike price—the part of the trade that is not at risk in either the long call or the married put. On this portion of the invested capital, the trader pays interest with the married put (whether actually or in the form of opportunity cost). This interest component is a pricing consideration that adds cost to the married put and not the long call.

So if the married put is a more expensive endeavor than the long call because of the interest paid on the investment portion that is below the strike, why would anyone buy a married put? Wouldn't traders instead buy the less expensive—less capital intensive—long call? Given the additional interest expense, they would rather buy the call. This relates to the concept of arbitrage. Given two effectively identical choices, rational traders will choose to buy the less expensive alternative. The market as a whole would buy the calls, creating demand which would cause upward price pressure on the call. The price of the call would rise until its interest advantage over the married put was gone. In a robust market with many savvy traders, arbitrage opportunities don't exist for very long.

It is possible to mathematically state the equilibrium point toward which the market forces the prices of call and put options by use of the put-call parity. As shown in Chapter 2, the put-call parity states

$$c + PV(x) = p + s$$

where c is the call premium, $PV(x)$ is the present value of the strike price, p is the put premium and s is the stock price.

Another, less academic and more trader-friendly way of stating this equation is

$$Call + Strike - Interest = Put + Stock$$

where Interest is calculated as

$$Interest = Strike \times Interest\ Rate \times (Days\ to\ Expiration/365)^1$$

The two versions of the put-call parity stated here hold true for European options on non-dividend-paying stocks.

Dividends

Another difference between call and married-put values is dividends. A call option does not extend to its owner the right to receive a dividend payment. Traders, however, who are long a put and long stock are entitled to a dividend if it is the corporation's policy to distribute dividends to its shareholders.

An adjustment must be made to the put-call parity to account for the possibility of a dividend payment. The equation must be adjusted to account for the absence of dividends paid to call holders. For a dividend-paying stock, the put-call parity states

$$Call + Strike - Interest + Dividend = Put + Stock$$

The interest advantage and dividend disadvantage of owning a call is removed from the market by arbitrageurs. Ultimately, that is what is expressed in the put-call parity. It's a way to measure the point at which the arbitrage opportunity ceases to exist. When interest and dividends are factored in, a long call is an equal position to a long put paired with long stock. In options nomenclature, a long put with long stock is a synthetic long call. Algebraically rearranging the above equation:

$$Call = Put + Stock - Strike + Interest - Dividend$$

The interest and dividend variables in this equation are often referred to as the basis. From this equation, other synthetic relationships can be algebraically derived, like the synthetic long put.

$$Put = Call - Stock + Strike - Interest + Dividend$$

A synthetic long put is created by buying a call and selling (short) stock. The at-expiration diagrams in Exhibit 6.2 show identical payouts for these two trades.

The concept of synthetics can become more approachable when studied from the perspective of delta as well. Take the 50-strike put and call listed on a $50 stock. A general rule of thumb in the put-call pair is that the call delta plus the put delta equals 1.00 when the signs are ignored. If the 50 put in this example has a −0.45 delta, the 50 call will have a 0.55 delta. By combining the long call (0.55 delta) with short stock (−1.00 delta), we get a synthetic long put with a −0.45 delta, just like the actual put. The directional risk is the same for the synthetic put and the actual put.

EXHIBIT 6.2   Long put vs. long call + short stock.

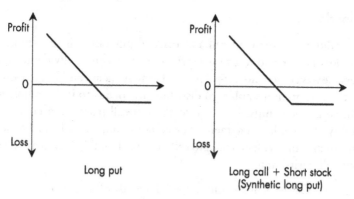

A synthetic short put can be created by selling a call of the same month and strike and buying stock on a share-for-share basis (i.e., a covered call). This is indicated mathematically by multiplying both sides of the put-call parity equation by −1:

$$-\text{Put} = -\text{Call} + \text{Stock} - \text{Strike} + \text{Interest} - \text{Dividend}$$

The at-expiration diagrams, shown in Exhibit 6.3, are again conceptually the same.

A short (negative) put is equal to a short (negative) call plus long stock, after the basis adjustment. Consider that if the put is sold instead of buying stock and selling a call, the interest that would otherwise be paid on the cost of the stock up to the strike price is a savings to the put seller. To balance the equation, the interest benefit of the short put must be added to the call side (or subtracted from the put side). It is the same with dividends. The dividend benefit of owning the stock must be subtracted from the call side to make it equal to the short put side (or added to the put side to make it equal the call side).

The same delta concept applies here. The short 50-strike put in our example would have a 0.45 delta. The short call would have a −0.55 delta. Buying one hundred shares along with selling the call gives the synthetic short put a net delta of 0.45 (−0.55 + 1.00).

Similarly, a synthetic short call can be created by selling a put and selling (short) one hundred shares of stock. Exhibit 6.4 shows a conceptual overview of these two positions at expiration.

EXHIBIT 6.3 Short put vs. short call + long stock.

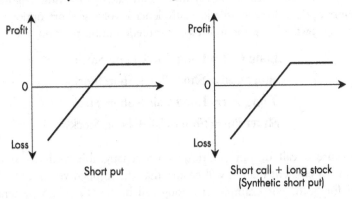

EXHIBIT 6.4 Short call vs. short put + short stock.

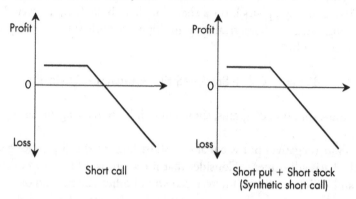

Put-call parity can be manipulated as shown here to illustrate the composition of the synthetic short call.

$$-\text{Call} = -\text{Put} - \text{Stock} + \text{Strike} - \text{Interest} + \text{Dividend}$$

Most professional traders earn a short stock rebate on the proceeds they receive when they short stock—an advantage to the short-put–short-stock side of the equation. Additionally, short-stock sellers must pay dividends on the shares they are short—a liability to the married-put seller. To make all things equal, one subtracts interest and adds dividends to the put side of the equation.

Comparing Synthetic Calls and Puts

The common thread among the synthetic positions explained above is that, for a put-call pair, long options have synthetic equivalents involving long options, and short options have synthetic equivalents involving short options. After accounting for the basis, the four basic synthetic option positions are:

Long Call = **Long** Put + Long Stock
Short Call = **Short** Put + Short Stock
Long Put = **Long** Call + Short Stock
Short Put = **Short** Call + Long Stock

Because a call or put position is interchangeable with its synthetic position, an efficient market will ensure that the implied volatility is closely related for both. For example, if a long call has an IV of 25 percent, the corresponding put should have an IV of about 25 percent, because the long put can easily be converted to a synthetic long call and vice versa. The greeks will be similar for synthetically identical positions, too. The long options and their synthetic equivalents will have positive gamma and vega with negative theta. The short options and their synthetics will have negative gamma and vega with positive theta.

American-Exercise Options

Put-call parity was designed for European-style options. The early exercise possibility of American-style options gums up the works a bit. Because a call (put) and a synthetic call (put) are functionally the same, it is logical to assume that the implied volatility and the greeks for both will be exactly the same. This is not necessarily true with American-style options. However, put-call parity may still be useful with American options when the limitations of the equation are understood. With at-the-money American-exercise options, the differences in the greeks for a put-call pair are subtle. Exhibit 6.5 is a comparison of the greeks for the 50-strike call and the 50-strike put with the underlying at $50 and 66 days until expiration.

The examples used earlier in this chapter in describing the deltas of synthetics were predicated on the rule of thumb that the absolute values of call and put deltas add up to 1.00. To be a bit more realistic, consider that because of American exercise, the absolute delta values of put-call pairs don't always add up to 1.00. In fact, Exhibit 6.5 shows that the call has closer to a 0.554 delta. The put struck at the same price then has a 0.457 delta. By selling 100 shares against the long call, we can create a combined-position delta (call delta plus stock delta) that is very close to the put's delta. The delta of this synthetic put is −0.446 (0.554 − 1.00). The delta of a put will

EXHIBIT 6.5 Greeks for a 50-strike put-call pair on a $50 stock.

	Call	Put
Delta	0.554	0.457
Gamma	0.075	0.078
Theta	0.020	0.013
Vega	0.084	0.084

always be similar to the delta of its corresponding synthetic put. This is also true with call–synthetic-call deltas. This relationship mathematically is

$$\Delta \text{put} \approx \Delta \text{synthetic put}$$
$$\Delta \text{call} \approx \Delta \text{synthetic call}$$

This holds true whether the options are in-, at-, or out-of-the-money. For example, with a stock at \$54, the 50-put would have a −0.205 delta and the call would have a 0.799 delta. Selling 100 shares against the call to create the synthetic put yields a net delta of −0.201.

$$-0.205 \approx -0.201$$

If long or short stock is added to a call or put to create a synthetic, delta will be the only greek affected. With that in mind, note the other greeks displayed in Exhibit 6.5—especially theta. Proportionally, the biggest difference in the table is in theta. The disparity is due in part to interest. When the effects of the interest component outweigh the effects of the dividend, the time value of the call can be higher than the time value of the put. Because the call must lose more premium than the put by expiration, the theta of the call must be higher than the theta of the put.

American exercise can also cause the option prices in put-call parity to not add up. Deep in-the-money (ITM) puts can trade at parity while the corresponding call still has time value. The put-call equation can be unbalanced. The same applies to calls on dividend-paying stocks as the dividend date approaches. When the date is imminent, calls can trade close to parity while the puts still have time value. The role of dividends will be discussed further in Chapter 8.

Synthetic Stock

Not only can synthetic calls and puts be derived by manipulation of put-call parity, but synthetic positions for the other security in the equation—stock—can be derived, as well. By isolating stock on one side of the equation, the formula becomes

$$\text{Stock} = \text{Call} - \text{Put} + \text{Strike} - \text{Interest} + \text{Dividend}$$

After accounting for interest and dividends, buying a call and selling a put of the same strike and time to expiration creates the equivalent of a long stock position. This is called a synthetic stock position, or a combo. After accounting for the basis, the equation looks conceptually like this:

$$Stock = Call - Put + Strike$$

This is easy to appreciate when put-call parity is written out as it is here. It begins to make even more sense when considering at-expiration diagrams and the greeks.

Exhibit 6.6 illustrates a long stock position compared with a long call combined with a short put position.

A quick glance at these two strategies demonstrates that they are the same, but think about why. Consider the synthetic stock position if both options are held until expiration. The long call gives the trader the right to buy the stock at the strike price. The short put gives the trader the obligation to buy the stock at the same strike price. It doesn't matter what the strike price is. As long as the strike is the same for the call and the put, the trader will have a long position in the underlying at the shared strike at expiration when exercise or assignment occurs.

The options in this example are 50-strike options. At expiration, the trader can exercise the call to buy the underlying at $50 if the stock is above the strike. If the underlying is below the strike at expiration, he'll get assigned on the put and buy the stock at $50. If the stock is bought, whether by exercise or assignment, the *effective price* of the potential stock purchase, however, is not necessarily $50.

For example, if the trader bought one 50-strike call at 3.50 and sold one 50-strike put at 1.50, he will effectively purchase the underlying at $52 upon

EXHIBIT 6.6 Long stock vs. long call + short put.

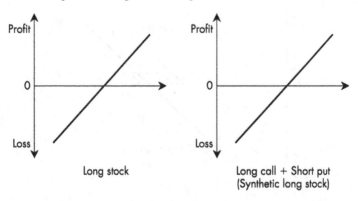

exercise or assignment. Why? The trader paid a net of $2 to get a long position in the stock synthetically (3.50 of call premium debited minus 1.50 of put premium credited). Whether the call or the put is ITM, the effective purchase price of the stock will always be the strike price plus or minus the cost of establishing the synthetic, in this case, $52.

The question that begs to be asked is: would the trader rather buy the stock or pay $2 to have the same market exposure as long stock? Arbitrageurs in the market (with the help of the put-call parity) ensure that neither position—long stock or synthetic long stock—is better than the other.

For example, assume a stock is trading at $51.54. With 71 days until expiration, 26.35 IV, a 5 percent interest rate, and no dividends, the 50-strike call is theoretically worth 3.50, and the 50-strike put is theoretically worth 1.50. Exhibit 6.7 charts the synthetic stock versus the actual stock when there are 71 days until expiration.

Looking at this exhibit, it appears that being long the actual stock outperforms being long the stock synthetically. If the stock is purchased at $51.54, it need only rise a penny higher to profit (in the theoretical world where traders do not pay commissions on transactions). If the synthetic is purchased for $2, the stock needs to rise $0.46 to break even—an apparent disadvantage. This figure, however, does not include interest.

EXHIBIT 6.7 Long stock and synthetic long stock with 71 days to expiration.

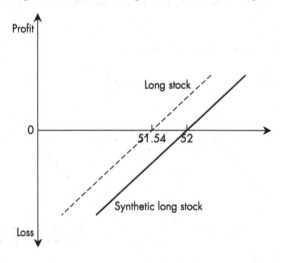

The synthetic stock offers the same risk/reward as actually being long the stock. There is a benefit, from the perspective of interest, to paying only $2 for this exposure rather than $51.54. The interest benefit here is about $0.486. We can find this number by calculating the interest as we did earlier in the chapter. Interest, again, is computed as the strike price times the interest rate times the number of days to expiration divided by the number of days in a year. The formula is as follows:

$$Interest = Strike \times Interest\ Rate \times (Days\ to\ Expiration/365)$$

Inputting the numbers from this example:

$$0.486 = 50 \times 0.05 \times (71/365)$$

The $0.486 of interest is about equal to the $0.46 disparity between the diagrams of the stock and the synthetic stock with 71 days until expiration. The difference is due mainly to rounding and the early-exercise potential of the American put. In mathematical terms

$$51.54 \approx 3.50 - 1.50 + 50 - 0.486 + 0$$

The synthetic long stock is approximately equal to the long stock position when considering the effect of interest. The two lines in Exhibit 6.7—representing stock and synthetic stock—would converge with each passing day as the calculated interest decreases.

This equation works as well for a synthetic short stock position; reversing the signs reveals the synthetic for short stock.

$$-Stock = -Call + Put - Strike + Interest - Dividend$$

Or, in this case,

$$-51.54 \approx -3.50 + 1.50 - 50 + 0.486 - 0$$

Shorting stock at $51.54 is about equal to selling the 50 call and buying the 50 put for a $2 credit based on the interest of 0.486 computed on the 50 strike. Again, the $0.016 disparity between the calculated interest and the actual difference between the synthetic value and the stock price is a function of rounding and early exercise. More on this in the "Conversions and Reversals" section.

Synthetic Stock Strategies

Ultimately, when we roll up our sleeves and get down to the nitty-gritty, options trading is less about having another alternative for trading the direction of the underlying than it is about trading the greeks. Different strategies allow traders to exploit different facets of option pricing. Some strategies allow traders to trade volatility. Some focus mainly on theta. Many of the strategies discussed in this section present ways for a trader to distill risk down mostly to interest rate exposure.

Conversions and Reversals

When calls and puts are combined to create synthetic stock, the main differences are the interest rate and dividends. This is important because the risks associated with interest and dividends can be isolated, and ultimately traded, when synthetic stock is combined with the underlying. There are two ways to combine synthetic stock with its underlying security: a conversion and a reversal.

Conversion

A conversion is a three-legged position in which a trader is long stock, short a call, and long a put. The options share the same month and strike price. By most metrics, this is a very flat position. A trader with a conversion is long the stock and, at the same time, synthetically short the same stock. Consider this from the perspective of delta. In a conversion, the trader is long 1.00 deltas (the long stock) and short very close to 1.00 deltas (the synthetic short stock). Conversions have net flat deltas.

The following is a simple example of a typical conversion and the corresponding deltas of each component.

Short one 35-strike call: −0.63 delta
Long one 35-strike put: −0.37 delta
Long 100 shares: <u>1.00 delta</u>
0.00 delta

The short call contributes a negative delta to the position, in this case, −0.63. The long put also contributes a negative delta, −0.37. The combined delta of the synthetic stock is −1.00 in this example, which is like being short 100 shares of stock. When the third leg of the spread is added, the long 100 shares, it counterbalances the synthetic. The total delta for the conversion is zero.

Most of the conversion's other greeks are pretty flat as well. Gamma, theta, and vega are similar for the call and the put in the conversion, because they have the same expiration month and strike price. Because the trader is selling one option and buying another—a call and a put, respectively—with the same month and strike, the greeks come very close to offsetting each other. For all intents and purposes, the trader is out of the primary risks of the position as measured by greeks when a position is converted. Let's look at a more detailed example.

A trader executes the following trade (for the purposes of this example, we assume the stock pays no dividend and the trade is executed at fair value):

Sell one 71-day 50 call at 3.50
Buy one 71-day 50 put at 1.50
Buy 100 shares at $51.54

The trader buys the stock at $51.54 and synthetically sells the stock at $52. The synthetic price is computed as $-3.50 + 1.50 - 50$. Therefore, the stock is sold synthetically at $0.46 over the actual stock price.

Exhibit 6.8 shows the analytics for the conversion.

This position has very subtle sensitivity to the greeks. The net delta for the spread has a very slightly negative bias. The bias is so small it is negligible to most traders, except professionals trading very large positions.

Why does this negative delta bias exist? Mathematically, the synthetic's delta can be higher with American options than with their European counterparts because of the possibility of early exercise of the put. This anomaly becomes more tangible when we consider the unique directional risk associated with this trade.

In this example, the stock is synthetically sold at $0.46 over the price at which the stock is bought. If the stock declines significantly in value before

EXHIBIT 6.8 Conversion greeks.

	Delta	Gamma	Theta	Vega	Rho
Sell 1 50 call	−0.654	−0.060	+0.020	−0.084	−0.059
Buy 1 50 put	−0.354	+0.062	−0.013	+0.084	−0.031
Buy 100 shares	+1.00	−0−	−0−	−0−	−0−
Total	−0.008	+0.002	+0.007	−0−	−0.090

expiration, the put will, at some point, trade at parity while the call loses all its time value. In this scenario, the value of the synthetic stock will be short at effectively the same price as the actual stock price. For example, if the stock declines to $35 per share then the numbers are as follows:

$$Stock = Call - Put + Strike$$

or

$$35 = 0 - 15 + 50$$

With American options, a put this far in-the-money with less than 71 days until expiry will be all intrinsic value. Interest, in this case, will not factor into the put's value, because the put can be exercised. By exercising the put, both the long stock leg and the long put leg can be closed for even money, leaving only the theoretically worthless call. The stock-synthetic spread is sold at 0.46 and essentially bought at zero when the put is exercised. If the put is exercised before expiration, the profit potential is 0.46 minus the interest calculated between the trade date and the day the put is exercised. If, however, the conversion is held until expiration, the $0.46 is negated by the $0.486 of interest incurred from holding long stock over the entire 71-day period, hence the trader's desire to see the stock decline before expiration, and thus the negative bias toward delta.

This is, incidentally, why the synthetic price (0.46 over the stock price) does not exactly equal the calculated value of the interest (0.486). The trader can exercise the put early if the stock declines and capitalize on the disparity between the interest calculated when the conversion was traded and the actual interest calculation given the shorter time frame. The model values the synthetic at a little less than the interest value would indicate—in this case $0.46 instead of $0.486.

The gamma of this trade is fairly negligible. The theta is slightly positive. Rho is the figure that deserves the most attention. Rho is the change in an option's price given a change in the interest rate.

The −0.090 rho of the conversion indicates that if the interest rate rises one percentage point, the position as a whole loses $0.09. Why? The financing of the position gets more expensive as the interest rate rises. The trader would have to pay more in interest to carry the long stock. In this example, if interest rises by one percentage point, the synthetic stock, which had an effective short price of $0.46 over the price of the long stock before the interest rate increase, will be $0.55 over the price of the long stock afterward. If, however, the interest rate declines by one percentage point, the trader profits $0.09, as the synthetic is repriced by the market to $0.37

over the stock price. The lower the interest rate, the less expensive it is to finance the long stock. This is proven mathematically by put-call parity. Negative rho indicates a bearish position on the interest rate; the trader wants it to go lower. Positive rho is a bullish interest rate position.

But a one-percentage-point change in the interest rate in one day is a big and uncommon change. The question is: is rho relevant? That depends on the type of position and the type of trader. A 0.090 rho would lead to a 0.0225 profit-and-loss (P&(L)) change per one lot conversion on a 25-basis-point, or quarter percent, change. That's just $2.25 per spread. This incremental profit or loss, however, can be relevant to professional traders like market makers. They trade very large positions with the aspiration of making small incremental profits on each trade. A market maker with a 5,000-lot conversion would stand to make or lose $11,250, given a quarter-percentage-point change in interest rate and a 0.090 rho.

The Mind of a Market Maker

Market makers are among the only traders who can trade conversions and reversals profitably, because of the size of their trades and the fact that they can buy the bid and sell the offer. Market makers often attempt to leg into and out of conversions (and reversals). Given the conversion in this example, a market maker may set out to sell calls and in turn buy stock to hedge the call's delta risk (this will be covered in Chapters 12 and 17), then buy puts and the rest of the stock to create a balanced conversion: one call to one put to one hundred shares. The trader may try to put on the conversion in the previous example for a total of $0.50 over the price of the long stock instead of the $0.46 it's worth. He would then try to leg out of the trade for less, say $0.45 over the stock, with the goal of locking in a $0.05 profit per spread on the whole trade.

Reversal

A reversal, or reverse conversion, is simply the opposite of the conversion: buy call, sell put, and sell (short) stock. A reversal can be executed to close a conversion, or it can be an opening transaction. Using the same stock and options as in the previous example, a trader could establish a reversal as follows:

Buy one 71-day 50 call at 3.50
Sell one 71-day 50 put at 1.50
Sell 100 shares at 51.54

The trader establishes a short position in the stock at $51.54 and a long synthetic stock position effectively at $52.00. He buys the stock synthetically at $0.46 over the stock price, again assuming the trade can be executed at fair value. With the reversal, the trader has a bullish position on interest rates, which is indicated by a positive rho.

In this example, the rho for this position is 0.090. If interest rates rise one percentage point, the synthetic stock (which the trader is long) gains nine cents in value relative to the stock. The short stock rebate on the short stock leg earns more interest at a higher interest rate. If rates fall one percentage point, the synthetic long stock loses $0.09. The trader earns less interest being short stock given a lower interest rate.

With the reversal, the fact that the put can be exercised early is a risk. Since the trader is short the put and short stock, he hopes not to get assigned. If he does, he misses out on the interest he planned on collecting when he put on the reversal for $0.46 over.

Pin Risk

Conversions and reversals are relatively low-risk trades. Rho and early exercise are relevant to market makers and other arbitrageurs, but they are among the lowest-risk positions they are likely to trade. There is one indirect risk of conversions and reversals that can be of great concern to market makers around expiration: pin risk. Pin risk is the risk of not knowing for certain whether an option will be assigned. To understand this concept, let's revisit the mind of a market maker.

Recall that market makers have two primary functions:

1. Buy the bid or sell the offer.
2. Manage risk.

When institutional or retail traders send option orders to an exchange (through a broker), market makers are usually the ones with whom they trade. Customers sell the bid; the market makers buy the bid. Customers buy the offer; the market makers sell the offer. The first and arguably easier function of market makers is accomplished whenever a marketable order is sent to the exchange.

Managing risk can get a bit hairy. For example, once the market makers buy April 40 calls, their first instinct is to hedge by selling stock to become delta neutral. Market makers are almost always delta neutral, which mitigates the direction risk. The next step is to mitigate theta, gamma, and vega risk by selling options. The ideal options to sell are the same calls that were bought—that is, get out of the trade. The next best thing is to sell the April 40 puts and sell more stock. In this case, the market makers have established a reversal and thereby have very little risk. If they can lock in the reversal for a small profit, they have done their job.

What happens if the market makers still have the reversal in inventory at expiration? If the stock is above the strike price—40, in this case—the puts expire, the market makers exercise the calls, and the short stock is consequently eliminated. The market makers are left with no position, which is good. They're delta neutral. If the stock is below 40, the calls expire, the puts get assigned, and the short stock is consequently eliminated. Again, no position. But what if the stock is exactly at $40? Should the calls be exercised? Will the puts get assigned? If the puts are assigned, the traders are left with no short stock and should let the calls expire without exercising so as not to have a long delta position after expiration. If the puts are not assigned, they should exercise the calls to get delta flat. It's also possible that only some of the puts will be assigned.

Because they don't know how many, if any, of the puts will be assigned, the market makers have pin risk. To avoid pin risk, market makers try to eliminate their position if they have conversions or reversals close to expiration.

Boxes and Jelly Rolls

There are two other uses of synthetic stock positions that form conventional strategies: boxes and rolls.

Boxes

When long synthetic stock is combined with short synthetic stock on the same underlying within the same expiration cycle but with a different strike price, the resulting position is known as a box. With a box, a trader is synthetically both long and short the stock. The two positions, for all intents and purposes, offset each other directionally. The risk of stock-price movement is almost entirely avoided. A study of the greeks shows that the delta is close to zero. Gamma, theta, vega, and rho are also negligible. Here's an example of a 60–70 box for April options:

Short 1 April 60 call
Long 1 April 60 put
Long 1 April 70 call
Short 1 April 70 put

EXHIBIT 6.9 Box greeks.

	Delta	Gamma	Theta	Vega	Rho
Buy 1 April 60 call	+0.787	+0.029	−0.022	+0.094	+0.109
Sell 1 April 60 put	+0.218	−0.030	+0.013	−0.094	+0.032
Sell 1 April 70 call	−0.419	−0.039	+0.026	−0.128	−0.061
Buy 1 April 70 put	−0.608	+0.042	−0.016	+0.128	−0.074
Total	−0.022	+0.002	+0.001	−0−	+0.006

In this example, the trader is synthetically short the 60-strike and, at the same time, synthetically long the 70-strike. Exhibit 6.9 shows the greeks.

Aside from the risks associated with early exercise implications, this position is just about totally flat. The near-1.00 delta on the long synthetic stock struck at 60 is offset by the near-negative-1.00 delta of the short synthetic struck at 70. The tiny gammas and thetas of both combos are brought closer to zero when they are spread against each another. Vega is zero. And the bullish interest rate sensitivity of the long combo is nearly all offset by the bearish interest sensitivity of the short combo. The stock can move, time can pass, volatility and interest can change, and there will be very little effect on the trader's P&(L). The question is: Why would someone trade a box?

Market makers accumulate positions in the process of buying bids and selling offers. But they want to eliminate risk. Ideally, they try to be *flat the strike*—meaning have an equal number of calls and puts at each strike price, whether through a conversion or a reversal. Often, they have a conversion at one strike and a reversal at another. The stock positions for these cancel each other out and the trader is left with only the four option legs—that is, a box. They can eliminate pin risk on both strikes by trading the box as a single trade to close all four legs. Another reason for trading a box has to do with capital.

Borrowing and Lending Money

The first thing to consider is how this spread is priced. Let's look at another example of a box, the October 50–60 box.

> Long 1 October 60 call
> Short 1 October 60 put
> Short 1 October 70 call
> Long 1 October 70 put

A trader with this position is synthetically long the stock at $60 and short the stock at $70. That sounds like $10 in the bank. The question is: How much would a trader be willing to pay for the right to $10? And for how much would someone be willing to sell it? At face value, the obvious answer is that the equilibrium point is at $10, but there is one variable that must be factored in: time.

In this example, assume that the October call has 90 days until expiration and the interest rate is 6 percent. A rational trader would not pay $10 today for the right to have $10 90 days from now. That would effectively be like loaning the $10 for 90 days and not receiving interest—A losing proposition! The trader on the other side of this box would be happy to enter into the spread for $10. He would have interest-free use of $10 for 90 days. That's free money! Certainly, there is interest associated with the cost of carrying the $10. In this case, the interest would be $0.15.

$$\$10 \times 0.06 \times (90/360)$$

This $0.15 is discounted from the price of the $10 box. In fact, the combined net value of the options composing the box should be about 9.85—with differences due mainly to rounding and the early exercise possibility for American options.

A trader buying this box—that is, buying the more ITM call and more ITM put—would expect to pay $0.15 below the difference between the strike prices. Fair value for this trade is $9.85. The seller of this box—the trader selling the meatier options and buying the cheaper ones—would concede up to $0.15 on the credit.

Jelly Rolls

A jelly roll, or simply a roll, is also a spread with four legs and a combination of two synthetic stock trades. In a box, the difference between the synthetics is the strike price; in a roll, it's the contract month. Here's an example:

Long 1 April 50 call
Short 1 April 50 put
Short 1 May 50 call
Long 1 May 50 put

The options in this spread all share the same strike price, but they involve two different months—April and May. In this example, the trader is long synthetic stock in April and short synthetic stock in May. Like the conversion, reversal, and box, this is a mostly flat position. Delta, gamma, theta, vega, and even rho have only small effects on a jelly roll, but like the others, this spread serves a purpose.

A trader with a conversion or reversal can roll the option legs of the position into a month with a later expiration. For example, a trader with an April 50 conversion in his inventory (short the 50 call, long the 50 put, long stock) can avoid pin risk as April expiration approaches by trading the roll from the above example. The long April 50 call and short April 50 put cancel out the current option portion of the conversion leaving only the stock. Selling the May 50 calls and buying the May 50 puts reestablishes the conversion a month farther out.

Another reason for trading a roll has to do with interest. The roll in this example has positive exposure to rho in April and negative exposure to rho in May. Based on a trader's expectations of future changes in interest rates, a position can be constructed to exploit opportunities in interest.

Theoretical Value and the Interest Rate

The main focus of the positions discussed in this chapter is fluctuations in the interest rate. But which interest rate? That of 30-year bonds? That of 10- or 5-year notes? Overnight rates? The federal funds rate? In the theoretical world, the answer to this question is not really that important. Professors simply point to the riskless rate and continue with their lessons. But when putting strategies like these into practice, choosing the right rate makes a big difference. To answer the question of which interest rate, we must consider exactly what the rates represent from the standpoint of an economist. Therefore, we must understand how an economist makes arguments—by making assumptions.

Take the story of the priest, the physicist, and the economist stranded on a desert island with nothing to eat except a can of beans. The problem is, the can is sealed. In order to survive, they must figure out how to open the can. The priest decides he will pray for the can to be opened by means of a miracle. He prays for hours, but, alas, the can remains sealed tight. The physicist devises a complex system of wheels and pulleys to pop the top off the can. This crude machine unfortunately fails as well. After watching the lack of success of his fellow strandees, the economist announces that he has the solution: "Assume we have a can opener."

In the spirit of economists' logic, let's imagine for a moment a theoretical economic microcosm in which a trader has two trading accounts at the same firm. The assumptions here are that a trader can borrow 100 percent of a stock's value to finance the purchase of the security and that there are no legal, moral, or other limitations on trading. In one account the trader is long 100 shares, fully leveraged. In the other, the trader is short 100 shares of the same stock, in which case the trader earns a short-stock rebate.

In the long run, what is the net result of this trade? Most likely, this trade is a losing proposition for the trader, because the interest rate at which the trader borrows capital is likely to be higher than the interest rate earned on the short-stock proceeds. In this example, interest is the main consideration.

But interest matters in the real world, too. Professional traders earn interest on proceeds from short stock and pay interest on funds borrowed. Interest rates may vary slightly from firm to firm and trader to trader. Interest rates are personal. The interest rate a trader should use when pricing options is specific to his or her situation.

A trader with no position in a particular stock who is interested in trading a conversion should consider that he will be buying the stock. This implies borrowing funds to open the long stock position. The trader should price his options according to the rate he will pay to borrow funds. Conversely, a trader trading a reversal should consider the fact that he is shorting the stock and will receive interest at the rate of the short-stock rebate. This trader should price his options at the short-stock rate.

A Call Is a Put

The idea that "a put is a call, a call is a put" is an important one, indeed. It lays the foundation for more advanced spreading strategies. The concepts in this chapter in one way or another enter into every spread strategy that will be discussed in this book from here on out.

Note

1. Note, for simplicity, simple interest is used in the computation.

CHAPTER 7

Rho

Interest is one of the six inputs of an option-pricing model for American options. Although interest rates can remain constant for long periods, when interest rates do change, call and put values can be positively or negatively affected. Some options are more sensitive to changes in the interest rate than others. To the unaware trader, interest-rate changes can lead to unexpected profits or losses. But interest rates don't have to be a wild-card risk. They're one that experienced traders watch closely to avoid unnecessary risk and increase profitability. To monitor the effect of changes in the interest rate, it is important to understand the quiet greek—rho.

Rho and Interest Rates

Rho is a measurement of the sensitivity of an option's value to a change in the interest rate. To understand how and why the interest rate is important to the value of an option, recall the formula for put-call parity stated in Chapter 6.

$$\text{Call} + \text{Strike} - \text{Interest} = \text{Put} + \text{Stock}^1$$

From this formula, it's clear that as the interest rate rises, put prices must fall and call prices must rise to keep put-call parity balanced. With a little algebra, the equation can be restated to better illustrate this concept:

$$\uparrow \textbf{Call} = \text{Stock} + \text{Put} + \uparrow \textbf{Interest} - \text{Strike}$$

and

$$\downarrow \textbf{Put} = \text{Call} + \text{Strike} + \uparrow \textbf{Interest} - \text{Stock}$$

If interest rates fall,

$$\downarrow \textbf{Call} = \text{Stock} + \text{Put} + \downarrow \textbf{Interest} - \text{Strike}$$

and

$$\uparrow \textbf{Put} = \text{Call} + \text{Strike} - \downarrow \textbf{Intererst} - \text{Stock}$$

Rho helps quantify this relationship. Calls have positive rho, and puts have negative rho. For example, a call with a rho of +0.08 will gain $0.08 with each one-percentage-point rise in interest rates and fall $0.08 with each one-percentage-point fall in interest rates. A put with a rho of −0.08 will lose $0.08 with each one-point rise and gain $0.08 in value with a one-point fall.

The effect of changes in the interest variable of put-call parity on call and put values is contingent on three factors: the strike price, the interest rate, and the number of days until expiration.

$$\text{Interest} = \text{Strike} \times \text{Interest Rate} \times (\text{Days to Expiration}/365)^2$$

Interest, for our purposes, is a function of the strike price. The higher the strike price, the greater the interest and, consequently the more changes in the interest rate will affect the option. The higher the interest rate is, the higher the interest variable will be. Likewise, the more time to expiration, the greater the effect of interest. Rho measures an option's sensitivity to the end results of these three influences.

To understand how changes in interest affect option prices, consider a typical at-the-money (ATM) conversion on a non-dividend-paying stock.

Short 1 May 50 call at 1.92
Long 1 May 50 put at 1.63
Long 100 shares at $50

With 43 days until expiration at a 5 percent interest rate, the interest on the 50 strike will be about $0.29. Put-call parity ensures that this $0.29 shows up in option prices. After rearranging the equation, we get

$$\text{Call} - \text{Put} = \text{Stock} - \text{Strike} + \text{Interest}$$

In this example, both options are exactly ATM. There is no intrinsic value. Therefore, the difference between the extrinsic values of the call and the put must equal interest. If one option were in-the-money (ITM), the intrinsic value on the left side of the equation would be offset by the Stock − Strike on the right side. Still, it would be the difference in the time value of the call and put that equals the interest variable.

This is shown by the fact that the synthetic stock portion of the conversion is short at $50.29 (call − put + strike). This is $0.29 above the stock price. The synthetic stock equals the Stock + Interest, or

$$\text{Call} - \text{Put} + \text{Strike} = \text{Stock} + \text{Interest}$$

Certainly, if the interest rate were higher, the interest on the synthetic stock would be a higher number. At a 6 percent interest rate, the effective short price of the synthetic stock would be about $50.35. The call would be valued at about 1.95, and the put would be 1.60—a net of $0.35.

A one-percentage-point rise in the interest rate causes the synthetic stock position to be revalued by $0.06—a $0.03 gain in the call value and a $0.03 decline in the put. Therefore, by definition, the call has a +0.03 rho and the put has a −0.03 rho.

Rho and Time

The time component of interest has a big impact on the magnitude of an option's rho, because the greater the number of days until expiration, the greater the interest. Long-term options will be more sensitive to changes in the interest rate and, therefore, have a higher rho.

Take a stock trading at about $120 per share. The July, October, and January ATM calls have the following rhos with the interest rate at 5.5 percent.

Option	Rho
July (38-day) 120 calls	+0.068
October (130-day) 120 calls	+0.226
January (221-day) 120 calls	+0.385

If interest rates rise 25 basis points, or a quarter of a percentage point, the July calls with only 38 days until expiration will gain very little: only $0.017 (0.068 × 0.25). The October 120 calls with 130 days until expiration gain more: $0.057 (0.226 × 0.25). The January calls that have 221 days until they expire make $0.096 theoretically (0.385 × 0.25). If all else is held constant, the more time to expiration, the higher the option's rho, and therefore, the more interest will affect the option's value.

Considering Rho When Planning Trades

Just having an opinion on a stock is only half the battle in options trading. Choosing the best way to trade a forecast can make all the difference to the success of a trade. Options give traders choices. And one of the choices a trader has is the month in which to trade. When trading LEAPS—Long-Term Equity AnticiPation Securities—delta, gamma, theta, and vega are important, as always, but rho is also a valuable part of the strategy.

LEAPS

Options buyers have time working against them. With each passing day, theta erodes the value of their assets. Buying a long-term option, or a LEAPS, helps combat erosion because long-term options can decay at a slower rate. In environments where there is interest rate uncertainty, however, LEAPS traders have to think about more than the rate of decay.

Consider two traders: Jason and Susanne. Both are bullish on XYZ Corp. (XYZ), which is trading at $59.95 per share. Jason decides to buy a May 60 call at 1.60, and Susanne buys a LEAPS 60 call at 7.60. In this example, May options have 44 days until expiration, and the LEAPS have 639 days.

EXHIBIT 7.1 XYZ short-term call vs. LEAPS call.

44-Day 60 Calls		639-Day 60 Calls	
Delta	0.55	Delta	0.71
Gamma	0.115	Gamma	0.03
Theta	−0.02	Theta	−0.01
Vega	0.08	Vega	0.27
Rho	0.039	Rho	0.638

Both of these trades are bullish, but the traders most likely had slightly different ideas about time, volatility, and interest rates when they decided which option to buy. Exhibit 7.1 compares XYZ short-term at-the-money calls with XYZ LEAPS ATM calls.

To begin with, it appears that Susanne was allowing quite a bit of time for her forecast to be realized—almost two years. Jason, however, was looking for short-term price appreciation. Concerns about time decay may have been a motivation for Susanne to choose a long-term option—her theta of 0.01 is half Jason's, which is 0.02. With only 44 days until expiration, the theta of Jason's May call will begin to rise sharply as expiration draws near.

But the trade-off of lower time decay is lower gamma. At the current stock price, Susanne has a higher delta. If the XYZ stock price rises $2, the gamma of the May call will cause Jason's delta to creep higher than Susanne's. At $62, the delta for the May 60s would be about 0.78, whereas the LEAPS 60 call delta is about 0.77. This disparity continues as XYZ moves higher.

Perhaps Susanne had implied volatility (IV) on her mind as well as time decay. These long-term ATM LEAPS options have vegas more than three times the corresponding May's. If IV for both the May and the LEAPS is at a yearly low, LEAPS might be a better buy. A one- or two-point rise in volatility if IV reverts to its normal level will benefit the LEAPS call much more than the May.

Theta, delta, gamma, and vega are typical considerations with most trades. Because this option is long term, in addition to these typical considerations, Susanne needs to take a good hard look at rho. The LEAPS rho is significantly higher than that of its short-term counterpart. A one-percentage-point change in the interest rate will change Susanne's P&(L) by $0.64— that's about 8.5 percent of the value of her option—and she has nearly two years of exposure to interest rate fluctuations. Certainly, when the Federal Reserve Board has great concerns about growth or inflation, rates can rise or fall by more than one percentage point in one year's time.

It is important to understand that, like the other greeks, rho is a snapshot at a particular price, volatility level, interest rate, and moment in time. If interest rates were to fall by one percentage point today, it would cause Susanne's call to decline in value by $0.64. If that rate drop occurred over the life of the option, it would have a much smaller effect. Why? Rate changes closer to expiration have less of an effect on option values.

Assume that on the trade date, when the LEAPS has 639 days until expiration, interest rates fall by 25 basis points. The effect will be a decline in the value of the call of 0.16—one-fourth of the 0.638 rho. If the next rate cut occurs six months later, the rho of the LEAPS will be smaller, because it will have less time until expiration. In this case, after six months, the rho will be only 0.46. Another 25-basis-point drop will hurt the call by $0.115. After another six months, the option will have a 0.26 rho. Another quarter-point cut costs Susanne only $0.065. Any subsequent rate cuts in ensuing months will have almost no effect on the now short-term option value.

Pricing in Interest Rate Moves

In the same way that volatility can get priced in to an option's value, so can the interest rate. When interest rates are expected to rise or fall, those expectations can be reflected in the prices of options. Say current interest rates are at 8 percent, but the Fed has announced that the economy is growing at too fast of a pace and that it may raise interest rates at the next Federal Open Market Committee meeting. Analysts expect more rate hikes to follow. The options with expiration dates falling after the date of the expected rate hikes will have higher interest rates priced in. In this situation, the higher interest rates in the longer-dated options will be evident when entering parameters into the model.

Take options on Already Been Chewed Bubblegum Corp. (ABC). A trader, Kyle, enters parameters into the model for ABC options and notices that the prices don't line up. To get the theoretical values of the ATM calls for all the expiration months to sit in the middle of the actual market values, Kyle may have to tinker with the interest rate inputs.

Assume the following markets for the ATM 70-strike calls in ABC options:

	Calls	Puts
Aug 70 calls	1.75–1.85	1.30–1.40
Sep 70 calls	2.65–2.75	1.75–1.85
Dec 70 calls	4.70–4.90	2.35–2.45
Mar 70 calls	6.50–6.70	2.65–2.75

ABC is at $70 a share, has a 20 percent IV in all months, and pays no dividend. August expiration is one month away.

Entering the known inputs for strike price, stock price, time to expiration, volatility, and dividend and using an 8 percent interest rate yields the following theoretical values for ABC options:

	Calls	Puts	Interest Rate
Aug 70 calls	1.80	1.35	8%
Sep 70 calls	**2.65**	**1.78**	8%
Dec 70 calls	**4.72**	**2.50**	8%
Mar 70 calls	**6.41**	**2.84**	8%

The theoretical values, in bold type, are those that don't line up in the middle of the call and put markets. These values are wrong. The call theoretical values are too low, and the put theoretical values are too high. They are the product of an interest rate that is too low being applied to the model. To generate values that are indicative of market prices, Kyle must change the interest input to the pricing model to reflect the market's expectations of future interest rate changes.

Using new values for the interest rate yields the following new values:

	Calls	Puts	Interest Rate
Aug 70 calls	1.80	1.35	8%
Sep 70 calls	2.67	1.77	8.25%
Dec 70 calls	4.80	2.43	8.50%
Mar 70 calls	6.60	2.71	8.75%

After recalculating, the theoretical values line up in the middle of the call and put markets. Using higher interest rates for the longer expirations raises the call values and lowers the put values for these months. These interest rates were inferred from, or backed out of, the option-market prices by use of the option-pricing model. In practice, it may take some trial and error to find the correct interest values to use.

In times of interest rate uncertainty, rho can be an important factor in determining which strategy to select. When rates are generally expected to continue to rise or fall over time, they are normally priced in to the options, as shown in the previous example. When there is no consensus among analysts and traders, the rates that are priced in may change as economic data are made available. This can cause a revision of option values. In long-term options that have higher rhos, this is a bona fide risk. Short-term options are a safer play in this environment. But as all traders know, risk also implies opportunity.

Trading Rho

While it's possible to trade rho, most traders forgo this niche for more dynamic strategies with greater profitability. The effects of rho are often overshadowed by the more profound effects of the other greeks. The opportunity to profit from rho is outweighed by other risks. For most traders, rho is hardly ever even looked at.

Because LEAPS have higher rho values than corresponding short-term options, it makes sense that these instruments would be appropriate for interest-rate plays. But even with LEAPS, rho exposure usually pales in comparison with that of delta, theta, and vega.

It is not uncommon for the rho of a long-term option to be 5 to 8 percent of the option's value. For example, Exhibit 7.2 shows a two-year LEAPS on a $70 stock with the following pricing-model inputs and outputs:

The rho is +0.793, or about 5.8 percent of the call value. That means a 25-basis-point rise in rates contributes to only a 20-cent profit on the call. That's only about 1.5 percent of the call's value. On one hand, 1.5 percent is not a very big profit on a trade. On the other hand, if there are more rate rises at following Fed meetings, the trader can expect further gains on rho.

Even if the trader is compelled to wait until the next Fed meeting to make another $0.20—or less, as rho will get smaller as time passes—from a

EXHIBIT 7.2 Long 70-strike LEAPS call.

Inputs		Outputs	
Stock price	70	Call value	13.60
Strike price	70	Delta	+0.760
Time to expiry	2 yrs	Gamma	+0.016
Interest rate	8%	Theta	−0.013
Dividends	0	Vega	+0.308
Volatility	20%	Rho	+0.793

second 25-basis-point rate increase, other influences will diminish rho's significance. If over the six-week period between Fed meetings, the underlying declines by just $0.60, the $0.40 that the trader hoped to make on rho is wiped out by delta loss. With the share price $0.60 lower, the 0.760 delta costs the trade about $0.46. Furthermore, the passing of six weeks (42 days) will lead to a loss of about $0.55 from time decay because of the −0.013 theta. There is also the risk from the fat vegas associated with LEAPS. A 1.5 percent drop in implied volatility completely negates any hopes of rho profits.

Aside from the possibility that delta, theta, and vega may get in the way of profits, the bid-ask spread with these long-term options tends to be wider than with their short-term counterparts. If the bid-ask spread is more than $0.40 wide, which is often the case with LEAPS, rho profits are canceled out by this cost of doing business. Buying the offer and selling the bid negative scalps away potential profits.

With LEAPS, rho is always a concern. It will contribute to prosperity or peril and needs to be part of the trade plan from forecast to implementation. Buying or selling a LEAPS call or put, however, is not a practical way to speculate on interest rates.

To take a position on interest rates in the options market, risk needs to be distilled down to rho. The other greeks need to be spread off. This is accomplished only through the conversions, reversals, and jelly rolls described in Chapter 6. However, the bid-ask can still be a hurdle to trading these strategies for non−market makers. Generally, rho is a greek that for most traders is important to understand but not practical to trade.

Notes

1. Please note, for simplification, dividends are not included.
2. Note, for simplicity, simple interest is used in the calculation.

CHAPTER 8

Dividends and Option Pricing

Much of this book studies how to break down and trade certain components of option prices. This chapter examines the role of dividends in the pricing structure. There is no greek symbol that measures an option's sensitivity to changes in the dividend. And in most cases, dividends are not "traded" by means of options in the same way that volatility, interest, and other option price influences are. Dividends do, though, affect option prices, and therefore a trader's P&(L), so they deserve attention.

There are some instances where dividends provide ample opportunity to the option trader, and there some instances where a change in dividend policy can have desirable, or undesirable, effects on the bottom line. Despite the fact that dividends do not technically involve greeks, they need to be monitored in much the same way as do delta, gamma, theta, vega, and rho.

Dividend Basics

Let's start at the beginning. When a company decides to pay a dividend, there are four important dates the trader must be aware of:

1. Declaration date
2. Ex-dividend date
3. Record date
4. Payable date

The first date chronologically is the declaration date. This date is when the company formally declares the dividend. It's when the company lets its shareholders know when and in what amount it will pay the dividend. Active traders, however, may buy and sell the same stock over and over again. How does the corporation know exactly who collects the dividend when it is opening up its coffers?

Dividends are paid to shareholders of record who are on the company's books as owning the stock at the opening of business on another important date: the record date. Anyone long the stock at this moment is entitled to the dividend. Anyone with a short stock position on the opening bell on the record date is required to make payment in the amount of the dividend. Because the process of stock settlement takes time, the important date is actually not the record date. For all intents and purposes, the key date is two days before the record date. This is called the ex-dividend date, or the ex-date.

Traders who have earned a dividend by holding a stock in their account on the morning of the ex-date have one more important date they need to know—the date they get paid. The date that the dividend is actually paid is called the payable date. The payable date can be a few weeks after the ex-date.

Let's walk through an example. ABC Corporation announces on March 21 (the declaration date) that it will pay a 25-cent dividend to shareholders of record on April 3 (the record date), payable on April 23 (the payable date). This means market participants wishing to receive the dividend must own the stock on the open on April 1 (the ex-date). In practice, they must buy the stock before the closing bell rings on March 31 in order to have it for the open the next day.

This presents a potential quandary. If a trader only needs to have the stock on the open on the ex-date, why not buy the stock just before the close on the day before the ex-date, in this case March 31, and sell it the next morning after the open? Could this be an opportunity for riskless profit?

Unfortunately, no. There are a couple of problems with that strategy. First, as far as the riskless part is concerned, stock prices can and often do change overnight. Yesterday's close and today's open can sometimes be significantly different. When they are, it is referred to as a gap open. Whenever a stock is held (long or short), there is risk. The second problem with this strategy to earn riskless profit is with the profit part. On the ex-date, the opening stock price reflects the dividend. Say ABC is trading at $50 at the close on March 31. If the market for the stock opens unchanged the next morning—that is, a zero net change on the day on—ABC will be trading at $49.75 ($50 minus the $0.25 dividend). Alas, the quest for riskless profit continues.

Dividends and Option Pricing

The preceding discussion demonstrated how dividends affect stock traders. There's one problem: we're option traders! Option holders or writers do not receive or pay dividends, but that doesn't mean dividends aren't relevant to the pricing of these securities. Observe the behavior of a conversion or a reversal before and after an ex-dividend date. Assuming the stock opens unchanged on the ex-date, the relationship of the price of the synthetic stock to the actual stock price will change. Let's look at an example to explore why.

At the close on the day before the ex-date of a stock paying a $0.25 dividend, a trader has an at-the-money (ATM) conversion. The stock is trading right at $50 per share. The 50 puts are worth 2.34, and the 50 calls are worth 2.48. Before the ex-date, the trader is

Long 100 shares at $50
Long one 50 put at 2.34
Short one 50 call at 2.48

Here, the trader is long the stock at $50 and short stock synthetically at $50.14—50 + (2.48 − 2.34). The trader is synthetically short $0.14 over the price at which he is long the stock.

Assume that the next morning the stock opens unchanged. Since this is the ex-date, that means the stock opens at $49.75—$0.25 lower than the previous day's close. The theoretical values of the options will change very little. The options will be something like 2.32 for the put and 2.46 for the call.

After the ex-date, the trader is

Long 100 shares at $49.75
Long one 50 put at 2.32
Short one 50 call at 2.46

Each option is two cents lower. Why? The change in the option prices is due to theta. In this case, it's $0.02 for each option. The synthetic stock is still short from an effective price of $50.14. With the stock at $49.75, the synthetic short price is now $0.39 over the stock. Incidentally, $0.39 is $0.25 more than the $0.14 difference before the ex-date.

Did the trader who held the conversion overnight from before the ex-date to after it make or lose money? Neither. Before the ex-date, he had an asset worth $50 per share (the stock) and he shorted the asset synthetically at \$50.14. After the ex-date, he still has assets totaling \$50 per share—the stock at \$49.75 plus the 0.25 dividend—and he is still synthetically short the stock at \$50.14. Before the ex-date, the \$0.14 difference between the synthetic and the stock is interest minus the dividend. After the ex-date, the \$0.39 difference is all interest.

Dividends and Early Exercise

As the ex-date approaches, in-the-money (ITM) calls on equity options can often be found trading at parity, regardless of the dividend amount and regardless of how far off expiration is. This seems counterintuitive. What about interest? What about dividends? Normally, these come into play in option valuation.

But option models designed for American options take the possibility of early exercise into account. It is possible to exercise American-style calls and exchange them for the underlying stock. This would give traders, now stockholders, the right to the dividend—a right for which they would not be eligible as call holders. Because of the impending dividend, the call becomes an exercise just before the ex-date. For this reason, the call can trade for parity before the ex-date.

Let's look at an example of a reversal on a \$70 stock that pays a \$0.40 dividend. The options in this reversal have 24 days until expiration, which makes the interest on the 60 strike roughly \$0.20, given a 5 percent interest rate. The day before the ex-date, a trader has the following position at the stated prices:

Short 100 shares at \$70
Long one 60 call at 10.00
Short one 60 put at 0.05

To understand how American calls work just before the ex-date, it is helpful first to consider what happens if the trader holds the position until the ex-date. Making the assumption that the stock is unchanged on the ex-dividend date, it will open at \$69.60, lower by the amount of the dividend—in this case, \$0.40. The put, being so far out-of-the-money (OTM) as to have a negligible delta, will remain unchanged. But what about the call? With no dividend left in the stock, the put call-parity states

$$Call = Put + Stock - Strike + Interest$$

In this case,

$$Call = 0.05 + 69.60 - 60 + 0.20$$
$$Call = 9.85$$

Before the ex-date, the model valued the call at parity. Now it values the same call at $0.25 over parity (9.85 − [69.60 − 60]). Another way to look at this is that the time value of the call is now made up of the interest plus the put premium. Either way, that's a gain of $0.25 on the call. That sounds good, but because the trader is short stock, if he hasn't exercised, he will owe the $0.40 dividend—a net loss of $0.15. The new position will be

Short 100 shares at $69.60
Owe $0.40 dividend
Long one 60 call at 9.85
Short one 60 put at 0.05

At the end of the trading day before the ex-date, this trader must exercise the call to capture the dividend. By doing so, he closes two legs of the trade—the call and the stock. The $10 call premium is forfeited, the stock that is short at $70 is bought at $60 (from the call exercise) for a $10 profit. The transaction leads to neither a profit nor a loss. The purpose of exercising is to avoid the $0.15 loss ($0.25 gain in call time value minus the $0.40 loss in dividends owed).

The other way the trader could achieve the same ends is to sell the long call and buy in the short stock. This is tactically undesirable because the trader may have to sell the bid in the call and buy the offer in the stock. Furthermore, when legging a trade in this manner, there is the risk of slippage. If the call is sold first, the stock can move before the trader has a chance to buy it at the necessary price. It is generally better and less risky to exercise the call rather than leg out of the trade.

In this transaction, the trader begins with a fairly flat position (short stock/long synthetic stock) and ends with a short put that is significantly out-of-the-money. For all intents and purposes, exercising the call in this trade is like synthetically selling the put. But at what price? In this case, it's $0.15. This again is the cost benefit of saving $0.40 by avoiding the dividend obligation versus the $0.25 gain in call time value. Exercising the call is effectively like selling the put at 0.15 in this example. If the dividend is lower or the interest is higher, it may not be worth it to the trader to exercise the call to capture the dividend. How do traders know if their calls should be exercised?

The traders must do the math before each ex-dividend date in option classes they trade. The traders have to determine if the benefit from exercising—or the price at which the synthetic put is essentially being sold—is more or less than the price at which they can sell the put. The math used here is adopted from put-call parity:

$$\text{If Dividend} - \text{Interest} > \text{Put Bid Price, then} \ldots$$

This shows the case where the traders can effectively synthetically sell the put (by exercising) for more than the current put value. Tactically, it's appropriate to use the bid price for the put in this calculation since that is the price at which the put can be sold.

$$\text{If Dividend} - \text{Interest} < \text{Put Bid Price, then} \ldots$$

In this case, the traders would be inclined to not exercise. It would be theoretically more beneficial to sell the put if the trader is so inclined.

$$\text{If Dividend} - \text{Interest} \approx \text{Put Bid Price, then} \ldots$$

Here, the traders, from a valuation perspective, are indifferent as to whether or not to exercise. The question then is simply: do they want to sell the put at this price?

Professionals and big retail traders who are long (ITM) calls—whether as part of a reversal, part of another type of spread, or because they are long the calls outright—must do this math the day before each ex-dividend date to maximize profits and minimize losses. Not exercising, or forgetting to exercise, can be a costly mistake. Traders who are short ITM dividend-paying calls, however, can reap the benefits of those sleeping on the job. It works both ways.

Traders who are long stock and short calls at parity before the ex-date may stand to benefit if some of the calls do not get assigned. Any shares of long stock remaining on the ex-date will result in the traders receiving dividends. If the dividends that will be received are greater in value than the interest that will subsequently be paid on the long stock, the traders may stand reap an arbitrage profit because of long call holders' forgetting to exercise.

Dividend Plays

The day before an ex-dividend date in a stock, option volume can be unusually high. Tens of thousands of contracts sometimes trade in names that usually have average daily volumes of only a couple thousand. This spike in volume often has nothing to do with the market's opinion on direction after the dividend. The heavy trading has to do with the revaluation of the relationship of exercisable options to the underlying expected to occur on the ex-dividend date.

Traders that are long ITM calls and short ITM calls at another strike just before an ex-dividend date have a potential liability and a potential benefit. The potential liability is that they can forget to exercise. This is a liability over which the traders have complete control. The potential benefit is that some of the short calls may not get assigned. If traders on the other side of the short calls (the longs) forget to exercise, the traders that are short the call make out by not having to pay the dividend on short stock.

Professionals and big retail traders who have very low transaction costs will sometimes trade ITM call spreads during the afternoon before an ex-dividend date. This consists of buying one call and selling another call with a different strike price. Both calls in the dividend-play strategy are ITM and have corresponding puts with little or no value (to be sure, the put value is less than the dividend minus the interest). The traders trade the spreads, fairly indifferent as to whether they buy or sell the spreads, in hope of skating—or not getting assigned—on some of their short calls. The more they don't get assigned the better.

This usually occurs in options that have high open interest, meaning there are a lot of outstanding contracts already. The more contracts in existence, the better the possibility of someone forgetting to exercise. The greatest volume also tends to occur in the front month.

Strange Deltas

Because American calls become an exercise possibility when the ex-date is imminent, the deltas can sometimes look odd. When the calls are trading at parity, they have a 1.00 delta. They are a substitute for the stock. They, in fact, will be stock if and when they are exercised just before the ex-date. But if the puts still have some residual time value, they may also have a small delta, of 0.05 or perhaps more.

In this unique scenario, the delta of the synthetic can be greater than +1.00 or less than −1.00. It is not uncommon to see the absolute values of the call and put deltas add up to 1.07 or 1.08. When the dividend comes out of the options model on the ex-date, synthetics go back to normal. The delta of the synthetic again approaches 1.00. Because of the out-of-whack deltas, delta-neutral traders need to take extra caution in their analytics when ex-dates are near. A little common sense should override what the computer spits out.

Inputting Dividend Data into the Pricing Model

Often dividend payments are regular and predictable. With many companies, the dividend remains constant quarter after quarter. Some corporations have a track record of incrementally increasing their dividends every year. Some companies pay dividends in a very irregular fashion, by paying special dividends that are often announced as a surprise to investors. In a truly capitalist society, there are no restrictions and no rules on when, whether, or how corporations pay dividends to their shareholders. Unpredictability of dividends, though, can create problems in options valuation.

When a company has a constant, reasonably predictable dividend, there is not a lot of guesswork. Take Exelon Corp. (EXC). From November 2008 to the time of this writing, Exelon has paid a regular quarterly dividend of $0.525. During that period, a trader has needed simply to enter 0.525 into the pricing calculator for all expected future dividends to generate the theoretical value. Based on recent past performance, the trader could feel confident that the computed analytics were reasonably accurate. If the trader believed the company would continue its current dividend policy, there would be little options-related dividend risk—unless things changed.

When there is uncertainty about when future dividends will be paid in what amounts, the level of dividend-related risk begins to increase. The more uncertainty, the more risk. Let's examine an interesting case study: General Electric (GE).

For a long time, GE was a company that has had a history of increasing its dividends at fairly regular intervals. In fact, there was more than a 30-year stretch in which GE increased its dividend every year. During most of the first decade of the 2000s, increases in GE's dividend payments were around one to six cents and tended to occur toward the end of December, after December expiration. The dividends were paid four times per year but not exactly quarterly. For several years, the ex-dates were in February, June, September, and December. Option traders trading GE options had a pretty easy time estimating their future dividend streams, and consequently evaded valuation problems that could result from using wrong dividend data. Traders would simply adjust the dividend data in the model to match their expectations for predictably increasing future dividends in order to achieve an accurate theoretical value. Let's look back at GE to see how a trader might have done this.

The following shows dividend-history data for GE.

Ex-Date	Dividend*
12/27/02	$0.19
02/26/03	$0.19
06/26/03	$0.19
09/25/03	$0.19
12/29/03	$0.20
02/26/04	$0.20
06/24/04	$0.20
09/23/04	$0.20
12/22/04	$0.22
02/24/05	$0.22
06/23/05	$0.22
09/22/05	$0.22
12/22/05	$0.25
02/23/06	$0.25
06/22/06	$0.25
09/21/06	$0.25
12/21/06	$0.28
02/22/07	$0.28
06/21/07	$0.28

*These data are taken from the following Web page on GE's web site: www.ge.com/investors/stock_info/dividend_history.html.

At the end of 2006, GE raised its dividend from $0.25 to $0.28. A trader trading GE options at the beginning of 2007 would have logically anticipated the next increase to occur again in the following December unless there was reason to believe otherwise. Options expiring before this anticipated next dividend increase would have the $0.28 dividend priced into their values. Options expiring after December 2007 would have a higher dividend priced into them—possibly an additional three cents to 0.31 (which indeed it was). Calls would be adversely affected by this increase, and puts would be favorably affected. A typical trader would have anticipated those changes. The dividend data a trader pricing GE options would have entered into the model in January 2007 would have looked something like this.

Ex-Date	Dividend*
02/22/07	$0.28
06/21/07	$0.28
09/20/07	$0.28
12/20/07	$0.31
02/21/08	$0.31
06/19/08	$0.31
09/18/08	$0.31

*These data are taken from the following Web page on GE's web site: www.ge.com/investors/stock_info/dividend_history.html.

The trader would have entered the anticipated future dividend amount in conjunction with the anticipated ex-dividend date. This trader projection goes out to February 2008, which would aid in valuing options expiring in 2007 as well as the 2008 LEAPS. Because the declaration dates had yet to occur, one could not know with certainty when the dividends would be announced or in what amount. Certainly, there would be some estimation involved for both the dates and the amount. But traders would probably get it pretty close—close enough.

Then, something particularly interesting happened. Instead of raising the dividend going into December 2008 as would be a normal pattern, GE kept it the same. As shown, the 12/24/08 ex-dated dividend remained $0.31.

Ex-Date	Dividend*
02/22/07	$0.28
06/21/07	$0.28

09/20/07	$0.28
12/20/07	$0.31
02/21/08	$0.31
06/19/08	$0.31
09/18/08	$0.31
12/24/08	$0.31

*These data are taken from the following Web page on GE's web site: www.ge.com/investors/stock_info/dividend_history.html.

The dividend stayed at $0.31 until the June 2009 dividend, which held another jolt for traders pricing options. Around this time, GE's stock price had taken a beating. It fell from around $42 a share in the fall of 2007 ultimately to about $6 in March 2009. GE had its first dividend cut in more than three decades. The dividend with the ex-date of 06/18/09 was $0.10.

12/24/08	$0.31
02/19/09	$0.31
06/18/09	$0.10
09/17/09	$0.10
12/23/09	$0.10
02/25/10	$0.10
06/17/10	$0.10
09/16/10	$0.12
12/22/10	$0.14
02/24/11	$0.14
06/16/11	$0.15
09/15/11	$0.15

Though the company gave warnings in advance, the drastic dividend change had a significant impact on option prices. Call prices were helped by the dividend cut (or anticipated dividend cut) and put prices were hurt.

The break in the pattern didn't stop there. The dividend policy remained $0.10 for five quarters until it rose to $0.12 in September 2010, then to $0.14 in December 2010, then to $0.15 in June 2011. These irregular changes in the historically predictable dividend policy made it tougher for traders to attain accurate valuations. If the incremental changes were bigger, the problem would have been even greater.

Good and Bad Dates with Models

Using an incorrect date for the ex-date in option pricing can lead to unfavorable results. If the ex-dividend date is not known because it has yet to be declared, it must be estimated and adjusted as need be after it is formally announced. Traders note past dividend history and estimate the expected dividend stream accordingly. Once the dividend is declared, the ex-date is known and can be entered properly into the pricing model. Not executing due diligence to find correct known ex-dates can lead to trouble. Using a bad date in the model can yield dubious theoretical values that can be misleading or worse—especially around the expiration.

Say a call is trading at 2.30 the day before the ex-date of a $0.25 dividend, which happens to be thirty days before expiration. The next day, of course, the stock may have moved higher or lower. Assume for illustrative purposes, to compare apples to apples as it were, that the stock is trading at the same price—in this case, $76.

If the trader is using the correct date in the model, the option value will adjust to take into account the effect of the dividend expiring, or reaching its ex-date, when the number of days to expiration left changes from 30 to 29. The call trading postdividend will be worth more relative to the same stock price. If the dividend date the trader is using in the model is wrong, say one day later than it should be, the dividend will still be an input of the theoretical value. The calculated value will be too low. It will be wrong.

Exhibit 8.1 compares the values of a 30-day call on the ex-date given the right and the wrong dividend.

At the same stock price of $76 per share, the call is worth $0.13 more after the dividend is taken out of the valuation. Barring any changes in implied volatility (IV) or the interest rate, the market prices of the options should reflect this change. A trader using an ex-date in the model that is farther in the future than the actual ex-date will still have the dividend as part of the generated theoretical value. With the ex-date just one day later, the call would be worth 2.27. The difference in option value is due to the effect of theta—in this case, $0.03.

With a bad date, the value of 2.27 would likely be significantly below market price, causing the market value of the option to look more expensive

EXHIBIT 8.1 Comparison of 30-day call values.

Call Value 1 Day Before Ex-Date		Call Value on Ex-Date with the "Right" Dividend		Call Value on Ex-Date with the "Wrong" Dividend	
Price	76	Price	76	Price	76
Strike	75	Strike	75	Strike	75
Days to Exp.	30	Days to Exp.	29	Days to Exp.	29
Volatility	20%	Volatility	20%	Volatility	20%
Interest	5.25%	Interest	5.25%	Interest	5.25%
Dividend	0.25	Dividend	−0−	Dividend	**0.25**
Call Theo.	2.30	Call Theo.	2.43	Call Theo.	2.27

than it actually is. If the trader did not know the date was wrong, he would need to raise IV to make the theoretical value match the market. This option has a vega of 0.08, which translates into a difference of about two IV points for the theoretical values 2.43 and 2.27. The trader would perceive the call to be trading at an IV two points higher than the market indicates.

Dividend Size

It's not just the date but also the size of the dividend that matters. When companies change the amount of the dividend, options prices follow in step. In 2004, when Microsoft (MSFT) paid a special dividend of $3 per share, there were unexpected winners and losers in the Microsoft options. Traders who were long calls or short puts were adversely affected by this change in dividend policy. Traders with short calls or long puts benefited. With long-term options, even less anomalous changes in the size of the dividend can have dramatic effects on options values.

Let's study an example of how an unexpected rise in the quarterly dividend of a stock affects a long call position. Extremely Yellow Zebra Corp. (XYZ) has been paying a quarterly dividend of $0.10. After a steady rise in stock price to $61 per share, XYZ declares a dividend payment of $0.50. It is expected that the company will continue to pay $0.50 per quarter. A trader, James, owns the 528-day 60-strike calls, which were trading at 9.80 before the dividend increase was announced.

EXHIBIT 8.2 Effect of change in quarterly dividend on call value.

Call Value with 0.10 Dividend		Call Value with 0.50 Dividend	
Price	61	Price	61
Strike	60	Strike	60
Days to Exp.	528	Days to Exp.	528
Volatility	25.5%	Volatility	25.5%
Interest	5.00%	Interest	5.00%
Dividend	0.10	Dividend	0.50
Call Theo.	9.65	Call Theo.	8.13

EXHIBIT 8.3 Effect of change in quarterly dividend on put value.

Put Value with 0.10 Dividend		Put Value with 0.50 Dividend	
Price	61	Price	61
Strike	60	Strike	60
Days to Exp.	528	Days to Exp.	528
Volatility	25.5%	Volatility	25.5%
Interest	5.00%	Interest	5.00%
Dividend	0.10	Dividend	0.50
Call Theo.	5.42	Call Theo.	6.08

Exhibit 8.2 compares the values of the long-term call using a $0.10 quarterly dividend and using a $0.50 quarterly dividend.

This $0.40 dividend increase will have a big effect on James's calls. With 528 days until expiration, there will be six dividends involved. Because James is long the calls, he loses 1.52 per option. If, however, he were short the calls, 1.52 would be his profit on each option.

Put traders are affected as well. Another trader, Marty, is long the 60-strike XYZ puts. Before the dividend announcement, Marty was running his values with a $0.10 dividend, giving his puts a value of 5.42. Exhibit 8.3 compares the values of the puts with a $0.10 quarterly dividend and with a $0.50 quarterly dividend.

When the dividend increase is announced, Marty will benefit. His puts will rise because of the higher dividend by $0.66 (all other parameters held constant). His long-term puts with six quarters of future expected dividends will benefit more than short-term XYZ puts of the same strike would. Of course, if he were short the puts, he would lose this amount.

The dividend inputs to a pricing model are best guesses until the dates and amounts are announced by the company. How does one find dividend information? Regularly monitoring the news and press releases on the companies one trades is a good way to stay up to date on dividend information, as well as other company news. Dividend announcements are widely disseminated by the major news services. Most companies also have an investor-relations phone number and section on their web sites where dividend information can be found.

PART II

Spreads

CHAPTER 9

Vertical Spreads

Risk—it is the focal point around which all trading revolves. It may seem as if profit should be occupying this seat, as most important to trading options, but without risk, there would be no profit! As traders, we must always look for ways to mitigate, eliminate, preempt, and simply avoid as much risk as possible in our pursuit of success without diluting opportunity. Risk must be controlled. Trading vertical spreads takes us one step further in this quest.

The basic strategies discussed in Chapters 4 and 5 have strengths when compared with pure linear trading in the equity markets. But they have weaknesses, too. Consider the covered call, one of the most popular option strategies.

A covered call is best used as an augmentation to an investment plan. It can be used to generate income on an investment holding, as an entrance strategy into a stock, or as an exit strategy out of a stock. But from a trading perspective, one can often find better ways to trade such a forecast.

If the forecast on a stock is neutral to moderately bullish, accepting the risk of stock ownership is often unwise. There is always the chance that the stock could collapse. In many cases, this is an unreasonable risk to assume.

To some extent, we can make the same case for the long call, short put, naked call, and the like. In certain scenarios, each of these basic strategies is accompanied with unwanted risks that serve no beneficial purpose to the trader but can potentially cause harm. In many situations, a vertical spread is a better alternative to these basic spreads. Vertical spreads allow a trader to limit potential directional risk, limit theta and vega risk, free up margin, and generally manage capital more efficiently.

Vertical Spreads

Vertical spreads involve buying one option and selling another. Both are on the same underlying and expire the same month, and both are either calls or puts. The difference is in the strike prices of the two options. One is higher than the other, hence the name *vertical spread*. There are four vertical spreads: bull call spread, bear call spread, bear put spread, and bull put spread. These four spreads can be sliced and diced into categories a number of ways: call spreads and put spreads, bull spreads and bear spreads, debit spreads and credit spreads. There is overlap among the four verticals in how and when they are used. The end of this chapter will discuss how the spreads are interrelated.

Bull Call Spread

A bull call spread is a long call combined with a short call that has a higher strike price. Both calls are on the same underlying and share the same expiration month. Because the purchased call has a lower strike price, it costs more than the call being sold. Establishing the trade results in a debit to the trader's account. Because of this debit, it's called a debit spread.

Below is an example of a bull call spread on Apple Inc. (AAPL):

Buy 1 Apple February 395 call @ 14.60
Sell 1 Apple February 405 call @ 10.20
Net debit 4.40

In this example, Apple is trading around $391. With 40 days until February expiration, the trader buys the 395–405 call spread for a net debit of $4.40, or $440 in actual cash. Or one could simply say the trader paid $4.40 for the 395–405 call.

Consider the possible outcomes if the spread is held until expiration. Exhibit 9.1 shows an at-expiration diagram of the bull call spread.

Before discussing the greeks, consider the bull call spread from an at-expiration perspective. Unlike the long call, which has two possible outcomes at expiration—above or below the strike—this spread has three possibilities: below both strikes, between the strikes, or above both strikes.

In this example, if Apple is below $395 at expiration, both calls expire worthless. The rights and obligations of the options are gone, as is the cash spent on the trade. In this case, the entire debit of $4.40 is lost.

EXHIBIT 9.1 AAPL bull call spread.

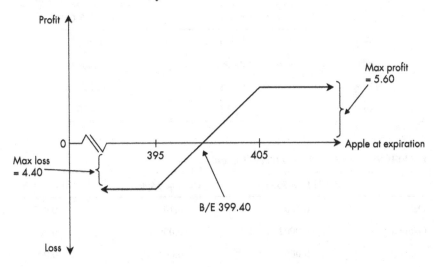

If Apple is between the strikes at expiration, the 405-strike call expires worthless. The trader is long stock at an effective price of $399.40. This is the $395-strike price at which the stock would be purchased if the call is exercised, plus the $4.40 premium spent on the spread. The break-even price of the trade is $399.40. If Apple is above $399.40 at expiration, the trade is profitable; below $399.40, it is a loser. The aptly named bull call spread requires the stock to rise to reach its profit potential. But unlike an outright long call, profits are capped with the spread.

If Apple is above $405 at expiration, both calls are in-the-money (ITM). If the 395-strike calls are exercised, the trader buys 100 shares of Apple at $395 and these shares, in turn, would be sold at $405 when the 405-strike calls are assigned, for a $10 gain per share. Subtract from that $10 the $4.40 debit spent on the trade and the net profit is $5.60 per share.

There are some other differences between the 395–405 call spread and the outright purchase of the 395 call. The absolute risk is lower. To buy the 395-strike call costs 14.60, versus 4.40 for the spread—a big difference. Because the debit is lower, the margin for the spread is lower at most option-friendly brokers, as well.

If we dig a little deeper, we find some other differences between the bull call spread and the outright call. Long options are haunted by the specter of time. Because the spread involves both a long and a short option, the time-decay risk is lower than that associated with owning an option outright.

EXHIBIT 9.2 Apple call versus bull call spread (Apple @ $391).

	395 Call	395–405 Call
Delta	0.484	0.100
Gamma	0.0097	0.0001
Theta	−0.208	−0.014
Vega	0.513	0.020

EXHIBIT 9.3 AAPL 395–405 bull call spread.

	AAPL @ $395	AAPL @ $400	AAPL @ $405
Delta	0.100	0.101	0.097
Gamma	0.0002	−0.0001	−0.0002
Theta	−0.009	0.001	0.004
Vega	0.010	−0.006	−0.035

Implied volatility (IV) risk is lower, too. Exhibit 9.2 compares the greeks of the long 395 call with those of the 395–405 call spread.

The positive deltas indicate that both positions are bullish, but the outright call has a higher delta. Some of the 395 call's directional sensitivity is lost when the 405 call is sold to make a spread. The negative delta of the 405 call somewhat offsets the positive delta of the 395 call. The spread delta is only about 20 percent of the outright call's delta. But for a trader wanting to focus on trading direction, the smaller delta can be a small sacrifice for the benefit of significantly reduced theta and vega. Theta spread's risk is about 7 percent that of the outright. The spread's vega risk is also less than 4 percent that of the outright 395 call. With the bull call spread, a trader can spread off much of the exposure to the unwanted risks and maintain a disproportionately higher greeks in the wanted exposure (delta).

These relationships change as the underlying moves higher. Remember, at-the-money (ATM) options have the greatest sensitivity to theta and vega. With Apple sitting at around the long strike, gamma and vega have their greatest positive value, and theta has its most negative value. Exhibit 9.3 shows the spread greeks given other underlying prices.

As the stock moves higher toward the 405 strike, the 395 call begins to move away from being at-the-money, and the 405 call moves toward being at-the-money. The at-the-money is the dominant strike when it comes to the characteristics of the spread greeks. Note the greeks position when the underlying is directly between the two strike prices: The long call has ceased to be the dominant influence on these metrics. Both calls influence the analytics pretty evenly. The time-decay risk has been entirely spread off. The volatility risk is mostly spread off. Gamma remains a minimal concern. When the greeks of the two calls balance each other, the result is a directional play.

As AAPL continues to move closer to the 405-strike, it becomes the at-the-money option, with the dominant greeks. The gamma, theta, and vega of the 405 call outweigh those of the ITM 395 call. Vega is more negative. Positive theta now benefits the trade. The net gamma of the spread has turned negative. Because of the negative gamma, the delta has become smaller than it was when the stock was at $400. This means that the benefit of subsequent upward moves in the stock begins to wane. Recall that there is a maximum profit threshold with a vertical spread. As the stock rises beyond $405, negative gamma makes the delta smaller and time decay becomes less beneficial. But at this point, the delta has done its work for the trader who bought this spread when the stock was trading around $395. The average delta on a move in the stock from $395 to $405 is about 0.10 in this case.

When the stock is at the 405 strike, the characteristics of the trade are much different than they are when the stock is at the 395 strike. Instead of needing movement upward in the direction of the delta to combat the time decay of the long calls, the position can now sit tight at the short strike and reap the benefits of option decay. The key with this spread, and with all vertical spreads, is that the stock needs to move in the direction of the delta to the short strike.

Strengths and Limitations

There are many instances when a bull call spread is superior to other bullish strategies, such as a long call, and there are times when it isn't. Traders must consider both price and time.

A bull call spread will always be cheaper than the outright call purchase. That's because the cost of the long-call portion of the spread is partially offset by the premium of the higher-strike short call. Spending less for the same exposure is always a better choice, but the exposure of the vertical is not exactly the same as that of the long call. The most obvious trade-off is the fact that profit is limited. For smaller moves—up to the price of the short strike—vertical spreads tend to be better trades than outright call purchases. Beyond the strike? Not so much.

But time is a trade-off, too. There have been countless times that I have talked with new traders who bought a call because they thought the stock was going up. They were right and still lost money. As the adage goes, timing is everything. The more time that passes, the more advantageous the lower-theta vertical spread becomes. When held until expiration, a vertical spread can be a better trade than an outright call in terms of percentage profit.

In the previous example, when Apple is at $391 with 40 days until expiration, the 395 call is worth 14.60 and the spread is worth 4.40. If Apple were to rise to be trading at $405 at expiration, the call rises to be worth 10, for a loss of 4.60 on the 14.60 debit paid. The spread also is worth 10. It yields a gain of about 127 percent on the initial $4.40 per share debit.

But look at this same trade if the move occurs before expiration. If Apple rallies to $405 after only a couple weeks, the outcome is much different. With four weeks still left until expiration, the 395 call is worth 19.85 with the underlying at $405. That's a 36 percent gain on the 14.60. The spread is worth 5.70. That's a 30 percent gain. The vertical spread must be held until expiration to reap the full benefits, which it accomplishes through erosion of the short option.

The long-call-only play (with a significantly larger negative theta) is punished severely by time passing. The long call benefits more from a quick move in the underlying. And of course, if the stock were to rise to a price greater than $405, in a short amount of time—the best of both worlds for the outright call—the outright long 395 call would be emphatically superior to the spread.

Bear Call Spread

The next type of vertical spread is called a *bear call spread*. A bear call spread is a short call combined with a long call that has a higher strike price. Both calls are on the same underlying and share the same expiration month. In this case, the call being sold is the option of higher value. This call spread results in a net credit when the trade is put on and, therefore, is called a credit spread.

The bull call spread and the bear call spread are two sides of the same coin. The difference is that with the bull call spread, one is buying the call spread, and with the bear call spread, one is selling the call spread.

EXHIBIT 9.4   Apple bear call spread.

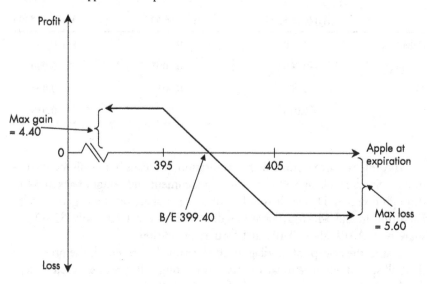

An example of a bear call spread can be shown using the same trade used earlier.

Sell 1 Apple February 395 call @ 14.60
Buy 1 Apple February 405 call @ 10.20
Net credit   4.40

Here we are selling one AAPL February (40-day) 395 call at 14.60 and buying the 405 call at 10.20. We are selling the 395–405 call at $4.40 per share, or $440.

Exhibit 9.4 is an at-expiration diagram of the trade.

The same three at-expiration outcomes are possible here as with the bull call spread: the stock can be above both strikes, between both strikes, or below both strikes. If the stock is below both strikes at expiration, both calls will expire worthless. The rights and obligations cease to exist. In this case, the entire credit of $440 is profit.

If AAPL is between the two strike prices at expiration, the 395-strike call will be in-the-money. The short call will get assigned and result in a short stock position at expiration. The break-even price falls at $399.40—the short strike plus the $4.40 net premium. This is the price at which the stock will effectively be sold if assignment occurs.

EXHIBIT 9.5 Apple 395–405 bear call spread.

	Apple @ $395	Apple @ $400	Apple @ $405
Delta	−0.100	−0.101	−0.097
Gamma	−0.0002	0.0001	0.0002
Theta	0.009	−0.001	−0.004
Vega	−0.010	0.006	0.035

If Apple is above both strikes at expiration, it means both calls are in-the-money. Stock is sold at $395 because of assignment and bought back at $405 through exercise. This leads to a loss of $10 per share on the negative scalp. Factoring in the $4.40-per-share credit makes the net loss only $5.60 per share with AAPL above $405 at February expiration.

Just as the at-expiration diagram is the same but reversed, the greeks for this call spread will be similar to those in the bull call spread example except for the positive and negative signs. See Exhibit 9.5.

A credit spread is commonly traded as an income-generating strategy. The idea is simple: sell the option closer-to-the-money and buy the more out-of-the-money (OTM) option—that is, sell volatility—and profit from nonmovement (above a certain point). In this example, with Apple at $391, a neutral to slightly bearish trader would think about selling this spread at 4.40 in hopes that the stock will remain below $395 until expiration. The best-case scenario is that the stock is below $395 at expiration and both options expire, resulting in a $4.40-per-share profit.

The strategy profits as long as Apple is under its break-even price, $399.40, at expiration. But this is not so much a bearish strategy as it is a nonbullish strategy. The maximum gain with a credit spread is the premium received, in this case $4.40 per share. Traders who thought AAPL was going to decline sharply would short it or buy a put. If they thought it would rise sharply, they'd use another strategy.

From a greek perspective, when the trade is executed it's very close to its highest theta price point—the 395 short strike price. This position theoretically collects $0.90 a day with Apple at around $395. As time passes, that theta rises. The key is that the stock remains at around $395 until the short option is just about worthless. The name of the game is sit and wait.

Although the delta is negative, traders trading this spread to generate income want the spread to expire worthless so they can pocket the $4.40 per share. If Apple declines, profits will be made on delta, and theta profits will be foregone later. All that matters is the break-even point. Essentially, the idea is to sell a naked call with a maximum potential loss. Sell the 395s and buy the 405s for protection.

If the underlying decreases enough in the short term and significant profits from delta materialize, it is logical to consider closing the spread early. But it often makes more sense to close part of the spread. Consider that the 405-strike call is farther out-of-the-money and will lose its value before the 395 call.

Say that after two weeks a big downward move occurs. Apple is trading at $325 a share; the 405s are 0.05 bid at 0.10, and the 395s are 0.50 bid at 0.55. At this point, the lion's share of the profits can be taken early. A trader can do so by closing only the 395 calls. Closing the 395s to eliminate the risk of negative delta and gamma makes sense. But does it make sense to close the 405s for 0.05? Usually not. Recouping this residual value accomplishes little. It makes more sense to leave them in your position in case the stock rebounds. If the stock proves it can move down $70; it can certainly move up $70. Because the majority of the profits were taken on the 395 calls, holding on to the 405s is like getting paid to own calls. In scenarios where a big move occurs and most of the profits can be taken early, it's often best to hold the long calls, just in case. It's a win-win situation.

Credit and Debit Spread Similarities

The credit call spread and the debit call spread appear to be exactly opposite in every respect. Many novice traders perceive credit spreads to be fundamentally different from debit spreads. That is not necessarily so. Closer study reveals that these two are not so different after all.

What if Apple's stock price was higher when the trade was put on? What if the stock was at $405? First, the spread would have had more value. The 395 and 405 calls would both be worth more. A trader could have sold the spread for a $5.65-per-share credit. The at-expiration diagram would look almost the same. See Exhibit 9.6.

Because the net premium is much higher in this example, the maximum gain is more—it is $5.65 per share. The breakeven is $400.65. The price points on the at-expiration diagram, however, have nothing to do with the greeks. The analytics from Exhibit 9.5 are the same either way.

The motivation for a trader selling this call spread, which has both options in-the-money, is different from that for the typical income generator. When the spread is sold in this context, the trader is buying volatility. Long gamma, long vega, negative theta. The trader here has a trade more like

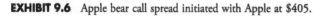

EXHIBIT 9.6 Apple bear call spread initiated with Apple at $405.

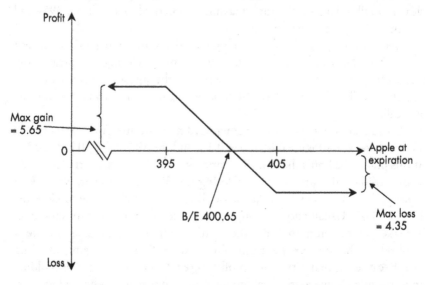

the one in the bull call spread example—except that instead of needing a rally, the trader needs a rout. The only difference is that the bull call spread has a bullish delta, and the bear call spread has a bearish delta.

Bear Put Spread

There is another way to take a bearish stance with vertical spreads: the bear put spread. A bear put spread is a long put plus a short put that has a lower strike price. Both puts are on the same underlying and share the same expiration month. This spread, however, is a debit spread because the more expensive option is being purchased.

Imagine that a stock has had a good run-up in price. The chart shows a steady march higher over the past couple of months. A study of technical analysis, though, shows that the run-up may be pausing for breath. An oscillator, such as slow stochastics, in combination with the relative strength index (RSI), indicates that the stock is overbought. At the same time, the average directional movement index (ADX) confirms that the uptrend is slowing.

For traders looking for a small pullback, a bear put spread can be an excellent strategy. The goal is to see the stock drift down to the short strike. So, like the other members of the vertical spread family, strike selection is important.

EXHIBIT 9.7 ExxonMobil bear put spread.

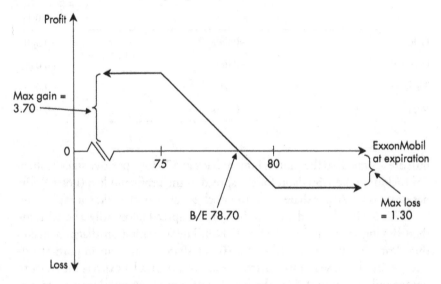

Let's look at an example of ExxonMobil (XOM). After the stock has rallied over a two-month period to $80.55, a trader believes there will be a short-term temporary pullback to $75. Instead of buying the June 80 puts for 1.75, the trader can buy the 75–80 put spread of the same month for 1.30 because the 75 put can be sold for 0.45.[1]

> Buy 1 ExxonMobil June 80 put @ 1.75
> Sell 1 ExxonMobil June 75 put @ 0.45
> Net debit   1.30

In this example, the June put has 40 days until expiration. Exhibit 9.7 illustrates the payout at expiration.

If the trader is wrong and ExxonMobil is still above 80 at expiry, both puts expire and the 1.30 premium is lost. If ExxonMobil is between the two strikes, the 80 puts are ITM, resulting in an exercise, and the 75 puts are OTM and expire. The net effect is short stock at an effective price of $78.70. The effective sale price is found by taking the price at which the short stock is established when the puts are exercised—$80—minus the net 1.30 paid for the spread. This is the spread's breakeven at expiration.

If the trader is right and ExxonMobil is below both strikes at expiration, both puts are ITM, and the result is a 3.70 profit and no position. Why a 3.70 profit? The 80 puts are exercised, making the trader short at $80, and the 75

EXHIBIT 9.8 ExxonMobil put vs. bear put spread (ExxonMobil @ $80.55).

	80 Put	75–80 Put
Delta	−0.445	−0.300
Gamma	+0.080	+0.041
Theta	−0.018	−0.006
Vega	+0.110	+0.046

puts are assigned, so the short is bought back at $75 for a positive stock scalp of $5. Including the 1.30 debit for the spread in the profit and loss (P&(L)), the net profit is $3.70 per share when the stock is below both strikes at expiration.

This is a bearish trade. But is the bear put spread necessarily a better trade than buying an outright ATM put? No. The at-expiration diagram makes this clear. Profits are limited to $3.70 per share. This is an important difference. But because in this particular example, the trader expects the stock to retrace only to around $75, the benefits of lower cost and lower theta and vega risk can be well worth the trade-off of limited profit. The trader's objectives are met more efficiently by buying the spread. The goal is to profit from the delta move down from $80 to $75. Exhibit 9.8 shows the differences between the greeks of the outright put and the spread when the trade is put on with ExxonMobil at $80.55.

As in the call-spread examples discussed previously, the spread delta is smaller than the outright put's. It appears ironic that the spread with the smaller delta is a better trade in this situation, considering that the intent is to profit from direction. But it is the relative differences in the greeks besides delta that make the spread worthwhile given the trader's goal. Gamma, theta, and vega are proportionately much smaller than the delta in the spread than in the outright put. While the spread's delta is two thirds that of the put, its gamma is half, its theta one third, and its vega around 42 percent of the put's.

Retracements such as the one called for by the trader in this example can happen fast, sometimes over the course of a week or two. It's not necessarily bad if this move occurs quickly. If ExxonMobil drops by $5 right away, the short delta will make the position profitable. Exhibit 9.9 shows how the spread position changes as the stock declines from $80 to $75.

The delta of this trade remains negative throughout the stock's descent to $75. Assuming the $5 drop occurs in one day, a delta averaging around −0.36 means about a 1.80 profit, or $180 per spread, for the $5 move (0.36 times $5 times 100). This is still a far cry from the spread's $3.70 potential

EXHIBIT 9.9 75–80 bear put spread as ExxonMobil declines.

	ExxonMobil @ $75	ExxonMobil @ $76	ExxonMobil @ $77	ExxonMobil @ $78	ExxonMobil @ $79	ExxonMobil @ $80
Delta	−0.364	−0.383	−0.388	−0.378	−0.355	−0.321
Gamma	−0.026	−0.012	0.003	0.017	0.029	0.037
Theta	0.016	0.013	0.009	0.004	0.000	−0.004
Vega	−0.038	−0.023	−0.006	0.012	0.027	0.040

profit. Although the stock is at $75, the maximum profit potential has yet to be reached, and it won't be until expiration. How does the rest of the profit materialize? Time decay.

The price the trader wants the stock to reach is $75, but the assumption here is that the move happens very fast. The trade went from being a long-volatility play—long gamma and vega—to a short-vol play: short gamma and vega. The trader wanted movement when the stock was at $80 and wants no movement when the stock is at $75. When the trade changes characteristics by moving from one strike to another, the trader has to reconsider the stock's outlook. The question is: if I didn't have this position on, would I want it now?

The trader has a choice to make: take the $180 profit—which represents a 138 percent profit on the 1.30 debit—or wait for theta to do its thing. The trader looking for a retracement would likely be inclined to take a profit on the trade. Nobody ever went broke taking a profit. But if the trader thinks the stock will sit tight for the remaining time until expiration, he will be happy with this income-generating position.

Although the trade in the last, overly simplistic example did not reap its full at-expiration potential, it was by no means a bad trade. Holding the spread until expiration is not likely to be part of a trader's plan. Buying the 80 put outright may be a better play if the trader is expecting a fast move. It would have a bigger delta than the spread. Debit and credit spreads can be used as either income generators or as delta plays. When they're used as delta plays, however, time must be factored in.

Bull Put Spread

The last of the four vertical spreads is a bull put spread. A bull put spread is a short put with one strike and a long put with a lower strike. Both puts are on

EXHIBIT 9.10   ExxonMobil bull put spread.

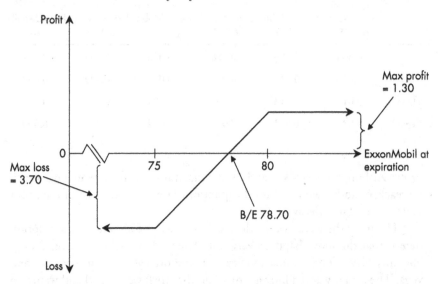

the same underlying and in the same expiration cycle. A bull put spread is a credit spread because the more expensive option is being sold, resulting in a net credit when the position is established. Using the same options as in the bear put example:

> Sell 1 ExxonMobil June 80 put @ 1.75
> Buy 1 ExxonMobil June 75 put @ 0.45
> Net credit   1.30

With ExxonMobil at $80.55, the June 80 puts are sold for 1.75 and the June 75 puts are bought at 0.45. The trade is done for a credit of 1.30. Exhibit 9.10 shows the payout of this spread if it is held until expiration.

The sale of this spread generates a 1.30 net credit, which is represented by the maximum profit to the right of the 80 strike. With ExxonMobil above $80 per share at expiration, both options expire OTM and the premium is all profit. Between the two strike prices, the 80 put expires in the money. If the ITM put is still held at expiration, it will be assigned. Upon assignment, the put becomes long stock, profiting with each tick higher up to $80, or losing with each tick lower to $75. If the 80 put is assigned, the effective price of the long stock will be $78.70. The assignment will "hit your sheets" as a buy at $80, but the 1.30 credit lowers the effective net cost to $78.70.

EXHIBIT 9.11 Greeks for ExxonMobil 75–80 bull put spread.

	ExxonMobil @ $75	ExxonMobil @ $76	ExxonMobil @ $77	ExxonMobil @ $78	ExxonMobil @ $79	ExxonMobil @ $80
Delta	0.364	0.383	0.388	0.378	0.355	0.321
Gamma	0.026	0.012	−0.003	−0.017	−0.029	−0.037
Theta	−0.016	−0.013	−0.009	−0.004	0.000	0.004
Vega	0.038	0.023	0.006	−0.012	−0.027	−0.040

If the stock is below $75 at option expiration, both puts will be ITM. This is the worst case scenario, because the higher-struck put was sold. At expiration, the 80 puts would be assigned, the 75 puts exercised. That's a negative scalp of $5 on the resulting stock. The initial credit lessens the pain by 1.30. The maximum possible loss with ExxonMobil below both strikes at expiration is $3.70 per spread.

The spread in this example is the flip side of the bear put spread of the previous example. Instead of buying the spread, as with the bear put, the spread in this case is sold.

Exhibit 9.11 shows the analytics for the bull put spread.

Instead of having a short delta, as with the bear spread, the bull spread is long delta. There is negative theta with positive gamma and vega as XOM approaches the long strike—the 75s, in this case. There is also positive theta with negative gamma and vega around the short strike—the 80s.

Exhibit 9.11 shows the characteristics that define the vertical spread. If one didn't know which particular options were being traded here, this could almost be a table of greeks for either a 75–80 bull put spread or a 75–80 bull call spread.

Like the other three verticals, this spread can be a delta play or a theta play. A bullish trader may sell the spread if both puts are in-the-money. Imagine that XOM is trading at around $75. The spread will have a positive 0.364 delta, positive gamma, and negative theta. The spread as a whole is a decaying asset. It needs the underlying to rally to combat time decay.

A bullish trader may also sell this spread if XOM is between the two strikes. In this case, with XOM at, say, $77, the delta is +0.388, and all other greeks are negligible. At this particular price point in the underlying, the trader has almost pure leveraged delta exposure. But this trade would be positioned for only a small move, not much above $80. A speculator wanting to trade direction for a small move while eliminating theta and vega risks achieves her objectives very well with a vertical spread.

A bullish-to-neutral trader would be inclined to sell this spread if ExxonMobil were around $80 or higher. Day by day, the 1.30 premium would start to come in. With 40 days until expiration, theta would be small, only 0.004. But if the stock remained at $80, this ATM put would begin decaying faster and faster. The objective of trading this spread for a neutral trader is selling future realized volatility—selling gamma to earn theta. A trader can also trade a vertical spread to profit from IV.

Verticals and Volatility

The IV component of a vertical spread, although small compared with that of an outright call or put, is still important—especially for large traders with low margin and low commissions who can capitalize on small price changes efficiently. Whether it's a call spread or a put spread, a credit spread or a debit spread, if the underlying is at the short option's strike, the spread will have a net negative vega. If the underlying is at the long option's strike, the spread will have positive vega. Because of this characteristic, there are three possible volatility plays with vertical spreads: speculating on IV changes when the underlying remains constant, profiting from IV changes resulting from movement of the underlying, and special volatility situations.

Vertical spreads offer a limited-risk way to speculate on volatility changes when the underlying remains fairly constant. But when the intent of a vertical spread is to benefit from vega, one must always consider the delta—it's the bigger risk. Chapter 13 discusses ways to manage this risk by hedging with stock, a strategy called delta-neutral trading.

Non-delta-neutral traders may speculate on vol with vertical spreads by assuming some delta risk. Traders whose forecast is vega bearish will sell the option with the strike closest to where the underlying is trading—that is, the ATM option—and buy an OTM strike. Traders would lean with their directional bias by choosing either a call spread or a put spread. As risk managers, the traders balance the volatility stance being taken against the additional risk of delta. Again, in this scenario, delta can hurt much more than help.

In the ExxonMobil bull put spread example, the trader would sell the 80-strike put if ExxonMobil were around $80 a share. In this case, if the stock didn't move as time passed, theta would benefit from historical volatility being's low—that is, from little stock movement. At first, the benefit would be only 0.004 per day, speeding up as expiration nears. And if implied volatility decreased, the trader would profit 0.04 for every 1 percent decline in IV. Small directional moves upward help a little. But in the long run, those profits are leveled off by the fact that theta gets smaller as the stock moves higher above $80—more profit on direction, less on time.

For the delta player, bull call spreads and bull put spreads have a potential added benefit that stems from the fact that IV tends to decrease as stocks rise and increase when stocks fall. This offers additional opportunity to the bull spread player. With the bull call spread or the bull put spread, the trader gains on positive delta with a rally. Once the underlying comes close to the short option's strike, vega is negative. If IV declines, as might be anticipated, there is a further benefit of vega profits on top of delta profits. If the underlying declines, the trader loses on delta. But the pain can potentially be slightly lessened by vega profits. Vega will get positive as the underlying approaches the long strike, which will benefit from the firming of IV that often occurs when the stock drops. But this dual benefit is paid for in the volatility skew. In most stocks or indexes, the lower strikes—the ones being bought in a bull spread—have higher IVs than the higher strikes, which are being sold.

Then there are special market situations in which vertical spreads that benefit from volatility changes can be traded. Traders can trade vertical spreads to strategically position themselves for an expected volatility change. One example of such a situation is when a stock is rumored to be a takeover target. A natural instinct is to consider buying calls as an inexpensive speculation on a jump in price if the takeover is announced. Unfortunately, the IV of the call is often already bid up by others with the same idea who were quicker on the draw. Buying a call spread consisting of a long ITM call and a short OTM call can eliminate immediate vega risk and still provide wanted directional exposure.

Certainly, with this type of trade, the trader risks being wrong in terms of direction, time, and volatility. If and when a takeover bid is announced, it will likely be for a specific price. In this event, the stock price is unlikely to rise above the announced takeover price until either the deal is consummated or a second suitor steps in and offers a higher price to buy the company. If the takeover is a "cash deal," meaning the acquiring company is tendering cash to buy the shares, the stock will usually sit in a very tight range below the takeover price for a long time. In this event, implied volatility will often drop to very low levels. Being short an ATM call when the stock rallies will let the trader profit from collapsing IV through negative vega.

Say XYZ stock, trading at $52 a share, is a rumored takeover target at $60. When the rumors are first announced, the stock will likely rise, to say

$55, with IV rising as well. Buying the 50–60 call spread will give a trader a positive delta and a negligible vega. If the rumors are realized and a cash takeover deal is announced at $60, the trade gains on delta, and the spread will now have negative vega. The negative vega at the 60 strike gains on implied volatility declining, and the stock will sit close to $60, producing the benefits of positive theta. Win, win, win.

The Interrelations of Credit Spreads and Debit Spreads

Many traders I know specialize in certain niches. Sometimes this is because they find something they know well and are really good at. Sometimes it's because they have become comfortable and don't have the desire to try anything new. I've seen this strategy specialization sometimes with traders trading credit spreads and debit spreads. I've had serial credit spread traders tell me credit spreads are the best trades in the world, much better than debit spreads. Habitual debit spread traders have likewise said their chosen spread is the best. But credit spreads and debit spreads are not so different. In fact, one could argue that they are really the same thing.

Conventionally, credit-spread traders have the goal of generating income. The short option is usually ATM or OTM. The long option is more OTM. The traders profit from nonmovement via time decay. Debit-spread traders conventionally are delta-bet traders. They buy the ATM or just out-of-the-money option and look for movement away from or through the long strike to the short strike. The common themes between the two are that the underlying needs to end up around the short strike price and that time has to pass to get the most out of either spread.

With either spread, movement in the underlying may be required, depending on the relationship of the underlying price to the strike prices of the options. And certainly, with a credit spread or debit spread, if the underlying is at the short strike, that option will have the most premium. For the trade to reach the maximum profit, it will need to decay.

For many retail traders, debit spreads and credit spreads begin to look even more similar when margin is considered. Margin requirements can vary from firm to firm, but verticals in retail accounts at option-friendly brokerage firms are usually margined in such a way that the maximum loss is required to be deposited to hold the position (this assumes Regulation T margining). For all intents and purposes, this can turn the trader's cash position from a credit into a debit. From a cash perspective, all vertical spreads are spreads that require a debit under these margin requirements.

Professional traders and retail traders who are subject to portfolio margining are subject to more liberal margin rules.

Although margin is an important concern, what we really care about as traders is risk versus reward. A credit call spread and a debit put spread on the same underlying, with the same expiration month, sharing the same strike prices will also share the same theoretical risk profile. This is because call and put prices are bound together by put-call parity.

Building a Box

Two traders, Sam and Isabel, share a joint account. They have each been studying Johnson & Johnson (JNJ), which is trading at around $63.35 per share. Sam and Isabel, however, cannot agree on direction. Sam thinks Johnson & Johnson will rise over the next five weeks, and Isabel believes it will decline during that period.

Sam decides to buy the January 62.50 −65 call spread (January has 38 days until expiration in this example). Sam can buy this spread for 1.28. His maximum risk is 1.28. This loss occurs if Johnson & Johnson is below $62.50 at expiration, leaving both calls OTM. His maximum gain is 1.22, realized if Johnson & Johnson is above $65 (65−62.50−1.28). With Johnson & Johnson at $63.35, Sam's delta is long 0.29 and his other greeks are about flat.

Isabel decides to buy the January 62.50−65 put spread for a debit of 1.22. Isabel's biggest potential loss is 1.22, incurred if Johnson & Johnson is above $65 a share at expiration, leaving both puts OTM. Her maximum possible profit is 1.28, realized if the stock is below $62.50 at option expiration. With Johnson & Johnson at $63.35, Isabel has a delta that is short around 0.27 and is nearly flat gamma, theta, and vega.

Collectively, if both Sam and Isabel hold their trades until expiration, it's a zero-sum game. With Johnson & Johnson below $62.50, Sam loses his

EXHIBIT 9.12 Sam's long call spread in Johnson & Johnson.

	62.50−65 Call Spread
Delta	+0.290
Gamma	+0.001
Theta	−0.004
Vega	+0.006

EXHIBIT 9.13   Isabel's long put spread in Johnson & Johnson.

	62.50–65 Put Spread
Delta	−0.273
Gamma	−0.001
Theta	+0.005
Vega	−0.006

investment of 1.28, but Isabel profits. She cancels out Sam's loss by making 1.28. Above \$65, Sam makes 1.22 while Isabel loses the same amount, canceling out Sam's gains. Between the two strikes, Sam has gains on his 62.50 call and Isabel has gains on her 65 put. The gains on the two options will total 2.50, the combined total spent on the spreads—another draw.

These two spreads were bought for a combined total of 2.50. The collective position, composed of the four legs of these two spreads, forms a new strategy altogether.

> Long 1 January 62.50 call at 1.84
> Short 1 January 65 call at 0.56
> Long 1 January 65 put at 2.19
> Short 1 January 62.50 put at 0.97
> Net debit 2.50

The two traders together have created a box. This box, which is empty of both profit and loss, is represented by greeks that almost entirely offset each other. Sam's positive delta of 0.29 is mostly offset by Isabel's −0.273 delta. Gamma, theta, and vega will mostly offset each other, too.

Chapter 6 described a box as long synthetic stock combined with short synthetic stock having a different strike price but the same expiration month. It can also be defined, however, as two vertical spreads: a bull (bear) call spread plus a bear (bull) put spread with the same strike prices and expiration month.

The value of a box equals the present value of the distance between the two strike prices (American-option models will also account for early exercise potential in the box's value). This 2.50 box, with 38 days until expiration at a 1 percent interest rate, has less than a penny of interest affecting its value. Boxes with more time until expiration will have a higher interest rate component. If there was one year until expiration, the combined value of the two verticals would equal 2.475. This is simply the distance between the strikes minus interest (2.50−[2.50 × 0.01]).

Credit spreads are often made up of OTM options. Traders betting against a stock rising through a certain price tend to sell OTM call spreads. For a stock at $50 per share, they might sell the 55 calls and buy the 60 calls. But because of the synthetic relationship that verticals have with one another, the traders could buy an ITM put spread for the same exposure, after accounting for interest. The traders could buy the 60 puts and sell the 55 puts. An ITM call (put) spread is synthetically equal to an OTM put (call) spread.

Verticals and Beyond

Traders who want to take full advantage of all that options have to offer can do so strategically by trading spreads. Vertical spreads truncate directional risk compared with strategies like the covered call or single-legged option trades. They also reduce option-specific risk, as indicated by their lower gamma, theta, and vega. But lowering risk both in absolute terms and in the greeks has a trade-off compared with buying options: limited profit potential. This trade-off can be beneficial, depending on the trader's forecast. Debit spreads and credit spreads can be traded interchangeably to achieve the same goals. When a long (short) call spread is combined with a long (short) put spread, the product is a box. Chapter 10 describes other ways vertical spreads can be combined to form positions that achieve different trading objectives.

Note

1. Note that it is customary when discussing the purchase or sale of spreads to state the lower strike first, regardless of which is being bought or sold. In this case, the trader is buying the 75−80 put spread.

Wing Spreads

Condors and Butterflies

The "wing spread" family is a set of option strategies that is very popular, particularly among experienced traders. These strategies make it possible for speculators to accomplish something they could not possibly do by just trading stocks: They provide a means to profit from a truly neutral market in a security. Stocks that don't move one iota can earn profits month after month for income-generating traders who trade these strategies.

These types of spreads have a lot of moving parts and can be intimidating to newcomers. At their heart, though, they are rather straightforward break-even analysis trades that require little complex math to maintain. A simple at-expiration diagram reveals in black and white the range in which the underlying stock must remain in order to have a profitable position. However, applying the greeks and some of the mathematics discussed in previous chapters can help a trader understand these strategies on a deeper level and maximize the chance of success. This chapter will discuss condors and butterflies and how to put them into action most effectively.

Taking Flight

There are four primary wing spreads: the condor, the iron condor, the butterfly, and the iron butterfly. Each of these spreads involves trading multiple options with three or four strikes prices. We can take these spreads at face value, we can consider each option as an individual component of the spread, or we can view the spreads as being made up of two vertical spreads.

Condor

A condor is a four-legged option strategy that enables a trader to capitalize on volatility—increased or decreased. Traders can trade long or short iron condors.

Long Condor

Long one call (put) with strike A; short one call (put) with a higher strike, B; short one call (put) at strike C, which is higher than B; and long one call (put) at strike D, which is higher than C. The distance between strike price A and B is equal to the distance between strike C and strike D. The options are all on the same security, in the same expiration cycle, and either all calls or all puts.

Long Condor Example

> Buy 1 XYZ November 70 call (A)
> Sell 1 XYZ November 75 call (B)
> Sell 1 XYZ November 90 call (C)
> Buy 1 XYZ November 95 call (D)

Short Condor

Short one call (put) with strike A; long one call (put) with a higher strike, B; long one call (put) with a strike, C, that is higher than B; and short one call (put) with a strike, D, that is higher than C. The options must be on the same security, in the same expiration cycle, and either all calls or all puts. The differences in strike price between the vertical spread of strike prices A and B and the strike prices of the vertical spread of strikes C and D are equal.

Short Condor Example

> Sell 1 XYZ November 70 call (A)
> Buy 1 XYZ November 75 call (B)
> Buy 1 XYZ November 90 call (C)
> Sell 1 XYZ November 95 call (D)

Iron Condor

An iron condor is similar to a condor, but with a mix of both calls and puts. Essentially, the condor and iron condor are synthetically the same.

Short Iron Condor

Long one put with strike A; short one put with a higher strike, B; short one call with an even higher strike, C; and long one call with a still higher strike, D. The options are on the same security and in the same expiration cycle. The put credit spread has the same distance between the strike prices as the call credit spread.

Short Iron Condor Example

> Buy 1 XYZ November 70 put (A)
> Sell 1 XYZ November 75 put (B)
> Sell 1 XYZ November 90 call (C)
> Buy 1 XYZ November 95 call (D)

Long Iron Condor

Short one put with strike A; long one put with a higher strike, B; long one call with an even higher strike, C; and short one call with a still higher strike, D. The options are on the same security and in the same expiration cycle. The put debit spread (strikes A and B) has the same distance between the strike prices as the call debit spread (strikes C and D).

Long Iron Condor Example

> Sell 1 XYZ November 70 put (A)
> Buy 1 XYZ November 75 put (B)
> Buy 1 XYZ November 90 call (C)
> Sell 1 XYZ November 95 call (D)

Butterflies

Butterflies are wing spreads similar to condors, but there are only three strikes involved in the trade—not four.

Long Butterfly

Long one call (put) with strike A; short two calls (puts) with a higher strike, B; and long one call (put) with an even higher strike, C. The options are on the same security, in the same expiration cycle, and are either all calls or all puts. The difference in price between strikes A and B equals that between strikes B and C.

Long Butterfly Example

> Buy 1 XYZ December 50 call (A)
> Sell 2 XYZ December 60 call (B)
> Buy 1 XYZ December 70 call (C)

Short Butterfly

Short one call (put) with strike A; long two calls (puts) with a higher strike, B; and short one call (put) with an even higher strike, C. The options are on the same security, in the same expiration cycle, and are either all calls or all puts. The vertical spread made up of the options with strike A and strike B has the same distance between the strike prices of the vertical spread made up of the options with strike B and strike C.

Short Butterfly Example

> Sell 1 XYZ December 50 call
> Buy 2 XYZ December 60 call
> Sell 1 XYZ December 70 call

Iron Butterflies

Much like the relationship of the condor to the iron condor, a butterfly has its synthetic equal as well: the iron butterfly.

Short Iron Butterfly

Long one put with strike A; short one put with a higher strike, B; short one call with strike B; long one call with a strike higher than B, C. The options are on the same security and in the same expiration cycle. The distances between the strikes of the put spread and between the strikes of the call spread are equal.

Short Iron Butterfly Example

> Buy 1 XYZ December 50 put (A)
> Sell 1 XYZ December 60 put (B)
> Sell 1 XYZ December 60 call (B)
> Buy 1 XYZ December 70 call (C)

Long Iron Butterfly

Short one put with strike A; long one put with a higher strike, B; long one call with strike B; short one call with a strike higher than B, C. The options are on the same security and in the same expiration cycle. The distances between the strikes of the put spread and between the strikes of the call spread are equal. The put debit spread has the same distance between the strike prices as the call debit spread.

Long Iron Butterfly Example

Sell 1 XYZ December 50 put
Buy 1 XYZ December 60 put
Buy 1 XYZ December 60 call
Sell 1 XYZ December 70 call

These spreads were defined in terms of both long and short for each strategy. Whether the spread is classified as long or short depends on whether it was established at a credit or a debit. Debit condors or butterflies are considered long spreads. And credit condors or butterflies are considered short spreads.

The words long and short mean little, though in terms of the spread as a whole. The important thing is which strikes have long options and which have short options. A call debit spread is synthetically equal to a put credit spread on the same security, with the same expiration month and strike prices. That means a long condor is synthetically equal to a short iron condor, and a long butterfly is synthetically equal to a short iron butterfly, when the same strikes are used. Whichever position is constructed, the best-case scenario is to have debit spreads expire with both options in-the-money (ITM) and credit spreads expire with both options out-of-the-money (OTM).

Many retail traders prefer trading these spreads for the purpose of generating income. In this case, a trader would sell the guts, or middle strikes, and buy the wings, or outer strikes. When a trader is short the guts, low realized volatility is usually the objective. For long butterflies and short iron butterflies, the stock needs to be right at the middle strike for the maximum payout. For long condors and short iron condors, the stock needs to be between the short strikes at expiration for maximum payout. In both instances, the wings are bought to limit potential losses of the otherwise naked options.

Long Butterfly Example

A trader, Kathleen, has been studying United Parcel Service (UPS), which is trading at around $70.65. She believes UPS will trade sideways until July expiration. Kathleen buys the July 65–70–75 butterfly for 2.00. She executes the following legs:

Buy 1 July 65 call @ 6.60
Sell 2 July 70 calls @ 2.50 each
Buy 1 July 75 call @ 0.40
       Net debit   2.00

Kathleen looks at her trade as two vertical spreads, the 65–70 bull (debit) call spread and the 70–75 bear (credit) call spread. Intuitively, she would want UPS to be at or above $70 at expiration for her bull call spread to have maximum value. But she has the seemingly conflicting goal of also wanting UPS to be at or below $70 to get the most from her 70–75 bear call spread. The ideal price for the stock to be trading at expiration in this example is right at $70 per share—the best of both worlds. The at-expiration diagram, Exhibit 10.1, shows the profit or loss of all possible outcomes at expiration.

If the price of UPS shares declines below $65 at expiration, all these calls will expire. The entire 2.00 spent on the trade will be lost. If UPS is above $65 at expiration, the 65 call will be ITM and will be exercised. The call will profit like a long position in 100 shares of the underlying. The maximum profit is reached if UPS is at $70 at expiration. Kathleen makes a 5.00 profit from $65 to $70 on her 65 calls. But because she paid 2.00 initially for the

EXHIBIT 10.1 UPS 65–70–75 butterfly.

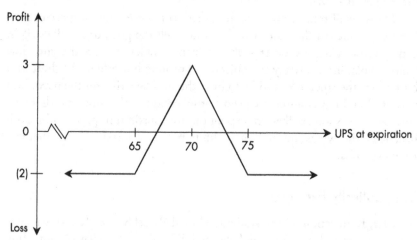

spread, her net profit at $70 is just 3.00. If UPS is above $70 a share at expiration in this example, the two 70 calls will be assigned. The assignment of one call will offset the long stock acquired by the 65 calls being exercised. Assignment of the other call will create a short position in the underlying. That short position loses as UPS moves higher up to $75 a share, eating away at the 3.00 profit. If UPS is above $75 at expiration, the 75 call can be exercised to buy back the short stock position that resulted from the 70's being assigned. The loss on the short stock between $70 and $75 will cost Kathleen 5.00, stripping her of her 3.00 profit and giving her a net loss of 2.00 to boot. End result? Above $75 at expiration, she has no position in the underlying and loses 2.00.

A butterfly is a *break-even analysis trade*. This name refers to the idea that the most important considerations in this strategy are the breakeven points. The at-expiration diagram, Exhibit 10.2, shows the break-even prices for this trade.

If the position is held until expiration and UPS is between $65 and $70 at that time, the 65 calls are exercised, resulting in long stock. The effective purchase price of that stock is $67. That's the strike price plus the cost of the spread; that's the lower break-even price. The other break-even is at $73. The net short position of 100 shares resulting from assignment of the 70 call loses more as the stock rises between $70 and $75. The entire 3.00 profit realized at the $70 share price is eroded when the stock reaches $73. Above $73, the trade produces a loss.

EXHIBIT 10.2   UPS 65–70–75 butterfly breakevens.

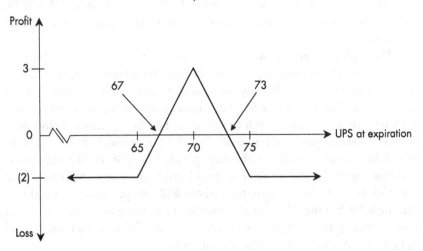

Kathleen's trading objective is to profit from UPS trading between $67 and $73 at expiration. The best-case scenario is that it declines only slightly from its price of $70.65 when the trade is established, to $70 per share.

Alternatives

Kathleen had other alternative positions she could have traded to meet her goals. An iron butterfly with the same strike prices would have shown about the same risk/reward picture, because the two positions are synthetically equivalent. But there may, in some cases, be a slight advantage to trading the iron butterfly over the long butterfly. The iron butterfly uses OTM put options instead of ITM calls, meaning the bid-ask spreads may be tighter. This means giving up less edge to the liquidity providers.

She could have also bought a condor or sold an iron condor. With condor-family spreads, there is a lower maximum profit potential but a wider range in which that maximum payout takes place. For example, Kathleen could have executed the following legs to establish an iron condor:

Buy 1 July 60 put @ 0.20
Sell 1 July 65 put @ 0.50
Sell 1 July 75 call @ 0.40
Buy 1 July 80 call @ 0.05
Net credit   0.65

Essentially, Kathleen would be selling two credit spreads: the July 60–65 put spread for 0.30 and the July 75–80 call spread for 0.35. Exhibit 10.3 shows the payout at expiration of the UPS July 60–65–75–80 iron condor.

Although the forecast and trading objectives may be similar to those for the butterfly, the payout diagram reveals some important differences. First, the maximum loss is significantly higher with a condor or iron condor. In this case, the maximum loss is 4.35. This unfortunate situation would occur if UPS were to drop to below $60 or rise above $80 by expiration. Below $60, the call spread expires, netting 0.35. But the put spread is ITM. Kathleen would lose a net of 4.70 on the put spread. The gain on the call spread combined with the loss on the put spread makes the trade a loser of 4.35 if the stock is below $60 at expiration. Above $80, the put spread is worthless, earning 0.30, but the call spread is a loser by 4.65. The gain on the put spread plus the loss on the call spread is a net loser of 4.35. Between $65 and $75, all options expire and the 0.65 credit is all profit.

EXHIBIT 10.3 UPS 60–65–75–80 iron condor.

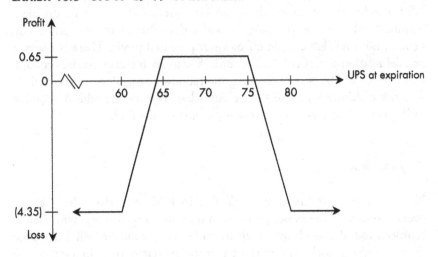

EXHIBIT 10.4 UPS 60–65–75–80 iron condor breakevens.

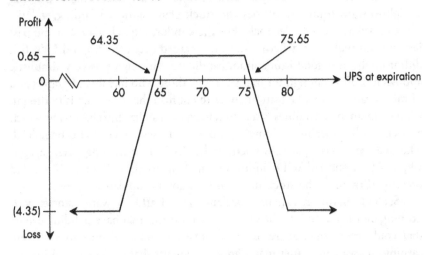

So far, this looks like a pretty lousy alternative to the butterfly. You can lose 4.35 but only make 0.65! Could there be any good reason for making this trade? Maybe. The difference is wiggle room. The breakevens are 2.65 wider in each direction with the iron condor. Exhibit 10.4 shows these prices on the graph.

The lower threshold for profit occurs at $64.35 and the upper at $75.65. With condor/iron condors, there can be a greater chance of producing a winning trade because the range is wider than that of the butterfly. This benefit, however, has a trade-off of lower potential profit. There is *always* a parallel relationship of risk and reward. When risk increases so does reward, and vice versa. This way of thinking should now be ingrained in your DNA. The risk of failure is less, so the payout is less. Because the odds of winning are higher, a trader will accept lower payouts on the trade.

Keys to Success

No matter which trade is more suitable to Kathleen's risk tolerance, the overall concept is the same: profit from little directional movement. Before Kathleen found a stock on which to trade her spread, she will have sifted through myriad stocks to find those that she expects to trade in a range. She has a few tools in her trading toolbox to help her find good butterfly and condor candidates.

First, Kathleen can use technical analysis as a guide. This is a rather straightforward litmus test: does the stock chart show a trending, volatile stock or a flat, nonvolatile stock? For the condor, a quick glance at the past few months will reveal whether the stock traded between $65 and $75. If it did, it might be a good iron condor candidate. Although this very simplistic approach is often enough for many traders, those who like lots of graphs and numbers can use their favorite analyses to confirm that the stock is trading in a range. Drawing trendlines can help traders to visualize the channel in which a stock has been trading. Knowing support and resistance is also beneficial. The average directional movement index (ADX) or moving average converging/diverging (MACD) indicator can help to show if there is a trend present. If there is, the stock may not be a good candidate.

Second, Kathleen can use fundamentals. Kathleen wants stocks with nothing on their agendas. She wants to avoid stocks that have pending events that could cause their share price to move too much. Events to avoid are earnings releases and other major announcements that could have an impact on the stock price. For example, a drug stock that has been trading in a range because it is awaiting Food and Drug Administration (FDA) approval, which is expected to occur over the next month, is not a good candidate for this sort of trade.

The last thing to consider is whether the numbers make sense. Kathleen's iron condor risks 4.35 to make 0.65. Whether this sounds like a good trade depends on Kathleen's risk tolerance and the general environment of UPS, the industry, and the market as a whole. In some environments, the 0.65/4.35 payout-to-risk ratio makes a lot of sense. For other people, other stocks, and other environments, it doesn't.

Greeks and Wing Spreads

Much of this chapter has been spent on how wing spreads perform if held until expiration, and little has been said of option greeks and their role in wing spreads. Greeks do come into play with butterflies and condors but not necessarily the same way they do with other types of option trades.

The vegas on these types of spreads are smaller than they are on many other types of strategies. For a typical nonprofessional trader, it's hard to trade implied volatility with condors or butterflies. The collective commissions on the four legs, as well as margin and capital considerations, put these out of reach for active trading. Professional traders and retail traders subject to portfolio margining are better equipped for volatility trading with these spreads.

The true strength of wing spreads, however, is in looking at them as break-even analysis trades much like vertical spreads. The trade is a winner if it is on the correct side of the break-even price. Wing spreads, however, are a combination of two vertical spreads, so there are two break-even prices. One of the verticals is guaranteed to be a winner. The stock can be either higher or lower at expiration—not both. In some cases, both verticals can be winners.

Consider an iron condor. Instead of reaping one premium from selling one OTM call credit spread, iron condor sellers double dip by additionally selling an OTM put credit spread. They collect a double credit, but only one of the credit spreads can be a loser at expiration. The trader, however, does have to worry about both directions independently.

There are two ways for greeks and volatility analysis to help traders trade wing spreads. One of them involves using delta and theta as tools to trade a directional spread. The other uses implied volatility in strike selection decisions.

Directional Butterflies

Trading a butterfly can be an excellent way to establish a low-cost, relatively low-risk directional trade when a trader has a specific price target in mind.

For example, a trader, Ross, has been studying Walgreen Co. (WAG) and believes it will rise from its current level of $33.50 to $36 per share over the next month. Ross buys a butterfly consisting of all OTM January calls with 31 days until expiration.

He executes the following legs:

Buy 1 January 35 call at 1.15
Sell 2 January 36 calls at 0.80 each
Buy 1 January 37 call at <u>0.55</u>
                Net debit 0.10

As a directional trade alternative, Ross could have bought just the January 35 call for 1.15. As a cheaper alternative, he could have also bought the 35−36 bull call spread for 0.35. In fact, Ross actually does buy the 35−36 spread, but he also sells the January 36−37 call spread at 0.25 to reduce the cost of the bull call spread, investing only a dime. The benefit of lower cost, however, comes with trade-offs. Exhibit 10.5 compares the bull call spread with a bullish butterfly.

The butterfly has lower nominal risk—only 0.10 compared with 0.35 for the call spread. The maximum reward is higher in nominal terms, too— 0.90 versus 0.65. The trade-off is what is given up. With both strategies, the goal is to have Walgreen Co. at $36 around expiration. But the bull call

EXHIBIT 10.5 Bull call spread vs. bull butterfly (Walgreen Co. at $33.50).

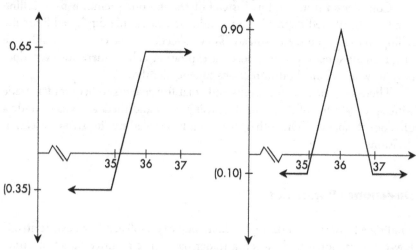

spread has more room for error to the upside. If the stock trades a lot higher than expected, the butterfly can end up being a losing trade.

Given Ross's expectations in this example, this might be a risk he is willing to take. He doesn't expect Walgreen Co. to close right at $36 on the expiration date. It could happen, but it's unlikely. However, he'd have to be wildly wrong to have the trade be a loser on the upside. It would be a much larger move than expected for the stock to rise significantly above $36. If Ross strongly believes Walgreen Co. can be around $36 at expiration, the cost benefit of 0.10 vs. 0.35 may offset the upside risk above $37. As a general rule, directional butterflies work well in trending, low-volatility stocks.

When Ross monitors his butterfly, he will want to see the greeks for this position as well. Exhibit 10.6 shows the trade's analytics with Walgreen Co. at $33.50.

When the trade is first put on, the delta is small—only +0.008. Gamma is slightly negative and theta is very slightly positive. This is important information if Walgreen Co.'s ascent happens sooner than Ross planned. The trade will show just a small profit if the stock jumps to $36 per share right away. Ross's theoretical gain will be almost unnoticeable. At $36 per share, the position will have its highest theta, which will increase as expiration approaches. Ross will have to wait for time to pass to see the trade reach its full potential.

This example shows the interrelation between delta and theta. We know from an at-expiration analysis that if Walgreen Co. moves from $33.50 to $36, the butterfly's profit will be 0.90 (the spread of $1 minus the 0.10 initial debit). If we distribute the 0.90 profit over the 2.50 move from $33.50 to $36, the butterfly gains about 0.36 per dollar move in Walgreen Co. (0.90/ (36 − 33.50). This implies a delta of about 0.36.

But the delta, with 31 days until expiration and Walgreen Co. at $33.50, is only 0.008, and because of negative gamma this delta will get even smaller as Walgreen Co. rises. Butterflies, like the vertical spreads of which

EXHIBIT 10.6   Walgreen Co. 35−36−37 butterfly greeks (stock at $33.50, 31 days to expiration).

Delta	+0.008
Gamma	−0.004
Theta	+0.001
Vega	−0.001

they are composed, can profit from direction but are never purely directional trades. Time is always a factor. It is theta, working in tandem with delta, that contributes to profit or peril.

A bearish butterfly can be constructed as well. One would execute the trade with all OTM puts or all ITM calls. The concept is the same: sell the guts at the strike at which the stock is expected to be trading at expiration, and buy the wings for protection.

Constructing Trades to Maximize Profit

Many traders who focus on trading iron condors trade exchange-traded funds (ETFs) or indexes. Why? Diversification. Because indexes are made up of many stocks, they usually don't have big gaps caused by surprise earnings announcements, takeovers, or other company-specific events. But it's not just selecting the right underlying to trade that is the challenge. A trader also needs to pick the right strike prices. Finding the right strike prices to trade can be something of an art, although science can help, as well.

Three Looks at the Condor

Strike selection is essential for a successful condor. If strikes are too close together or two far apart, the trade can become much less attractive.

Strikes Too Close

The QQQs are options on the ETFs that track the Nasdaq 100 (QQQ). They have strikes in $1 increments, giving traders a lot to choose from. With QQQ trading at around $55.95, consider the 54–55–57–58 iron condor. In this example, with 31 days until expiration, the following legs can be executed:

>   Buy 1 54 put at   0.80
>   Sell 1 55 put at 1.10
>   Sell 1 57 call at 0.75
>   Buy 1 58 call at 0.42
>   Total credit 0.63

In this trade, the maximum profit is 0.63. The maximum risk is 0.37. This isn't a bad profit-to-loss ratio. The break-even price on the downside is

$54.37 and on the upside is $57.63. That's a $3.26 range—a tight space for a mover like the QQQ to occupy in a month. The ETF can drop about only 2.8 percent or rise 3 percent before the trade becomes a loser. No one needs any fancy math to show that this is likely a losing proposition in the long run. While choosing closer strikes can lead to higher premiums, the range can be so constricting that it asphyxiates the possibility of profit.

Strikes Too Far

Strikes too far apart can make for impractical trades as well. Exhibit 10.7 shows an options chain for the Dow Jones Industrial Average Index (DJX). These prices are from around 2007 when implied volatility (IV) was historically low, making the OTM options fairly low priced. In this example, DJX is around $135.20 and there are 51 days until expiration.

If the goal is to choose strikes that are far enough apart to be unlikely to come into play, a trader might be tempted to trade the 120–123–142–145 iron condor. With this wingspan, there is certainly a good chance of staying between those strikes—you could drive a proverbial truck through that range.

This would be a great trade if it weren't for the prices one would have to accept to put it on. First, the 120 puts are offered at 0.25 and the 123 puts are 0.25 bid. This means that the put spread would be sold at zero! The maximum risk is 3.00, and the maximum gain is zero. Not a really good risk/reward. The 142–145 call spread isn't much better: it can be sold for a dime.

At the time, again a low-volatility period, many traders probably felt it was unlikely that the DJX will rise 5 percent in a 51-day period. Some traders may have considered trading a similarly priced iron condor (though of course they'd have to require some small credit for the risk). A little over a year later the DJX was trading around 50 percent lower. Traders must always be vigilant of the possibility of volatility, even unexpected volatility and structure their risk/reward accordingly. Most traders would say the risk/reward of this trade isn't worth it. Strikes too far apart have a greater chance of success, but the payoff just isn't there.

Strikes with High Probabilities of Success

So how does a trader find the happy medium of strikes close enough together to provide rich premiums but far enough apart to have a good chance of success? Certainly, there is something to be said for looking at the prices at

EXHIBIT 10.7 Options chain for DJIA.

Call Bid	Call Ask	Strike	Put Bid	Put Ask
16.10	16.30	120	0.15	0.25
15.10	15.30	121	0.20	0.30
14.10	14.40	122	0.20	0.30
13.20	13.40	123	0.25	0.35
12.20	12.50	124	0.30	0.40
11.30	11.50	125	0.35	0.45
10.30	10.60	126	0.40	0.50
9.40	9.70	127	0.50	0.60
8.50	8.80	128	0.55	0.65
7.60	7.90	129	0.65	0.75
6.80	7.00	130	0.80	0.90
5.90	6.10	131	0.95	1.05
5.10	5.30	132	1.10	1.20
4.40	4.50	133	1.35	1.40
3.60	3.80	134	1.60	1.65
2.95	3.10	135	1.90	2.00
2.30	2.45	136	2.25	2.35
1.75	1.90	137	2.75	2.80
1.30	1.40	138	3.10	3.20
0.95	1.00	139	3.70	4.00
0.60	0.70	140	4.40	4.70
0.35	0.45	141	5.20	5.40
0.20	0.30	142	6.00	6.30
0.10	0.20	143	6.90	7.10
0.05	0.10	144	7.80	8.00
0.00	0.10	145	8.80	9.00

which a trade can be done and having a subjective feel for whether the underlying is likely to move outside the range of the break-even prices. A little math, however, can help quantify this likelihood and aid in the decision-making process.

Recall that IV is read by many traders to be the market's consensus estimate of future realized volatility in terms of annualized standard deviation. While that is a mouthful to say—or in this case, rather, an eyeful to read—when broken down it is not quite as intimidating as it sounds. Consider a simplified example in which an underlying security is trading at $100 a share and the implied volatility of the at-the-money (ATM) options is 10 percent. That means, from a statistical perspective, that if the expected return for the stock is unchanged, the one-year standard deviations are at $90 and $110.[1] In this case, there is about a 68 percent chance of the stock trading between $90 and $110 one year from now. IV then is useful information to a trader who wants to quantify the chances of an iron condor's expiring profitable, but there are a few adjustments that need to be made.

First, because with an iron condor the idea is to profit from net short option premium, it usually makes more sense to sell shorter-term options to profit from higher rates of time decay. This entails trading condors composed of one- or two-month options. The IV needs to be deannualized and converted to represent the standard deviation of the underlying at expiration.

The first step is to compute the one-day standard deviation. This is found by dividing the implied volatility by the square root of the number of trading days in a year, then multiplying by the square root of the number of trading days until expiration. The result is the standard deviation () at the time of expiration stated as a percent. Next, multiply that percentage by the price of the underlying to get the standard deviation in absolute terms.

The formula[2] for calculating the shorter-term standard deviation is as follows:

$$\left(\frac{IV}{\sqrt{256}} \times \sqrt{\text{Trading days until expiration}} \right) \times \text{underlying price}$$

This value will be added to or subtracted from the price of the underlying to get the price points at which the approximate standard deviations fall.

Consider an example using options on the Standard & Poor's 500 Index (SPX). With 50 days until expiration, the SPX is at 1241 and the implied volatility is 23.2 percent. To find strike prices that are one standard deviation away from the current index price, we need to enter the values into the equation. We first need to know how many actual trading days are in the 50-day period. There are 35 business days during this particular 50-day period (there is one holiday and seven weekend days). We now have all the data we need to calculate which strikes to sell.

$$\left(\frac{0.232}{\sqrt{256}} \times \sqrt{35}\right) \times 1241 = 106.45$$

The lower standard deviation is 1134.55 (1241 − 106.45) and the upper is 1347.45 (1241 + 106.45). This means there would be about a 68 percent chance of SPX ending up between 1134.55 and 1347.45 at expiration. In this example, to have about a two-thirds chance of success, one would sell the 1135 puts and the 1350 calls as part of the iron condor.

Being Selective

There is about a two-thirds chance of the underlying staying between the upper and lower standard deviation points and about a one-third chance it won't. Reasonably good odds. But the maximum loss of an iron condor will be more than the maximum profit potential. In fact, the max-profit-to-max-loss ratio is usually less than 1 to 3. For every $1 that can be made, often $4 or $5 will be at risk.

The pricing model determines fair value of an option based on the implied volatility set by the market. Again, many traders consider IV to be the market's consensus estimate of future realized volatility. Assuming the market is generally right and options are efficiently priced, in the long run, future stock volatility should be about the same as the implied volatility from options prices. That means that if all of your options trades are executed at fair value, you are likely to break even in the long run. The caveat is that whether the options market is efficient or not, retail or institutional traders cannot generally execute trades at fair value. They have to sell the bid (sell below theoretical value) and buy the offer (buy above theoretical value). This gives the trade a statistical disadvantage, called giving up the edge, from an expected return perspective.

Even though you are more likely to win than to lose with each individual trade when strikes are sold at the one-standard-deviation point, the edge given up to the market in conjunction with the higher price tag on losers makes the trade a statistical loser in the long run. While this means for certain that the non-market-making trader is at a constant disadvantage, trading condors and butterflies is no different from any other strategy. Giving up the edge is the plight of retail and institutional traders. To profit in the long run, a trader needs to beat the market, which requires careful planning, selectivity, and risk management.

Savvy traders trade iron condors with strikes one standard deviation away from the current stock price only when they think there is more than a two-thirds chance of market neutrality. In other words, if you think the market will be less volatile than the prices in the options market imply, sell the iron condor or trade another such premium-selling strategy. As discussed above, this opinion should reflect sound judgment based on some combination of technical analysis, fundamental analysis, volatility analysis, feel, and subjectivity.

A Safe Landing for an Iron Condor

Although traders can't control what the market does, they can control how they react to the market. Assume a trader has done due diligence in studying a stock and feels it is a qualified candidate for a neutral strategy. With the stock at $90, a 16.5 percent implied volatility, and 41 days until expiration, the standard deviation is about 5. The trader sells the following iron condor:

> Buy ten 80 puts at 0.05
> Sell ten 85 puts at 0.35
> Sell ten 95 calls at 0.55
> Buy ten 100 calls at <u>0.05</u>
> Net credit 0.80 per contract (or $800)

With the stock at $90, directly between the two short strikes, the trade is direction neutral. The maximum profit is equal to the total premium taken in, which in this case is $800. The maximum loss is $4,200. There is about a two-thirds chance of retaining the $800 at expiration.

After one week, the overall market begins trending higher on unexpected bullish economic news. This stock follows suit and is now trading at $93, and concern is mounting that the rally will continue. The value of the spread now is about 1.10 per contract (we ignore slippage from trading on the bid-ask spreads of the four legs of the spread). This means the trade has lost $300 because it would cost $1,100 to buy back what the trader sold for a total of $800.

EXHIBIT 10.8 Greeks for iron condor with stock at $93.

		Premium	Cash	Delta	Gamma	Theta	Vega
+10	80 put	0	$0	0.000	0.010	0.000	0.020
−10	85 put	0.07	$70	0.340	−0.150	0.050	−0.220
−10	95 call	1.24	$1,240	−3.840	−0.810	0.310	−1.090
+10	100 call	0.21	−$210	0.960	0.360	−0.130	0.550
			$1,100	−2.54	−0.590	+0.230	−0.740

One strategy for managing this trade looking forward is inaction. The philosophy is that sometimes these trades just don't work out and you take your lumps. The philosophy is that the winners should outweigh the losers over the long term. For some of the more talented and successful traders with a proven track record, this may be a viable strategy, but there are more active options as well. A trader can either close the spread or adjust it.

The two sets of data that must be considered in this decision are the prices of the individual options and the greeks for the trade. Exhibit 10.8 shows the new data with the stock at $93.

The trade is no longer neutral, as it was when the underlying was at $90. It now has a delta of −2.54, which is like being short 254 shares of the underlying. Although the more time that passes the better—as indicated by the +0.230 theta—delta is of the utmost concern. The trader has now found himself short a market that he thinks may rally.

Closing the entire position is one alternative. To be sure, if you don't have an opinion on the underlying, you shouldn't have a position. It's like making a bet on a sporting event when you don't really know who you think will win. The spread can also be dismantled piecemeal. First, the 85 puts are valued at $0.07 each. Buying these back is a no-brainer. In the event the stock does retrace, why have the positive delta of that leg working against you when you can eliminate the risk inexpensively now?

The 80 puts are worthless, offered at 0.05, presumably. There is no point in trying to sell these. If the market does turn around, they may benefit, resulting in an unexpected profit.

The 80 and 85 puts are the least of his worries, though. The concern is a continuing rally. Clearly, the greater risk is in the 95−100 call spread. Closing the call spread for a loss eliminates the possibility of future losses and may be a wise choice, especially if there is great uncertainty. Taking a small loss now of only around $300 is a better trade than risking a total loss

EXHIBIT 10.9 Iron condor adjusted to strangle.

		$Premium	Delta	Gamma	Theta	Vega
+10	80 put	$0	0.000	0.010	0.000	0.020
+10	100 call	−$210	0.960	0.360	−0.130	0.550
Net spread cost		−$210	0.960	0.370	−0.130	0.570

of $4,200 when you think there is a strong chance of that total loss occurring.

But if the trader is not merely concerned that the stock will rally but truly believes that there is a good chance it will, the most logical action is to position himself for that expected move. Although there are many ways to accomplish this, the simplest way is to buy to close the 95 calls to eliminate the position at that strike. This eliminates the short delta from the 95 calls, leading to a now-positive delta for the position as a whole. The new position after adjusting by buying the 85 puts and the 95 calls is shown in Exhibit 10.9.

The result is a long strangle: a long call and a long put of the same month with two different strikes. Strangles will be discussed in subsequent chapters. The 80 puts are far enough out-of-the-money to be fairly irrelevant. Effectively, the position is long ten 100-strike calls. This serves the purpose of changing the negative 2.54 delta into a positive 0.96 delta. The trader now has a bullish position in the stock that he thinks will rally—a much smarter position, given that forecast.

The Retail Trader versus the Pro

Iron condors are very popular trades among retail traders. These days one can hardly go to a cocktail party and mention the word *options* without hearing someone tell a story about an iron condor on which he's made a bundle of money trading. Strangely, no one ever tells stories about trades in which he has lost a bundle of money.

Two of the strengths of this strategy that attract retail traders are its limited risk and high probability of success. Another draw of this type of strategy is that the iron condor and the other wing spreads offer something truly unique to the retail trader: a way to profit from stocks that don't move. In the stock-trading world, the only thing that can be traded is direction— that is, delta. The iron condor is an approachable way for a nonprofessional to dabble in nonlinear trading. The iron condor does a good job in eliminating delta—unless, of course, the stock moves and gamma kicks in. It is efficient in helping income-generating retail traders accomplish their goals. And when a loss occurs, although it can be bigger than the potential profits, it is finite.

But professional option traders, who have access to lots of capital and have very low commissions and margin requirements, tend to focus their efforts in other directions: they tend to trade volatility. Although iron condors are well equipped for profiting from theta when the stock cooperates, it is also possible to trade implied volatility with this strategy.

The examples of iron condors, condors, iron butterflies, and butterflies presented in this chapter so far have for the most part been from the perspective of the neutral trader: selling the guts and buying the wings. A trader focusing on vega in any of these strategies may do just the opposite—buy the guts and sell the wings—depending on whether the trader is bullish or bearish on volatility.

Say a trader, Joe, had a bullish outlook on volatility in Salesforce.com (CRM). Joe could sell the following condor 100 times.

> Sell 100 February 90 calls at 17.40
> Buy 100 February 95 calls at 13.75
> Buy 100 February 115 calls at   3.80
> Sell 100 February 120 calls at   2.55
> Total credit   2.40

In this example, February is 59 days from expiration. Exhibit 10.10 shows the analytics for this trade with CRM at $104.32.

As expected with the underlying centered between the two middle strikes, delta and gamma are about flat. As Salesforce.com moves higher or

EXHIBIT 10.10 Salesforce.com condor (Salesforce.com at $104.32).

		Premium	Delta	Gamma	Theta	Vega
Sell 100 February	90 calls	17.40	−78.5	−1.29	5.6	−12.3
Buy 100 February	95 calls	13.75	71.0	1.58	−6.3	14.4
Buy 100 February	115 calls	3.80	33.0	1.89	−5.9	15.3
Sell 100 February	120 calls	2.55	−24.8	−1.67	5.1	−13.4
			0.70	0.51	−1.50	4.0

lower, though, gamma and, consequently, delta will change. As the stock moves closer to either of the long strikes, gamma will become more positive, causing the delta to change favorably for Joe. Theta, however, is working against him with Salesforce.com at $104.32, costing $150 a day. In this instance, movement is good. Joe benefits from increased realized volatility. The best-case scenario would be if Salesforce.com moves through either of the long strikes to, or through, either of the short strikes.

The prime objective in this example, though, is to profit from a rise in IV. The position has a positive vega. The position makes or loses $400 with every point change in implied volatility. Because of the proportion of theta risk to vega risk, this should be a short-term play.

If Joe were looking for a small rise in IV, say five points, the move would have to happen within 13 calendar days, given the vega and theta figures. The vega gain on a rise of five vol points would be $2,000, and the theta loss over 13 calendar days would be $1,950. If there were stock movement associated with the IV increase, that delta/gamma gain would offset some of the havoc that theta wreaked on the option premiums. However, if Joe traded a strategy like a condor as a vol play, he would likely expect a bigger volatility move than the five points discussed here as well as expecting increased realized volatility.

A condor bullish vol play works when you expect something to change a stock's price action in the short term. Examples would be rumors of a new product's being unveiled, a product recall, a management change, or some other shake-up that leads to greater uncertainty about the company's future—good or bad. The goal is to profit from a rise in IV, so the trade needs to be put on before the announcement occurs. The motto in option-volatility trading is "Buy the rumor; sell the news." Usually, by the time the news is out, the increase in IV is already priced into option premiums. As uncertainty decreases, IV decreases as well.

Notes

1. It is important to note that in the real world, interest and expectations for future stock-price movement come into play. For simplicity's sake, they've been excluded here.
2. This is an approximate formula for estimating standard deviation. Although it is mathematically only an approximation, it is the convention used by many option traders. It is a traders' short cut.

CHAPTER 11

Calendar and Diagonal Spreads

Option selling is a niche that attracts many retail and professional traders because it's possible to profit from the passage of time. Calendar and diagonal spreads are practical strategies to limit risk while profiting from time. But these spreads are unique in many ways. In order to be successful with them, it is important to understand their subtle qualities.

Calendar Spreads

Definition: A calendar spread, sometimes called a *time spread* or a *horizontal spread,* is an option strategy that involves buying one option and selling another option with the same strike price but with a different expiration date.

At-expiration diagrams do a calendar-spread trader little good. Why? At the expiration of the short-dated option, the trader is left with another option that may have time value. To estimate what the position will be worth when the short-term option expires, the value of the long-term option must be analyzed using the greeks. This is true of the variants of the calendar—double calendars, diagonals, and double diagonals—as well. This chapter will show how to analyze strategies that involve options with different expirations and discuss how and when to use them.

Buying the Calendar

The calendar spread and all its variations are commonly associated with income-generating spreads. Using calendar spreads as income generators is popular among retail and professional traders alike. The process involves buying a longer-term at-the-money option and selling a shorter-term at-the-money (ATM) option. The options must be either both calls or both puts. Because this transaction results in a net debit—the longer-term option being purchased has a higher premium than the shorter-term option being sold—this is referred to as buying the calendar.

The main intent of buying a calendar spread for income is to profit from the positive net theta of the position. Because the shorter-term ATM option decays at a faster rate than the longer-term ATM option, the net theta is positive. As for most income spreads, the ideal outcome occurs when the underlying is at the short strike (in this case, shared strike) when the shorter-term option expires. At this strike price, the long option has its highest value, while the short option expires without the trader's getting assigned. As long as the underlying remains close to the strike price, the value of the spread rises as time passes, because the short option decreases in value faster than the long option.

For example, a trader, Richard, watches Bed Bath & Beyond Inc. (BBBY) on a regular basis. Richard believes that Bed Bath & Beyond will trade in a range around $57.50 a share (where it is trading now) over the next month. Richard buys the January–February 57.50 call calendar for 0.80. Assuming January has 25 days until expiration and February has 53 days, Richard will execute the following trade:

Sell 1 Bed Bath & Beyond January 57.50 call at 1.30
Buy 1 Bed Bath & Beyond February 57.50 call at 2.10
Net debit 0.80

Richard's best-case scenario occurs when the January calls expire at expiration and the February calls retain much of their value.

If Richard created an at-expiration P&(L) diagram for his position, he'd have trouble because of the staggered expiration months. A general representation would look something like Exhibit 11.1.

The only point on the diagram that is drawn with definitive accuracy is the maximum loss to the downside at expiration of the January call. The maximum loss if Bed Bath & Beyond falls low enough is 0.80—the debit paid for the spread. If Bed Bath & Beyond is below $57.50 at January expiration, the January 57.50 call expires worthless, and the February 57.50 call may or may not have residual value. If Bed Bath & Beyond declines enough, the February 57.50 call can lose all of its value,

EXHIBIT 11.1   Bed Bath & Beyond January–February 57.50 calendar.

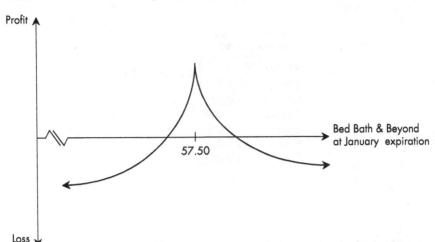

even with residual time until expiration. If the stock falls enough, the entire 0.80 debit would be a loss.

If Bed Bath & Beyond is above $57.50 at January expiration, the January 57.50 call will be trading at parity. It will be a negative-100-delta option, imitating short stock. If Bed Bath & Beyond is trading high enough, the February 57.50 call will become a positive-100-delta option trading at parity plus the interest calculated on the strike. The February deep-in-the-money option would imitate long stock. At a 2 percent interest rate, interest on the 57.50 strike is about 0.17. Therefore, Richard would essentially have a short stock position from $57.50 from the January 57.50 call and would be essentially long stock from $57.50 plus 0.28 from the February call. The maximum loss to the upside is about 0.63 (0.80 − 0.17).

The maximum loss if Bed Bath & Beyond is trading over $57.50 at expiration is only an estimate that assumes there is no time value and that interest and dividends remain constant. Ultimately, the maximum loss will be 0.80, the premium paid, if there is no time value or carry considerations.

The maximum profit is gained if Bed Bath & Beyond is at $57.50 at expiration. At this price, the February 57.50 call is worth the most it can be worth without having the January 57.50 call assigned and creating negative deltas to the upside. But how much precisely is the maximum profit? Richard would have to know what the February 57.50 call would be worth with Bed Bath & Beyond stock trading at $57.50 at February expiration before he can know the maximum profit potential. Although Richard can't know for sure

EXHIBIT 11.2 Bed Bath & Beyond January–February 57.50 call calendar greeks at January expiration.

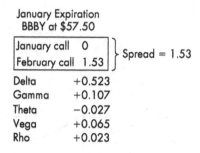

January Expiration
BBBY at $57.50

| January call | 0 |
| February call | 1.53 |

Spread = 1.53

Delta	+0.523
Gamma	+0.107
Theta	−0.027
Vega	+0.065
Rho	+0.023

EXHIBIT 11.3 Bed Bath & Beyond January–February 57.50 call calendar.

25 days until January
Expiration BBBY at $57.50

| January call | 1.30 |
| February call | 2.10 |

Spread = 0.80

Delta	+0.009
Gamma	−0.036
Theta	+0.009
Vega	+0.027
Rho	+0.022

at what price the calls will be trading, he can use a pricing model to estimate the call's value. Exhibit 11.2 shows analytics at January expiration.

With an unchanged implied volatility of 23 percent, an interest rate of two percent, and no dividend payable before February expiration, the February 57.50 calls would be valued at 1.53 at January expiration. In this best-case scenario, therefore, the spread would go from 0.80, where Richard purchased it, to 1.53, for a gain of 91 percent. At January expiration, with Bed Bath & Beyond at $57.50, the January call would expire; thus, the spread is composed of just the February 57.50 call.

Let's now go back in time and see how Richard figured this trade. Exhibit 11.3 shows the position when the trade is established.

A small and steady rise in the stock price with enough time to collect theta is the recipe for success in this trade. As time passes, delta will flatten out if Bed Bath & Beyond is still right at-the-money. The delta of the January call that Richard is short will move closer to exactly −0.50. The February call delta moves toward exactly +0.50.

Gamma and theta will both rise if Bed Bath & Beyond stays around the strike. As expiration approaches, there is greater risk if there is movement and greater reward if there is not.

Vega is positive because the long-term option with the higher vega is the long leg of the spread. When trading calendars for income, implied volatility (IV) must be considered as a possible threat. Because it is Richard's objective to profit from Bed Bath & Beyond being at $57.50 at expiration, he will try to avoid vega risk by checking that the implied volatility of the February call is in the lower third of the 12-month range. He will also determine if there are any impending events that could cause IV to change. The less likely IV is to drop, the better.

If there is an increase in IV, that may benefit the profitability of the trade. But a rise in IV is not really a desired outcome for two reasons. First, a rise in IV is often more pronounced in the front month than in the months farther out. If this happens, Richard can lose more on the short call than he makes on the long call. Second, a rise in IV can indicate anxiety and therefore a greater possibility for movement in the underlying stock. Richard doesn't want IV to rock the boat. "Buy low, stay low" is his credo.

Rho is positive also. A rise in interest rates benefits the position because the long-term call is helped by the rise more than the short call is hurt. With only a one-month difference between the two options, rho is very small. Overall, rho is inconsequential to this trade.

There is something curious to note about this trade: the gamma and the vega. Calendar spreads are the one type of trade where gamma can be negative while vega is positive, and vice versa. While it appears—at least on the surface— that Richard wants higher IV, he certainly wants low realized volatility.

Bed Bath & Beyond January–February 57.50 Put Calendar

Richard's position would be similar if he traded the January–February 57.50 put calendar rather than the call calendar. Exhibit 11.4 shows the put calendar.

The premium paid for the put spread is 0.75. A huge move in either direction means a loss. It is about the same gamma/theta trade as the 57.50 call calendar. At expiration, with Bed Bath & Beyond at $57.50 and IV unchanged, the value of the February put would be 1.45—a 93 percent gain. The position is almost exactly the same as the call calendar. The biggest

EXHIBIT 11.4   Bed Bath & Beyond January–February 57.50 put calendar.

25 days until January
Expiration BBBY at $57.50

| January put | 1.20 |
| February put | 1.95 |

} Spread = 0.75

Delta	−0.009
Gamma	−0.046
Theta	+0.004
Vega	+0.023
Rho	−0.020

EXHIBIT 11.5   20-Lot Bed Bath & Beyond January–February 57.50 call calendar.

25 days until January
Expiration BBBY at $57.50

| January call | 1.30 |
| February call | 2.10 |

} Spread = 0.80
Per contract

Delta	+0.180
Gamma	−0.720
Theta	+0.180
Vega	+0.540
Rho	+0.440

difference is that the rho is negative, but that is immaterial to the trade. As with the call spread, being short the front-month option means negative gamma and positive theta; being long the back month means positive vega.

Managing an Income-Generating Calendar

Let's say that instead of trading a one-lot calendar, Richard trades it 20 times. His trade in this case is

Sell 20 Bed Bath & Beyond January 57.50 calls at 1.30
Buy 20 Bed Bath & Beyond February 57.50 calls at 2.10
Net debit 0.80

His total cash outlay is $1,600 ($80 times 20). The greeks for this trade, listed in Exhibit 11.5, are also 20 times the size of those in Exhibit 11.3.

Note that Richard has a +0.18 delta. This means he's long the equivalent of about 18 shares of stock—still pretty flat. A gamma of −0.72 means that if Bed Bath & Beyond moves $1 higher, his delta will be starting to get short; and if it moves $1 lower he will be longer, long 90 deltas.

Richard can use the greeks to get a feel for how much the stock can move before negative gamma causes a loss. If Bed Bath & Beyond starts trending in either direction, Richard may need to react. His plan is to cover his deltas to continue the position.

Say that after one week Bed Bath & Beyond has dropped $1 to $56.50. Richard will have collected seven days of theta, which will have increased slightly from $18 per day to $20 per day. His average theta during that time is about $19, so Richard's profit attributed to theta is about $133.

With a big-enough move in either direction, Richard's delta will start working against him. Since he started with a delta of +0.18 on this 20-lot spread and a gamma of −0.72, one might think that his delta would increase to 0.90 with Bed Bath & Beyond a dollar lower (18 − [−0.072 × 1.00]). But because a week has passed, his delta would actually get somewhat more positive. The shorter-term call's delta will get smaller (closer to zero) at a faster rate compared to the longer-term call because it has less time to expiration. Thus, the positive delta of the long-term option begins to outweigh the negative delta of the short-term option as time passes.

In this scenario, Richard would have almost broken even because what would be lost on stock price movement, is made up for by theta gains. Richard can sell about 100 shares of Bed Bath & Beyond to eliminate his immediate directional risk and stem further delta losses. The good news is that if Bed Bath & Beyond declines more after this hedge, the profit from the short stock offsets losses from the long delta. The bad news is that if BBBY rebounds, losses from the short stock offset gains from the long delta.

After Richard's hedge trade is executed, his delta would be zero. His other greeks remain unchanged. The idea is that if Bed Bath & Beyond stays at its new price level of $56.50, he reaps the benefits of theta increasing with time from $18 per day. Richard is accepting the new price level and any profits or losses that have occurred so far. He simply adjusts his directional exposure to a zero delta.

Rolling and Earning a "Free" Call

Many traders who trade income-generating strategies are conservative. They are happy to sell low IV for the benefits afforded by low realized volatility. This is the problem-avoidance philosophy of trading. Due to risk aversion, it's common to trade calendar spreads by buying the two-month option and selling the one-month option. This can allow traders to avoid buying the calendar in earnings months, and it also means a shorter time horizon, signifying less time for something unwanted to happen.

But there's another school of thought among time-spread traders. There are some traders who prefer to buy a longer-term option—six months to a year—while selling a one-month option. Why? Because month after month, the trader can roll the short option to the next month. This is a simple tactic that is used by market makers and other professional traders as well as savvy retail traders. Here's how it works.

XYZ stock is trading at $60 per share. A trader has a neutral outlook over the next six months and decides to buy a calendar. Assuming that July has 29 days until expiration and December has 180, the trader will take the following position:

> Sell 1 XYZ July 60 call at 1.45
> Buy 1 XYZ December 60 call at 4.00
> Initial debit 2.55

The initial debit here is 2.55. The goal is basically the same as for any time spread: collect theta without negative gamma spoiling the party. There is another goal in these trades as well: to roll the spread.

At the end of month one, if the best-case scenario occurs and XYZ is sitting at $60 at July expiration, the July 60 call expires. The December 60 call will then be worth 3.60, assuming all else is held constant. The positive theta of the short July call gives full benefits as the option goes from 1.45 to zero. The lower negative theta of the December call doesn't bite into profits quite as much as the theta of a short-term call would.

The profit after month one is 1.05. Profit is derived from the December call, worth 3.60 at July expiry, minus the 2.55 initial spread debit. This works out to about a 41 percent return. The profit is hardly as good as it would have been if a short-term, less expensive August 60 call were the long leg of this spread.

Rolling the Spread

The July—December spread is different from short-term spreads, however. When the Julys expire, the August options will have 29 days until expiration. If volatility is still the same, XYZ is still at $60, and the trader's forecast is still neutral, the 29-day August 60 calls can be sold for 1.45. The trader can either wait until the Monday after July expiration and then sell the August 60s, or when the Julys are offered at 0.05 or 0.10, he can buy the Julys and

EXHIBIT 11.6 A "free" call.

	29 Days to July Exp	29 Days to Aug Exp	36 Days to Sep Exp	29 Days to Oct Exp	29 Days to Nov Exp
Credit from short call	1.45	1.45	1.60	1.45	1.45
Aggregate credit	1.45	2.90	**4.50**	**6.95**	**7.40**
Value of Dec call	4.00	3.60	3.20	2.70	2.20

sell the Augusts as a spread. In either case, it is called rolling the spread. When the August expires, he can sell the Septembers, and so on.

The goal is to get a credit month after month. At some point, the aggregate credit from the call sales each month is greater than the price initially paid for the long leg of the spread, thus eliminating the original net debit. Exhibit 11.6 shows how the monthly credits from selling the one-month calls aggregate over time.

After July has expired, 1.45 of premium is earned. After August expiration, the aggregate increases to 2.90. When the September calls, which have 36 days until expiration, are sold, another 1.60 is added to the total premium collected. Over three months—assuming the stock price, volatility, and the other inputs don't change—this trader collects a total of 4.50. That's 0.50 more than the price originally paid for the December 60 call leg of the spread.

At this point, he effectively owns the December call for free. Of course, this call isn't really free; it's earned. It's paid for with risk and maybe a few sleepless nights. At this point, even if the stock and, consequently, the December call go to zero, the position is still a profitable trade because of the continued month-to-month rolling. This is now a no-lose situation.

When the long call of the spread has been paid for by rolling, there are three choices moving forward: sell it, hold it, or continue writing calls against it. If the trader's opinion calls for the stock to decline, it's logical to sell the December call and take the residual value as profit. In this case, over three months the trade will have produced 4.50 in premium from the sale of three consecutive one-month calls, which is more than the initial purchase price of the December call. At September expiration, the premium that will be received for selling the December call is all profit, plus 0.50, which is the aggregate premium minus the initial cost of the December call.

If the outlook is for the underlying to rise, it makes sense to hold the call. Any appreciation in the value of the call resulting from delta gains as the underlying moves higher is good—$0.50 plus whatever the call can be sold for.

If the forecast is for XYZ to remain neutral, it's logical to continue selling the one-month call. Because the December call has been financed by the aggregate short call premiums already, additional premiums earned by writing calls are profit with "free" protection. As long as the short is closed at its expiration, the risk of loss is eliminated.

This is the general nature of rolling calls in a calendar spread. It's a beautiful plan when it works! The problem is that it is incredibly unlikely that the stock will stay right at $60 per share for five months. It's almost inevitable that it will move at some point. It's like a game of Russian roulette. At some point it's going to be a losing proposition—you just don't know when. The benefit of rolling is that if the trade works out for a few months in a row, the long call is paid for and the risk of loss is covered by aggregate profits.

If we step outside this best-case theoretical world and consider what is really happening on a day-to-day basis, we can gain insight on how to manage this type of trade when things go wrong. Effectively, a long calendar is a typical gamma/theta trade. Negative gamma hurts. Positive theta helps.

If we knew which way the stock was going, we would simply buy or sell stock to adjust to get long or short deltas. But, unfortunately, we don't. Our only tool is to hedge by buying or selling stock as mentioned above to flatten out when gamma causes the position delta to get more positive or negative.[1] The bottom line is that if the effect of gamma creates unwanted long deltas but the theta/gamma is still a desirable position, selling stock flattens out the delta. If the effect of gamma creates unwanted short deltas, buying stock flattens out the delta.

Trading Volatility Term Structure

There are other reasons for trading calendar spreads besides generating income from theta. If there is skew in the term structure of volatility, which was discussed in Chapter 3, a calendar spread is a way to trade volatility. The tactic is to buy the "cheap" month and sell the "expensive" month.

Selling the Front, Buying the Back

If for a particular stock, the February ATM calls are trading at 50 volatility and the May ATM calls are trading at 35 volatility, a vol-calendar trader would buy the Mays and sell the Februarys. Sounds simple, right? The devil is in the details. We'll look at an example and then discuss some common pitfalls with vol-trading calendars.

George has been studying the implied volatility of a $164.15 stock. George notices that front-month volatility has been higher than that of the other months for a couple of weeks. There is nothing in the news to indicate immediate risk of extraordinary movement occurring in this example.

George sees that he can sell the 22-day July 165 calls at a 45 percent IV and buy the 85-day September 165 calls at a 38 percent IV. George would like to buy the calendar spread, because he believes the July ATM volatility will drop down to around 38, where the September is trading. If he puts on this trade, he will establish the following position:

Sell 10 July 165 calls at   7.10   45% IV
Buy 10 Sep 165 calls at   12.60   38% IV
                Net debit   5.50

What are George's risks? Because he would be selling the short-term ATM option, negative gamma could be a problem. The greeks for this trade, shown in Exhibit 11.7, confirm this. The negative gamma means each dollar of stock price movement causes an adverse change of about 0.09 to delta. The spread's delta becomes shorter when the stock rises and longer when the stock falls. Because the position's delta is long 0.369 from the start, some price appreciation may be welcomed in the short term. The stock advance will yield profits but at a diminishing rate, as negative gamma reduces the delta.

But just looking at the net position greeks doesn't tell the whole story. It is important to appreciate the fact that long calendar spreads such as this have long vegas. In this case, the vega is +1.522. But what does this number

EXHIBIT 11.7   10-lot July–September 165 call calendar.

22 days until July Expiration
Stock at $164.15

July call	7.10
Sep call	12.60

Spread = 5.50
Per contract

Delta	+0.369
Gamma	−0.089
Theta	+0.945
Vega	+1.522
Rho	+1.357

really mean? This vega figure means that if IV rises or falls in both the July and the September calls by the same amount, the spread makes or loses $152 per vol point.

George's plan, however, is to see the July's volatility decline to converge with the September's. He hopes the volatilities of the two months will move independently of each other. To better gauge his risk, he needs to look at the vega of each option. With the stock at $164.15 the vegas are as follows:

	Vega
−10 July 50 calls	−1.604
+10 Sep 50 calls	+3.127

If George is right and July volatility declines 8 points, from 46 to 38, he will make $1,283 ($1.604 × 100 × 8).

There are a couple of things that can go awry. First, instead of the volatilities converging, they can diverge further. Implied volatility is a slave to the whims of the market. If the July IV continues to rise while the September IV stays the same, George loses $160 per vol point.

The second thing that can go wrong is the September IV declining along with the July IV. This can lead George into trouble, too. It depends the extent to which the September volatility declines. In this example, the vega of the September leg is about twice that of the July leg. That means that if the July volatility loses eight points while the September volatility declines four points, profits from the July calls will be negated by losses from the September calls. If the September volatility falls even more, the trade is a loser.

IV is a common cause of time-spread failure for market makers. When i in the front month rises, the volatility of the back-months sometimes does as well. When this happens, it's often because market makers who sold front-month options to retail or institutional buyers buy the back-month options to hedge their short-gamma risk. If the market maker buys enough back-month options, he or she will accumulate positive vega. But when the market sells the front-month volatility back to the market makers, the back months drop, too, because market makers no longer need the back months for a hedge.

Traders should study historical implied volatility to avoid this pitfall. As is always the case with long vega strategies, there is a risk of a decline in IV. Buying long-term options with implied volatility in the lower third of the 12-month IV range helps improve the chances of success, since the volatility being bought is historically cheap.

This can be tricky, however. If a trader looks back on a chart of IV for an option class and sees that over the past six months it has ranged between 20 and 30 but nine months ago it spiked up to, say, 55, there must be a reason. This solitary spike could be just an anomaly. To eliminate the noise from volatility charts, it helps to filter the data. News stories from that time period and historical stock charts will usually tell the story of why volatility spiked. Often, it is a one-time event that led to the spike. Is it reasonable to include this unique situation when trying to get a feel for the typical range of implied volatility? Usually not. This is a judgment call that needs to be made on a case-by-case basis. The ultimate objective of this exercise is to determine: "Is volatility cheap or expensive?"

Buying the Front, Selling the Back

All trading is based on the principle of "buy low, sell high"—even volatility trading. With time spreads, we can do both at once, but we are not limited to selling the front and buying the back. When short-term options are trading at a lower IV than long-term ones, there may be an opportunity to sell the calendar. If the IV of the front month is 17 and the back-month IV is 25, for example, it could be a wise trade to buy the front and sell the back. But selling time spreads in this manner comes with its own unique set of risks.

First, a short calendar's greeks are the opposite of those of a long calendar. This trade has negative theta with positive gamma. A sideways market hurts this position as negative theta does its damage. Each day of carrying the position is paid for with time decay.

The short calendar is also a short-vega trade. At face value, this implies that a drop in IV leads to profit and that the higher the IV sold in the back month, the better. As with buying a calendar, there are some caveats to this logic.

If there is an across-the-board decline in IV, the net short vega will lead to a profit. But an across-the-board drop in volatility, in this case, is probably not a realistic expectation. The front month tends to be more sensitive to volatility. It is a common occurrence for the front month to be "cheap" while the back month is "expensive."

The volatilities of the different months can move independently, as they can when one buys a time spread. There are a couple of scenarios that might lead to the back-month volatility's being higher than the front month. One is high complacency in the short term. When the market collectively sells options in expectation of lackluster trading, it generally prefers to sell the short-term options. Why? Higher theta. Because the trade has less time until expiration, the trade has a shorter period of risk. Because of this, selling pressure can push down IV in the front-month options more than in the back. Again, the front month is more sensitive to changes in implied volatility.

Because volatility has peaks and troughs, this can be a smart time to sell a calendar. The focus here is in seeing the "cheap" front month rise back up to normal levels, not so much in seeing the "expensive" back month fall. This trade is certainly not without risk. If the market doesn't move, the negative theta of the short calendar leads to a slow, painful death for calendar sellers.

Another scenario in which the back-month volatility can trade higher than the front is when the market expects higher movement after the expiration of the short-term option but before the expiration of the long-term option. Situations such as the expectation of the resolution of a lawsuit, a product announcement, or some other one-time event down the road are opportunities for the market to expect such movement. This strategy focuses on the back-month vol coming back down to normal levels, not on the front-month vol rising. This can be a more speculative situation for a volatility trade, and more can go wrong.

The biggest volatility risk in selling a time spread is that what goes up can continue to go up. The volatility disparity here is created by hedgers and speculators favoring long-term options, hence pushing up the volatility, in anticipation of a big future stock move. As the likely date of the anticipated event draws near, more buyers can be attracted to the market, driving up IV even further. Realized volatility can remain low as investors and traders lie in wait. This scenario is doubly dangerous when volatility rises and the stock doesn't move. A trader can lose on negative theta and lose on negative vega.

A Directional Approach

Calendar spreads are often purchased when the outlook for the underlying is neutral. Sell the short-term ATM option; buy the long-term ATM option; collect theta. But with negative gamma, these trades are never really neutral. The delta is constantly changing, becoming more positive or negative. It's like a rubber band: at times being stretched in either direction but always demanding a pull back to the strike. When the strike price being traded is not ATM, calendar spreads can be strategically traded as directional plays.

Buying a calendar, whether using calls or puts, where the strike price is above the current stock price is a bullish strategy. With calls, the positive delta of the long-term out-of-the-money (OTM) call will be greater than the negative delta of the short-term OTM call. For puts, the positive delta of the short-term in-the-money (ITM) put will be greater than the negative delta of the long-term ITM put.

Just the opposite applies if the strike price is below the current stock price. The negative delta of the short-term ITM call is greater than the positive delta of the long-term ITM call. The negative delta of the long-term OTM put is greater than the positive delta of the short-term OTM put.

When the position starts out with either a positive or negative delta, movement in the direction of the delta is necessary for the trade to be profitable. Negative gamma is also an important strategic consideration. Stock-price movement is needed, but not too much.

Buying calendar spreads is like playing outfield in a baseball game. To catch a fly ball, an outfielder must focus on both distance and timing. He must gauge how far the ball will be hit and how long it will take to get there. With calendars, the distance is the strike price—that's where the stock needs to be—and the time is the expiration day of the short month's option: that's when it needs to be at the target price.

For example, with Wal-Mart (WMT) at $48.50, a trader, Pete, is looking for a rise to about $50 over the next five or six weeks. Pete buys the August–September call calendar. In this example, August has 39 days until expiration and September has 74 days.

> Sell 10 August 50 calls at 0.60
> Buy 10 September 50 calls at 1.10
> Net debit 0.50

Exactly what does 50 cents buy Pete? The stock price sitting below the strike price means a net positive delta. This long time spread also has positive theta and vega. Gamma is negative. Exhibit 11.8 shows the specifics.

EXHIBIT 11.8   10-lot Wal-Mart August–September 50 call calendar.

39 days until August Expiration WMT at $48.50	
Aug call	0.60
Sep call	1.10
Delta	+0.563
Gamma	−0.323
Theta	+0.030
Vega	+0.214
Rho	+0.213

Spread = 0.50
Per contract

EXHIBIT 11.9 Stock price movement and greeks.

	$47.00	$47.50	$48.00	$48.50	$49.00	$49.50
Δ	0.871	0.816	0.707	0.563	0.390	0.196
Γ	−0.079	−0.171	−0.254	−0.323	−0.374	−0.392
Θ	0.002	0.012	0.021	0.030	0.037	0.042

	$50.00	$50.50	$51.00	$51.50	$52.00
Δ	0.002	−0.187	−0.351	−0.249	−0.603
Γ	−0.390	−0.362	−0.309	−0.498	−0.177
Θ	0.044	0.043	0.039	0.033	0.026

The delta of this trade, while positive, is relatively small with 39 days left until August expiration. It's not rational to expect a quick profit if the stock advances faster than expected. But ultimately, a rise in stock price is the goal. In this example, Wal-Mart needs to rise to $50, and timing is everything. It needs to be at that price in 39 days. In the interim, a move too big and too fast in either direction hurts the trade because of negative gamma. Starting with Wal-Mart at $48.50, delta/gamma problems are worse to the downside. Exhibit 11.9 shows the effects of stock price on delta, gamma, and theta.

If Wal-Mart moves lower, the delta gets more positive, racking up losses at a higher rate. To add to Pete's woes, theta becomes less of a benefit as the stock drifts lower. At $47 a share, theta is about flat. With Wal-Mart trading even lower than $47, the positive theta of the August call is overshadowed by the negative theta of the September. Theta can become negative, causing the position to lose value as time passes.

A big move to the upside doesn't help either. If Wal-Mart rises just a bit, the −0.323 gamma only lessens the benefit of the 0.563 delta. But above $50, negative gamma begins to cause the delta to become increasingly negative. Theta begins to wither away at higher stock prices as well.

The place to be is right at $50. The delta is flat and theta is highest. As long as Wal-Mart finds its way up to this price by the third Friday of August, life is good for Pete.

The In-or-Out Crowd

Pete could just as well have traded the Aug–Sep 50 put calendar in this situation. If he'd been bearish, he could have traded either the Aug–Sep 45 call spread or the Aug–Sep 45 put spread. Whether bullish or bearish, as mentioned earlier, the call calendar and the put calendar both function about the same. When deciding which to use, the important consideration is that one of them will be in-the-money and the other will be OTM. Whether you have an ITM spread or an OTM spread has potential implications for the success of the trade.

The bid-ask spreads tend to be wider for higher-delta, ITM options. Because of this, it can be more expensive to enter into an ITM calendar. Why? Trading options with wider markets requires conceding more edge. Take the following options series:

Call Bid-Ask	Call Theo.	Month/Strike	Put Bid-Ask	Put Theo.
3.00–3.20	3.10	May 50	0.90–1.00	0.95

By buying the May 50 calls at 3.20, a trader gives up 0.10 of theoretical edge (3.20 is 0.10 higher than the theoretical value). Buying the put at 1.00 means buying only 0.05 over theoretical.

Because a calendar is a two-legged spread, the double edge given up by trading the wider markets of two in-the-money options can make the out-of-the-money spread a more attractive trade. The issue of wider markets is compounded when rolling the spread. Giving up a nickel or a dime each month can add up, especially on nominally low-priced spreads. It can cut into a high percentage of profits.

Early assignment can complicate ITM calendars made up of American options, as dividends and interest can come into play. The short leg of the spread could get assigned before the expiration date as traders exercise calls to capture the dividend. Short ITM puts may get assigned early because of interest.

Although assignment is an undesirable outcome for most calendar spread traders, getting assigned on the short leg of the calendar spread may not necessarily create a significantly different trade. If a long put calendar, for example, has a short front-month put that is so deep in-the-money that it is likely to get assigned, it is trading close to a 100 delta. It is effectively a long stock position already. After assignment, when a long stock position is created, the resulting position is long stock with a deep ITM long put—a fairly delta-flat position.

Double Calendars

Definition: A double calendar spread is the execution of two calendar spreads that have the same months in common but have two different strike prices.

Example

> Sell 1 XYZ February 70 call
> Buy 1 XYZ March 70 call
> Sell 1 XYZ February 75 call
> Buy 1 XYZ March 75 call

Double calendars can be traded for many reasons. They can be vega plays. If there is a volatility-time skew, a double calendar is a way to take a position without concentrating delta or gamma/theta risk at a single strike.

This spread can also be a gamma/theta play. In that case, there are two strikes, so there are two potential focal points to gravitate to (in the case of a long double calendar) or avoid (in the case of a short double calendar).

Selling the two back-month strikes and buying the front-month strikes leads to negative theta and positive gamma. The positive gamma creates favorable deltas when the underlying moves. Positive or negative deltas can be covered by trading the underlying stock. With positive gamma, profits can be racked up by buying the underlying to cover short deltas and subsequently selling the underlying to cover long deltas.

Buying the two back-month strikes and selling the front-month strikes creates negative gamma and positive theta, just as in a conventional calendar. But the underlying stock has two target price points to shoot for at expiration to achieve the maximum payout.

Often double calendars are traded as IV plays. Many times when they are traded as IV plays, traders trade the lower-strike spread as a put calendar and the higher-strike spread a call calendar. In that case, the spread is sometimes referred to as a *strangle swap*. Strangles are discussed in Chapter 15.

Two Courses of Action

Although there may be many motivations for trading a double calendar, there are only two courses of action: buy it or sell it. While, for example, the trader's goal may be to capture theta, buying a double calendar comes with the baggage of the other greeks. Fully understanding the interrelationship of the greeks is essential to success. Option traders must take a holistic view of their positions.

Let's look at an example of buying a double calendar. In this example, Minnesota Mining & Manufacturing (MMM) has been trading in a range between about $85 and $97 per share. The current price of Minnesota Mining & Manufacturing is $87.90. Economic data indicate no specific reasons to anticipate that Minnesota Mining & Manufacturing will deviate from its recent range over the next month—that is, there is nothing in the news, no earnings anticipated, and the overall market is stable. August IV is higher than October IV by one volatility point, and October implied volatility is in line with 30-day historical volatility. There are 38 days until August expiration, and 101 days until October expiration.

The Aug–Oct 85–90 double calendar can be traded at the following prices:

> Sell 10 Minnesota Mining & Manufacturing August 85 calls at 4.30
> Sell 10 Minnesota Mining & Manufacturing August 90 calls at 1.50
> Buy 10 Minnesota Mining & Manufacturing October 85 calls at 5.90
> Buy 10 Minnesota Mining & Manufacturing October 90 calls at <u>3.10</u>
> Net Debit 3.20

Much like a traditional calendar spread, the price points cannot be definitively plotted on a P&(L) diagram. What is known for certain is that at August expiration, the maximum loss is $3,200. While it's comforting to know that there is limited loss, losing the entire premium that was paid for the spread is an outcome most traders would like to avoid. We also know the maximum gains occur at the strike prices; but not exactly what the maximum profit can be. Exhibit 11.10 provides an alternative picture of the position that is useful in managing the trade on a day-to-day basis.

These numbers are a good representation of the position's risk. Knowing that long calendars and long double calendars have maximum losses at the expiration of the short-term option equal to the net premiums paid, the max loss in this example is 3.20. Break-even prices are not relevant

EXHIBIT 11.10   10-lot Minnesota Mining & Manufacturing Aug–Oct 85–90 double call calendar.

38 days until August
Expiration MMM at $87.90

−Aug 85 call	4.30
−Aug 90 call	1.50
+Oct 85 call	5.90
+Oct 90 call	3.10

Spread = 3.20 debit
Per contract

Delta	0.043
Gamma	−0.468
Theta	0.189
Vega	1.471
Rho	1.568

to this position because they cannot be determined with any certainty. What is important is to get a feel for how much movement can hurt the position.

To make $19 a day in theta, a -0.468 gamma must be accepted. In the long run, $1 of movement is irrelevant. In fact, some movement is favorable because the ideal point for MMM to be at, at August expiration is either $85 or $90. So while small moves are acceptable, big moves are of concern. The negative gamma is an illustration of this warning.

The other risk besides direction is vega. A positive 1.471 vega means the calendar makes or loses about $147 with each one-point across-the-board change in implied volatility. Implied volatility is a risk in all calendar trades. Volatility was one of the criteria studied when considering this trade. Recall that the August IV was one point higher than the October and that the October IV was in line with the 30-day historical volatility at inception of the trade.

Considering the volatility data is part of the due diligence when considering a calendar or a double calendar. First, the (slightly) more expensive options (August) are being sold, and the cheaper ones are being bought (October). A study of the company reveals no news to lead one to believe that Minnesota Mining & Manufacturing should move at a higher realized volatility than it currently is in this example. Therefore, the front month's higher IV is not a red flag. Because the volatility of the October option (the month being purchased) is in line with the historical volatility, the trader could feel that he is paying a reasonable price for this volatility.

In the end, the trade is evaluated on the underlying stock, realized volatility, and IV. The trade should be executed only after weighing all the available data. Trading is both cerebral and statistical in nature. It's about gaining a statistically better chance of success by making rational decisions.

Diagonals

Definition: A diagonal spread is an option strategy that involves buying one option and selling another option with a different strike price and with a different expiration date. Diagonals are another strategy in the time spread family.

Diagonals enable a trader to exploit opportunities similar to those exploited by a calendar spread, but because the options in a diagonal spread have two different strike prices, the trade is more focused on delta. The name *diagonal* comes from the fact that the spread is a combination of a horizontal spread (two different months) and a vertical spread (two different strikes).

EXHIBIT 11.11 Apple January–February 400–420 call diagonal.

22 days until January
expiration AAPL at $405.10

Jan 420 call	5.35	
Feb 400 call	21.80	} Spread = 16.45

Delta	+0.255
Gamma	−0.005
Theta	+0.037
Vega	+0.239
Rho	+0.210

Say it's 22 days until January expiration and 50 days until February expiration. Apple Inc. (AAPL) is trading at $405.10. Apple has been in an uptrend heading toward the peak of its six-month range, which is around $420. A trader, John, believes that it will continue to rise and hit $420 again by February expiration. Historical volatility is 28 percent. The February 400 calls are offered at a 32 implied volatility and the January 420 calls are bid on a 29 implied volatility. John executes the following diagonal:

Sell 1 Apple January 420 call at   5.35
Buy 1 Apple February 400 call at 21.80
Net Debit 16.45

Exhibit 11.11 shows the analytics for this trade.

From the presented data, is this a good trade? The answer to this question is contingent on whether the position John is taking is congruent with his view of direction and volatility and what the market tells him about these elements.

John is bullish up to August expiration, and the stock in this example is in an uptrend. Any rationale for bullishness may come from technical or fundamental analysis, but techniques for picking direction, for the most part, are beyond the scope of this book. Buying the lower strike in the February option gives this trade a more positive delta than a straight calendar spread would have. The trader's delta is 0.255, or the equivalent of about 25.5 shares of Apple. This reflects the trader's directional view.

The volatility is not as easy to decipher. A specific volatility forecast was not stated above, but there are a few relevant bits of information that should be considered, whether or not the trader has a specific view on future volatility. First, the historical volatility is 28 percent. That's lower than either the January or the February calls. That's not ideal. In a perfect world, it's better to buy below historical and sell above. To that point, the February option that John is buying has a higher volatility than the January he is selling. Not so good either. Are these volatility observations deal breakers?

A Good Ex-Skews

It's important to take skew into consideration. Because the January calls have a higher strike price than the February calls, it's logical for them to trade at a lower implied volatility. Is this enough to justify the possibility of selling the lower volatility? Consider first that there is some margin for error. The bid-ask spreads of each of the options has a volatility disparity. In this case, both the January and February calls are 10 cents wide. That means with a January vega of 0.34 the bid-ask is about 0.29 vol points wide. The Februarys have a 0.57 vega. They are about 0.18 vol points wide. That accounts for some of the disparity. Natural vertical skew accounts for the rest of the difference, which is acceptable as long as the skew is not abnormally pronounced.

As for other volatility considerations, this diagonal has the rather unorthodox juxtaposition of positive vega and negative gamma seen with other time spreads. The trader is looking for a move upward, but not a big one. As the stock rises and Apple moves closer to the 420 strike, the positive delta will shrink and the negative gamma will increase. In order to continue to enjoy profits as the stock rises, John may have to buy shares of Apple to keep his positive delta. The risk here is that if he buys stock and Apple retraces, he may end up negative scalping stock. In other words, he may sell it back at a lower price than he bought it. Using stock to adjust the delta in a negative-gamma play can be risky business. Gamma scalping is addressed further in Chapter 13.

Making the Most of Your Options

The trader from the previous example had a time-spread alternative to the diagonal: John could have simply bought a traditional time spread at the 420 strike. Recall that calendars reap the maximum reward when they are at the shared strike price at expiration of the short-term option. Why would he choose one over the other?

The diagonal in that example uses a lower-strike call in the February than a straight 420 calendar spread and therefore has a higher delta, but it costs more. Gamma, theta, and vega may be slightly lower with the in-the-money call, depending on how far from the strike price the ITM call is and how much time until expiration it has. These, however, are less relevant differences.

The delta of the February 400 call is about 0.57. The February 420 call, however, has only a 0.39 delta. The 0.18 delta difference between the calls means the position delta of the time spread will be only about 0.07 instead of about 0.25 of the diagonal—a big difference. But the trade-off for lower delta is that the February 420 call can be bought for 12.15. That means a lower debit paid—that means less at risk. Conversely, though there is greater risk with the diagonal, the bigger delta provides a bigger payoff if the trader is right.

Double Diagonals

A double diagonal spread is the simultaneous trading of two diagonal spreads: one call spread and one put spread. The distance between the strikes is the same in both diagonals, and both have the same two expiration months. Usually, the two long-term options are more out-of-the-money than the two shorter-term options. For example

Buy 1 XYZ May 70 put
Sell 1 XYZ March 75 put
Sell 1 XYZ March 85 call
Buy 1 XYZ May 90 call

Like many option strategies, the double diagonal can be looked at from a number of angles. Certainly, this is a trade composed of two diagonal spreads—the March–May 70–75 put and the March–May 85–90 call. It is also two strangles—buying the May 70–90 strangle and selling the March 75–85 strangle. One insightful way to look at this spread is as an iron condor in which the guts are March options and the wings are May options.

Trading a double diagonal like this one, rather than a typically positioned iron condor, can offer a few advantages. The first advantage, of course, is theta. Selling short-term options and buying long-term options helps the trader reap higher rates of decay. Theta is the raison d'être of the iron condor. A second advantage is rolling. If the underlying asset stays in a range for a long period of time, the short strangle can be rolled month after month. There may, in some cases, also be volatility-term-structure discrepancies on which to capitalize.

A trader, Paul, is studying JPMorgan (JPM). The current stock price is $49.85. In this example, JPMorgan has been trading in a pretty tight range over the past few months. Paul believes it will continue to do so over the next month. Paul considers the following trade:

$$
\begin{array}{lll}
\text{Buy 10 September 55 calls at 0.30} & - & 19\% \text{ IV} \\
\text{Sell 10 August 52.50 call at 0.40} & - & 20.5\% \text{ IV} \\
\text{Sell 10 August 47.50 put at 0.50} & - & 24.4\% \text{ IV} \\
\text{Buy 10 September 45 put at } \underline{0.45} & - & 26\% \text{ IV} \\
\text{Net Credit } \overline{0.15}
\end{array}
$$

Paul considers volatility. In this example, the JPMorgan ATM call, the August 50 (which is not shown here), is trading at 22.9 percent implied volatility. This is in line with the 20-day historical volatility, which is 23 percent. The August IV appears to be reasonably in line with the September volatility, after accounting for vertical skew. The IV of the August 52.50 calls is 1.5 points above that of the September 55 calls and the August 47.50 put IV is 1.6 points below the September 45 put IV. It appears that neither month's volatility is cheap or expensive.

Exhibit 11.12 shows the trade's greeks.

The analytics of this trade are similar to those of an iron condor. Immediate directional risk is almost nonexistent, as indicated by the delta. But gamma and theta are high, even higher than they would be if this were a straight September iron condor, although not as high as if this were an August iron condor.

Vega is positive. Surely, if this were an August or a September iron condor, vega would be negative. In this example, Paul is indifferent as to

EXHIBIT 11.12 10-lot JPMorgan August–September 45–47.50–52.50–55 double diagonal.

33 days until August
expiration JPM at $49.85

−Aug 52.50 call	0.40	Spread = 0.15
−Aug 47.50 put	0.50	Per contract
+Sep 55 calls	0.30	
+Sep 45 puts	0.45	

Delta	−0.032
Gamma	−0.842
Theta	+0.146
Vega	+0.183
Rho	−0.003

whether vega is positive or negative because IV is fairly priced in terms of historical volatility and term structure. In fact, to play it close to the vest, Paul probably wants the smallest vega possible, in case of an IV move. Why take on the risk?

The motivation for Paul's double diagonal was purely theta. The volatilities were all in line. And this one-month spread can't be rolled. If Paul were interested in rolling, he could have purchased longer-term options. But if he is anticipating a sideways market for only the next month and feels that volatility could pick up after that, the one-month play is the way to go. After August expiration, Paul will have three choices: sell his Septembers, hold them, or turn them into a traditional iron condor by selling the September 47.50s and 52.50s. This depends on whether he is indifferent, expects high volatility, or expects low volatility.

The Strength of the Calendar

Spreads in the calendar-spread family allow traders to take their trading to a higher level of sophistication. More basic strategies, like vertical spreads and wing spreads, provide a practical means for taking positions in direction, realized volatility, and to some extent implied volatility. But because calendar-family spreads involve two expiration months, traders can take positions in the same market variables as with these more basic strategies and also in the volatility spread between different expiration months. Calendar-family spreads are veritable volatility spreads. This is a powerful tool for option traders to have at their disposal.

Note

1. Advanced hedging techniques are discussed in subsequent chapters.

PART III

Volatility

CHAPTER 12

Delta-Neutral Trading
Trading Implied Volatility

Many of the strategies covered so far have been option-selling strategies. Some had a directional bias; some did not. Most of the strategies did have a primary focus on realized volatility—especially selling it. These short volatility strategies require time. The reward of low stock volatility is theta. In general, most of the strategies previously covered were theta trades in which negative gamma was an unpleasant inconvenience to be dealt with.

Moving forward, much of the remainder of this book will involve more in-depth discussions of trading both realized and implied volatility (IV), with a focus on the harmonious, and sometimes disharmonious, relationship between the two types. Much attention will be given to how IV trades in the option market, describing situations in which volatility moves are likely to occur and how to trade them.

Direction Neutral versus Direction Indifferent

In the world of nonlinear trading, there are two possible nondirectional views of the underlying asset: direction neutral and direction indifferent. Direction neutral means the trader believes the stock will not trend either higher or lower. The trader is neutral in his or her assessment of the future direction of the asset. Short iron condors, long time spreads, and out-of-the-money (OTM) credit spreads are examples of direction-neutral strategies. These strategies generally have deltas close to zero. Because of negative gamma, movement is the bane of the direction-neutral trade.

Direction indifferent means the trader may desire movement in the underlying but is indifferent as to whether that movement is up or down. Some direction-indifferent trades are almost completely insulated from directional movement, with a focus on interest or dividends instead. Examples of these types of trades are conversions, reversals, and boxes, which are described in Chapter 6, as well as dividend plays, which are described in Chapter 8.

Other direction-indifferent strategies are long option strategies that have positive gamma. In these trades, the focus is on movement, but the direction of that movement is irrelevant. These are plays that are bullish on realized volatility. Yet other direction-indifferent strategies are volatility plays from the perspective of IV. These are trades in which the trader's intent is to take a bullish or bearish position in IV.

Delta Neutral

To be truly direction neutral or direction indifferent means to have a delta equal to zero. In other words, there are no immediate gains if the underlying moves incrementally higher or lower. This zero-delta method of trading is called *delta-neutral trading*.

A delta-neutral position can be created from any option position simply by trading stock to flatten out the delta. A very basic example of a delta-neutral trade is a long at-the-money (ATM) call with short stock.

Consider a trade in which we buy 20 ATM calls that have a 50 delta and sell stock on a delta-neutral ratio.

Buy 20 50-delta calls (long 1,000 deltas)
Short 1,000 shares (short 1,000 deltas)

In this position, we are long 1,000 deltas from the calls (20 × 50) and short 1,000 deltas from the short sale of stock. The net delta of the position is zero. Therefore, the immediate directional exposure has been eliminated from the trade. But intuitively, there are other opportunities for profit or loss with this trade.

The addition of short stock to the calls will affect only the delta, not the other greeks. The long calls have positive gamma, negative theta, and positive vega. Exhibit 12.1 is a simplified representation of the greeks for this trade.

EXHIBIT 12.1 20-lot delta-neutral long call.

Long 20 ATM calls	
Short 1,000 shares	
Delta	**0**
Gamma	+2.80
Theta	−0.50
Vega	+1.15

With delta not an immediate concern, the focus here is on gamma, theta, and vega. The +1.15 vega indicates that each one-point change in IV makes or loses $115 for this trade. Yet there is more to the volatility story. Each day that passes costs the trader $50 in time decay. Holding the position for an extended period of time can produce a loser even if IV rises. Gamma is potentially connected to the success of this trade, too. If the underlying moves in either direction, profit from deltas created by positive gamma may offset the losses from theta. In fact, a big enough move in either direction can produce a profitable trade, regardless of what happens to IV.

Imagine, for a moment, that this trade is held until expiration. If the stock is below the strike price at this point, the calls expire. The resulting position is short 1,000 shares of stock. If the stock is above the strike price at expiration, the calls can be exercised, creating 2,000 shares of long stock. Because the trade is already short 1,000 shares, the resulting net position is long 1,000 shares (2,000 − 1,000). Clearly, the more the underlying stock moves in either direction the greater the profit potential. The underlying has to move far enough above or below the strike price to allow the beneficial gains from buying or selling stock to cover the option premium lost from time decay. If the trade is held until expiration, the underlying needs to move far enough to cover the entire premium spent on the calls.

The solid lines forming a V in Exhibit 12.2 conceptually illustrate the profit or loss for this delta-neutral long call at expiration.

Because of gamma, some deltas will be created by movement of the underlying before expiration. Gamma may lead to this being a profitable trade in the short term, depending on time and what happens with IV. The dotted line illustrates the profit or loss of this trade at the point in time when the trade is established. Because the options may still have time value at this point—depending on how far from the strike price the stock is trading—the value of the position, as a whole, is higher than it will be if the calls are trading at parity at expiration. Regardless, the plan is for the stock to make a move in either direction. The bigger the move and the faster it happens, the better.

EXHIBIT 12.2 Profit-and-loss diagram for delta-neutral long-call trade.

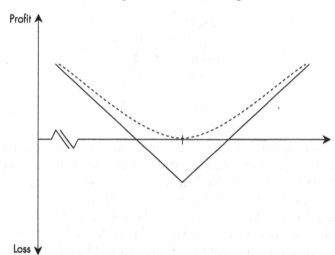

Why Trade Delta Neutral?

A few years ago, I was teaching a class on option trading. Before the seminar began, I was talking with one of the students in attendance. I asked him what he hoped to learn in the class. He said that he was really interested in learning how to trade delta neutral. When I asked him why he was interested in that specific area of trading, he replied, "I hear that's where all the big money is made!"

This observation, right or wrong, probably stems from the fact that in the past most of the trading in this esoteric discipline has been executed by professional traders. There are two primary reasons why the pros have dominated this strategy: high commissions and high margin requirements for retail traders. Recently, these two reasons have all but evaporated.

First, the ultracompetitive world of online brokers has driven commissions for retail traders down to, in some cases, what some market makers pay. Second, the oppressive margin requirements that retail option traders were subjected to until 2007 have given way to portfolio margining.

Portfolio Margining

Customer portfolio margining is a method of calculating customer margin in which the margin requirement is based on the "up and down risk" of the portfolio. Before the advent of portfolio margining, retail traders were subject to strategy-based margining, also called Reg. T margining, which in many cases required a significantly higher amount of capital to carry a position than portfolio margining does.

With portfolio margining, highly correlated securities can be offset against each other for purposes of calculating margin. For example, SPX options and SPY options—both option classes based on the Standard & Poor's 500 Index—can be considered together in the margin calculation. A bearish position in one and a bullish position in the other may partially offset the overall risk of the portfolio and therefore can help to reduce the overall margin requirement.

With portfolio margining, many strategies are margined in such a way that, from the point of view of this author, they are subject to a much more logical means of risk assessment. Strategy-based margining required traders of some strategies, like a protective put, to deposit significantly more capital than one could possibly lose by holding the position. The old rules require a minimum margin of 50 percent of the stock's value and up to 100 percent of the put premium. A portfolio-margined protective put may require only a fraction of what it would with strategy-based margining.

Even though Reg. T margining is antiquated and sometimes unreasonable, many traders must still abide by these constraints. Not all traders meet the eligibility requirements to qualify for portfolio-based margining. There is a minimum account balance for retail traders to be eligible for this treatment. A broker may also require other criteria to be met for the trader to benefit from this special margining. Ultimately, portfolio margining allows retail traders to be margined similarly to professional traders.

There are some traders, both professional and otherwise, who indeed have made "big money," as the student in my class said, trading delta neutral. But, to be sure, there are successful and unsuccessful traders in many areas of trading. The real motivation for trading delta neutral is to take a position in volatility, both implied and realized.

Trading Implied Volatility

With a typical option, the sensitivity of delta overshadows that of vega. To try and profit from a rise or fall in IV, one has to trade delta neutral to eliminate immediate directional sensitivity. There are many strategies that can be traded as delta-neutral IV strategies simply by adding stock. Throughout this chapter, I will continue using a single option leg with stock, since it provides a simple yet practical example. It's important to note that delta-neutral trading does not refer to a specific strategy; it refers to the fact that the trader is indifferent to direction. Direction isn't being traded, volatility is.

Volatility trading is fundamentally different from other types of trading. While stocks can rise to infinity or decline to zero, volatility can't. Implied volatility, in some situations, can rise to lofty levels of 100, 200, or even higher. But in the long-run, these high levels are not sustainable for most stocks. Furthermore, an IV of zero means that the options have no extrinsic value at all. Now that we have established that the thresholds of volatility are not as high as infinity and not as low as zero, where exactly are they? The limits to how high or low IV can go are not lines in the sand. They are more like tides that ebb and flow, but normally come up only so far onto the beach.

The volatility of an individual stock tends to trade within a range that can be unique to that particular stock. This can be observed by studying a chart of recent volatility. When IV deviates from the range, it is typical for it to return to the range. This is called *reversion to the mean,* which was discussed in Chapter 3. IV can get stretched in either direction like a rubber band but then tends to snap back to its original shape.

There are many examples of situations where reversion to the mean enters into trading. In some, volatility temporarily dips below the typical range, and in some, it rises beyond the recent range. One of the most common examples is the rush and the crush.

The Rush and the Crush

In this situation, volatility rises before and falls after a widely anticipated news announcement, of earnings, for instance, or of a Food and Drug Administration (FDA) approval. In this situation, option buyers rush in and bid up IV. The more uncertainty—the more demand for insurance—the higher vol rises. When the event finally occurs and the move takes place or doesn't, volatility gets crushed. The crush occurs when volatility falls very sharply— sometimes 10 points, 20 points, or more—in minutes. Traders with large vega positions appreciate the appropriateness of the term crush all too well. Volatility traders also affectionately refer to this sudden drop in IV by saying that volatility has gotten "whacked."

In order to have a feel for whether implied volatility is high or low for a particular stock, you need to know where it's been. It's helpful to have an idea of where realized volatility is and has been, too. To be sure, one analysis cannot be entirely separate from the other. Studying both implied and realized volatility and how they relate is essential to seeing the big picture.

The Inertia of Volatility

Sir Isaac Newton said that an object in motion tends to stay in motion unless acted upon by another force. Volatility acts much the same way. Most stocks tend to trade with a certain measurable amount of daily price fluctuations. This can be observed by looking at the stock's realized volatility. If there is no outside force—some pivotal event that fundamentally changes how the stock is likely to behave—one would expect the stock to continue trading with the same level of daily price movement. This means IV (the market's expectation of future stock volatility) should be the same as realized volatility (the calculated past stock volatility).

But just as in physics, it seems there is always some friction affecting the course of what is in motion. Corporate earnings, Federal Reserve Board reports, apathy, lulls in the market, armed conflicts, holidays, rumors, and takeovers, among other market happenings all provide a catalyst for volatility changes. Divergences of realized and implied volatility, then, are commonplace. These divergences can create tradable conditions, some of which are more easily exploited than others.

To find these opportunities, a trader must conduct a study of volatility. Volatility charts can help a trader visualize the big picture. This historical information offers a comparison of what is happening now in volatility with what has happened in the past. The following examples use a volatility chart to show how two different traders might have traded the rush and crush of an earnings report.

Volatility Selling

Susie Seller, a volatility trader, studies semiconductor stocks. Exhibit 12.3 shows the volatilities of a $50 chip stock. The circled area shows what happened before and after second-quarter earnings were reported in July. The black line is the IV, and the gray is the 30-day historical.

In mid-July, Susie did some digging to learn that earnings were to be announced on July 24, after the close. She was careful to observe the classic rush and crush that occurred to varying degrees around the last three earnings announcements, in October, January, and April. In each case, IV firmed up before earnings only to get crushed after the report. In mid-to-late July, she watched as IV climbed to the mid-30s (the rush) just before earnings. As the stock lay in wait for the report, trading came to a proverbial screeching halt, sending realized volatility lower, to about 13 percent. Susie waited for the end of the day just before the report to make her move. Before

EXHIBIT 12.3 Chip stock volatility before and after earnings reports.

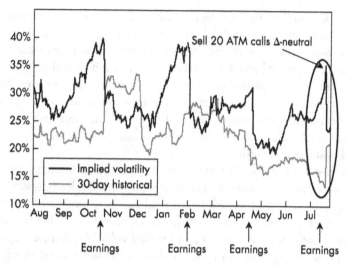

Source: Chart courtesy of iVolatility.com

EXHIBIT 12.4 Delta-neutral short ATM call, long stock position.

One month until expiration
stock at $50

| Short × @ 20 50 calls 2.10 |
| Long × @ 1,100 shrs 50 |

	Per cont.	Position
Delta	−0.540	+0.20
Gamma	−0.080	−1.60
Theta	+.0375	+0.75
Vega	−0.0575	−1.15

the closing bell, the stock was at $50. Susie sold 20 one-month 50-strike calls at 2.10 (a 35 volatility) and bought 1,100 shares of the underlying stock at $50 to become delta neutral.

Exhibit 12.4 shows Susie's position.

Her delta was just about flat. The delta for the 50 calls was 0.54 per contract. Selling a 20-lot creates 10.80 short deltas for her overall position. After buying 1,100 shares, she was left long 0.20 deltas, about the equivalence of being long 20 shares. Where did her risk lie? Her biggest concern was negative gamma. Without even seeing a chart of the stock's price, we can see from the volatility chart that this stock can have big moves on earnings. In October, earnings caused a more than 10-point jump in realized volatility, to its highest level during the year shown. Whether the stock rose or fell is irrelevant. Either event means risk for a premium seller.

The positive theta looks good on the surface, but in fact, theta provided Susie with no significant benefit. Her plan was "in and out and nobody gets hurt." She got into the trade right before the earnings announcement and out as soon as implied volatility dropped off. Ideally, she'd like to hold these types of trades for less than a day. The true prize is vega.

Susie was looking for about a 10-point drop in IV, which this option class had following the October and January earnings reports. April had a big drop in IV, as well, of about eight or nine points. Ultimately, what Susie is looking for is reversion to the mean.

She gauges the normal level of volatility by observing where it is before and after the surges caused by earnings. From early November to mid- to late-December, the stock's IV bounced around the 25 percent level. In the month of February, the IV was around 25. After the drop-off following April earnings and through much of May, the IV was closer to 20 percent. In June, IV was just above 25. Susie surmised from this chart that when no earnings event is pending, this stock's options typically trade at about a 25 percent IV. Therefore, anticipating a 10-point decline from 35 was reasonable, given the information available. If Susie gets it right, she stands to make $1,150 from vega (10 points × 1.15 vegas × 100).

As we can see from the right side of the volatility chart in Exhibit 12.3, Susie did get it right. IV collapsed the next morning by just more than ten points. But she didn't make $1,150; she made less. Why? Realized volatility (gamma). The jump in realized volatility shown on the graph is a function of the fact that the stock rallied $2 the day after earnings. Negative gamma contributed to negative deltas in the face of a rallying market. This negative delta affected some of Susie's potential vega profits.

So what was Susie's profit? On this trade she made $800. The next morning at the open, she bought back the 50-strike calls at 2.80 (25 IV) and sold the stock at $52. To compute her actual profit, she compared the prices of the spread when entering the trade with the prices of the spread when exiting. Exhibit 12.5 shows the breakdown of the trade.

After closing the trade, Susie knew for sure what she made or lost. But there are many times when a trader will hold a delta-neutral position for an extended period of time. If Susie hadn't closed her trade, she would have looked at her marks to see her P&(L) at that point in time. Marks are the prices at which the securities are trading in the actual market, either in

EXHIBIT 12.5 Profit breakdown of delta-neutral trade.

<u>**Calls**</u>
Sell 20 @ 2.10
<u>Buy 20 @ 2.80</u>
20 × (0.70) = ($1,400)
<u>**Stock**</u>
Buy 1,100 @ $50
<u>Sell 1,100 @ $52</u>
1,100 × $ 2 = <u>$2,200</u>
Position
P&(L) $ 800

EXHIBIT 12.6 Profit breakdown by greek.

Delta: 0.20 × 2 = 0.40
Gamma: (−1.60 × 2) × 2 ÷ 2 = −3.20
Theta: = 0.75
<u>Vega: −1.15 × −10 = 11.50</u>
Total P&(L):   + 9.45, or $945

real time or at end of day. With most online brokers' trading platforms or options-trading software, real-time prices are updated dynamically and always at their fingertips. The profit or loss is, then, calculated automatically by comparing the actual prices of the opening transaction with the current marks.

What Susie will want to know is why she made $800. Why not more? Why not less, for that matter? When trading delta neutral, especially with more complex trades involving multiple legs, a manual computation of each leg of the spread can be tedious. And to be sure, just looking at the profit or loss on each leg doesn't provide an explanation.

Susie can see where her profits or losses came from by considering the profit or loss for each influence contributing to the option's value. Exhibit 12.6 shows the breakdown.

Delta

Susie started out long 0.20 deltas. A $2 rise in the stock price yielded a $40 profit attributable to that initial delta.

Gamma

As the stock rose, the negative delta of the position increased as a result of negative gamma. The delta of the stock remained the same, but the negative delta of the 50 call grew by the amount of the gamma. Deriving an exact P&(L) attributable to gamma is difficult because gamma is a dynamic metric: as the stock price changes, so can the gamma. This calculation assumes that gamma remains constant. Therefore, the gamma calculation here provides only an estimate.

The initial position gamma of −1.6 means the delta decreases by 3.2 with a $2 rise in the stock (−1.60 times the $2 rise in the stock price). Susie, then, would multiply −3.2 by $2 to find the loss on −3.2 deltas over a $2 rise. But she wasn't short 3.2 deltas for the whole $2. She started out with zero deltas attributable to gamma and ended up being 3.2 shorter from gamma over that $2 move. Therefore, if she assumes her negative delta from gamma grew steadily from 0 to −3.2, she can estimate her average delta loss over that move by dividing by 2.

Theta

Susie held this trade one day. Her total theta contributed 0.75 or $75 to her position.

Vega

Vega is where Susie made her money on this trade. She was able to buy her call back 10 IV points lower. The initial position vega was −1.15. Multiplying −1.15 by the negative 10-point crush of volatility yields a vega profit of $1,150.

Conclusions

Studying her position's P&(L) by observing what happened in her greeks provides Susie with an alternate—and in some ways, better—method to evaluate her trade. The focus of this delta-neutral trade is less on the price at which Susie can buy the calls back to close the position than on the volatility level at which she can buy them back, weighed against the P&(L) from her other risks. Analyzing her position this way gives her much more information than just comparing opening and closing prices. Not only does she get a good estimate of how much she made or lost, but she can understand why as well.

The Imprecision of Estimation

It is important to notice that the P&(L) found by adding up the P&(L)'s from the greeks is slightly different from the actual P&(L). There are a couple of reasons for this. First, the change in delta resulting from gamma is only an estimate, because gamma changes as the stock price changes. For small moves in the underlying, the gamma change is less significant, but for larger moves, the rate of change of the gamma can be bigger, and it can be nonlinear. For example, as an option moves from being at-the-money (ATM) to being out-of-the-money (OTM), its gamma decreases. But as the option becomes more OTM, its gamma decreases at a slower rate.

Another reason that the P&(L) from the greeks is different from the actual P&(L) is that the greeks are derived from the option-pricing model and are therefore theoretical values and do not include slippage.

Furthermore, the volatility input in this example is rounded a bit for simplicity. For example, a volatility of 25 actually yielded a theoretical value of 2.796, while the call was bought at 2.80. Because some options trade at minimum price increments of a nickel, and none trade in fractions of a penny, IV is often rounded.

Caveat Venditor

Reversion to the mean holds the promise of profit in this trade, but Susie also knows that this strategy does not come without risks of loss. The mean to which volatility is expected to revert is not a constant. This benchmark can and does change. In this example, if the company had an unexpectedly terrible quarter, the stock could plunge sharply. In some cases, this would cause IV to find a new, higher level at which to reside. If that had happened here, the trade could have been a big loser. Gamma and vega could both have wreaked havoc. In trading, there is no sure thing, no matter what the chart looks like. Remember, every ship on the bottom of the ocean has a chart!

Volatility Buying

This same earnings event could have been played entirely differently. A different trader, Bobby Buyer, studied the same volatility chart as Susie. It is shown again here as Exhibit 12.7. Bobby also thought there would be a rush and crush of IV, but he decided to take a different approach.

EXHIBIT 12.7 Chip stock volatility before and after earnings reports.

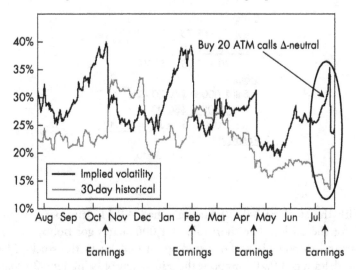

Source: Chart courtesy of iVolatility.com

EXHIBIT 12.8 Delta-neutral long call, short stock position.

33 days until expiration
stock at $49.70

| Long 20 50 calls 1.75 |
| Short 1,000 shrs 49.70 |

	Per cont.	Position
Delta	+0.510	+0.20
Gamma	+0.090	+1.80
Theta	−0.0321	−0.64
Vega	+0.060	+1.20

About an hour before the close of business on July 21, just three days before earnings announcements, Bobby saw that he could buy volatility at 30 percent. In Bobby's opinion, volatility seemed cheap with earnings so close. He believed that IV could rise at least five points over the next three days. Note that we have the benefit of 20/20 hindsight in the example.

Near the end of the trading day, the stock was at $49.70. Bobby bought 20 33-day 50-strike calls at 1.75 (30 volatility) and sold short 1,000 shares of the underlying stock at $49.70 to become delta neutral. Exhibit 12.8 shows Bobby's position.

EXHIBIT 12.9   Profit breakdown.

<u>**Calls**</u>
Buy 20 at 1.75
<u>Sell 20 at 2.10</u>
20 × 0.35 = $700
<u>**Stock**</u>
Sell 1,000 @ $49.70
<u>Buy 1,000 @ $50.00</u>
1,000 × $ (0.30) = ($300)
<u>**Position**</u>
P&(L) $400

With the stock at $49.70, the calls had +0.51 delta per contract, or +10.2 for the 20-lot. The short sale of 1,000 shares got Bobby as close to delta-neutral as possible without trading an odd lot in the stock. The net position delta was +0.20, or about the equivalent of being long 20 shares of stock. Bobby's objective in this case is to profit from an increase in implied volatility leading up to earnings.

While Susie was looking for reversion to the mean, Bobby hoped for a further divergence. For Bobby, positive gamma looked like a good thing on the surface. However, his plan was to close the position just before earnings were released—before the vol crush and before the potential stock-price move. With realized volatility already starting to drop off at the time the trade was put on, gamma offered little promise of gain.

As fate would have it, IV did indeed increase. At the end of the day before the July earnings report, IV was trading at 35 percent. Bobby closed his trade by selling his 20-lot of the 50 calls at 2.10 and buying his 1,000 shares of stock back at $50. Exhibit 12.9 shows the P&(L) for each leg of the spread.

The calls earned Bobby a total of $700, while the stock lost $300. Of course, with this type of trade, it is not relevant which leg was a winner and which a loser. All that matters is the bottom line. The net P&(L) on the trade was a gain of $400. The gain in this case was mostly a product of IV's rising. Exhibit 12.10 shows the P&(L) per greek.

Delta

The position began long 0.20 deltas. The 0.30-point rise earned Bobby a 0.06 point gain in delta per contract.

EXHIBIT 12.10 Profit breakdown by greek.

Delta:	$0.20 \times 0.30 = 0.06$
Gamma:	$(1.8 \times 0.30) \times 0.30 \div 2 = 0.08$
Theta:	$0.64 \times 3 = -1.92$
Vega:	$1.20 \times 5 = 6.00$
Total P&(L):	$+ 4.22$, or \$422

Gamma

Bobby had an initial gamma of +1.8. We will use 1.8 for estimating the P&(L) in this example, assuming gamma remained constant. A 0.30 rise in the stock price multiplied by the 1.8 gamma means that with the stock at \$50, Bobby was long an additional 0.54 deltas. We can estimate that over the course of the 0.30 rise in the stock price, Bobby was long an average of 0.27 (0.54 ÷ 2). His P&(L) due to gamma, therefore, is a gain of about 0.08 (0.27 × 0.30).

Theta

Bobby held this trade for three days. His total theta cost him 1.92 or \$192.

Vega

The biggest contribution to Bobby's profit on this trade was made by the spike in IV. He bought 30 volatility and sold 35 volatility. His 1.20 position vega earned him 6.00, or \$600.

Conclusions

The \$422 profit is not exact, but the greeks provide a good estimate of the hows and the whys behind it. Whether they are used for forecasting profits or for doing a postmortem evaluation of a trade, consulting the greeks offers information unavailable by just looking at the transaction prices.

By thinking about all these individual pricing components, a trader can make better decisions. For example, about two weeks earlier, Bobby could have bought an IV level closer to 26 percent. Being conscious of his theta, however, he decided to wait. The \$64-a-day theta would have cost him \$896 over 14 days. That's much more that the \$480 he could have made by buying volatility four points lower with his 1.20 vega.

Risks of the Trade

Like Susie's trade, Bobby's play was not without risk. Certainly theta was a concern, but in addition to that was the possibility that IV might not have played out as he planned. First, IV might not have risen enough to cover three days' worth of theta. It needed to rise, in this case, about 1.6 volatility points for the 1.20 vega to cover the 1.92 theta loss. It might even have dropped. An earlier-than-expected announcement that the earnings numbers were right on target could have spoiled Bobby's trade. Or the market simply might not have reacted as expected; volatility might not have risen at all, or might have fallen. Remember, IV is a function of the market. It does not always react as one thinks it should.

CHAPTER 13

Delta-Neutral Trading
Trading Realized Volatility

So far, we've discussed many option strategies in which realized volatility is an important component of the trade. And while the management of these positions has been the focus of much of the discussion, the ultimate gain or loss for many of these strategies has been from movement in a single direction. For example, with a long call, the higher the stock rallies the better.

But increases or decreases in realized volatility do not necessarily have an exclusive relationship with direction. Recall that realized volatility is the annualized standard deviation of daily price movements. Take two similarly priced stocks that have had a net price change of zero over a one-month period. Stock A had small daily price changes during that period, rising $0.10 one day and falling $0.10 the next. Stock B went up or down by $5 each day for a month. In this rather extreme example, Stock B was much more volatile than Stock A, regardless of the fact that the net price change for the period for both stocks was zero.

A stock's volatility—either high or low volatility—can be capitalized on by trading options delta neutral. Simply put, traders buy options delta neutral when they believe a stock will have more movement and sell options delta neutral when they believe a stock will move less.

Delta-neutral option sellers profit from low volatility through theta. Every day that passes in which the loss from delta/gamma movement is less than the gain from theta is a winning day. Traders can adjust their deltas by hedging. Delta-neutral option buyers exploit volatility opportunities through a trading technique called gamma scalping.

Gamma Scalping

Intraday trading is seldom entirely in one direction. A stock may close higher or lower, even sharply higher or lower, on the day, but during the day there is usually not a steady incremental rise or fall in the stock price. A typical intraday stock chart has peaks and troughs all day long. Delta-neutral traders who have gamma don't remain delta neutral as the underlying price changes, which inevitably it will. Delta-neutral trading is kind of a misnomer.

In fact, it is gamma trading in which delta-neutral traders engage. For long-gamma traders, the position delta gets more positive as the underlying moves higher and more negative as the underlying moves lower. An upward move in the underlying increases positive deltas, resulting in exponentially increasing profits. But if the underlying price begins to retrace downward, the gain from deltas can be erased as quickly as it was racked up.

To lock in delta gains, a trader can adjust the position to delta neutral again by selling short stock to cover long deltas. If the stock price declines after this adjustment, losses are curtailed thanks to the short stock. In fact, the delta will become negative as the underlying price falls, leading to growing profits. To lock in profits again, the trader buys stock to cover short deltas to once again become delta neutral.

The net effect is a stock scalp. Positive gamma causes the delta-neutral trader to sell stock when the price rises and buy when the stock falls. This adds up to a true, realized profit. So positive gamma is a money-making machine, right? Not so fast. As in any business, the profits must be great enough to cover expenses. Theta is the daily cost of running this gamma-scalping business.

For example, a trader, Harry, notices that the intraday price swings in a particular stock have been increasing. He takes a bullish position in realized volatility by buying 20 off the 40-strike calls, which have a 50 delta, and selling stock on a delta-neutral ratio.

Buy 20 40-strike calls (50 delta) (long 1,000 deltas)
Short 1,000 shares at $40 (short 1,000 deltas)

The immediate delta of this trade is flat, but as the stock moves up or down, that will change, presenting gamma-scalping opportunities. Gamma scalping is the objective here. The position greeks in Exhibit 13.1 show the relationship of the two forces involved in this trade: gamma and theta.

The relationship of gamma to theta in this sort of trade is paramount to its success. Gamma-scalping plays are not buy-and-hold strategies. This is

EXHIBIT 13.1   Greeks for 20-lot delta-neutral long call.

Gamma vs. Theta

Long 20 40-strike calls Short 1,000 shares at $40

Delta	0
Gamma	**+2.80**
Theta	**−0.50**
Vega	+1.15

active trading. These spreads need to be monitored intraday to take advantage of small moves in the underlying security. Harry will sell stock when the underlying rises and buy it when the underlying falls, taking a profit with each stock trade. The goal for each day that passes is to profit enough from positive gamma to cover the day's theta. But that's not always as easy as it sounds. Let's study what happens the first seven days after this hypothetical trade is executed. For the purposes of this example, we assume that gamma remains constant and that the trader is content trading odd lots of stock.

Day One

The first day proves to be fairly volatile. The stock rallies from $40 to $42 early in the day. This creates a positive position delta of 5.60, or the equivalent of being long about 560 shares. At $42, Harry covers the position delta by selling 560 shares of the underlying stock to become delta neutral again.

Later in the day, the market reverses, and the stock drops back down to $40 a share. At this point, the position is short 5.60 deltas. Harry again adjusts the position, buying 560 shares to get flat. The stock then closes right at $40.

The net result of these two stock transactions is a gain of $1,070. How? The gamma scalp minus the theta, as shown below.

$$\begin{array}{ll} \text{Sold} & 560 \text{ shares at } \$42 \\ \text{Bought} & 560 \text{ shares at } \$40 \\ \hline 560 & \times\ \$\ 2 = \ \$1,120 \\ -1 \text{ day theta} & \times\ \$50 = (\$\ \ 50) \\ \hline & \$1,070 \text{ profit} \end{array}$$

The volatility of day one led to it being a profitable day. Harry scalped 560 shares for a $2 profit, resulting from volatility in the stock. If the stock hadn't moved as much, the delta would have been smaller, and the dollar amount scalped would have been smaller, leading to an exponentially smaller profit. If there had been more volatility, profits would have been exponentially larger. It would have led to a bigger bite being taken out of the market.

Day Two

The next day, the market is a bit quieter. There is a $0.40 drop in the price of the stock, at which point the position delta is short 1.12. Harry buys 112 shares at $39.60 to get delta neutral.

Following Harry's purchase, the stock slowly drifts back up and is trading at $40 near the close. Harry decides to cover his deltas and sell 112 shares at $40. It is common to cover all deltas at the end of the day to get back to being delta neutral. Remember, the goal of gamma scalping is to trade volatility, not direction. Starting the next trading day with a delta, either positive or negative, means an often unwanted directional bias and unwanted directional risk. Tidying up deltas at the end of the day to get neutral is called going home flat.

Today was not a banner day. Harry did not quite have the opportunity to cover the decay.

$$
\begin{array}{ll}
\text{Bought} & \text{112 shares at } \$39.60 \\
\underline{\text{Sold} \quad \text{112 shares at } \$40.00} \\
\quad 112 \quad\quad \times \ \$ \ 0.40 = \ \$45 \\
\underline{-1 \text{ day theta} \times \$50 \quad = (\$50)} \\
\quad\quad\quad\quad\quad\quad\quad\quad\quad (\$5) \text{ loss}
\end{array}
$$

Day Three

On this day, the market trends. First, the stock rises $0.50, at which point Harry sells 140 shares of stock at $40.50 to lock in gains from his delta and to get flat. However, the market continues to rally. At $41 a share, Harry is long another 1.40 deltas and so sells another 140 shares. The rally continues, and at $41.50 he sells another 140 shares to cover the delta. Finally, at the end of the day, the stock closes at $42 a share. Harry sells a final 140 shares to get flat.

There was not any literal scalping of stock today. It was all selling. Nonetheless, gamma trading led to a profitable day.

Sold 140 shares at $40.50
$$140 \times \$\ 0.50 \div 2 = \$\ 35$$
Sold 140 shares at $41
$$140 \times \$\ 0.50 \div 2 = \$\ 35$$
Sold 140 shares at $41.50
$$140 \times \$\ 0.50 \div 2 = \$\ 35$$
Sold 140 shares at $42
$$140 \times \$\ 0.50 \div 2 = \underline{\$\ 35}$$
$$\$140$$
$$-1\ \text{day theta} \times \$50 = \underline{(\$\ 50)}$$
$$\$\ 90\ \text{profit}$$

As the stock rose from $40 to $40.50, 140 deltas were created from positive gamma. Because the delta was zero at $40 and 140 at $40.50, the estimated average delta is found by dividing 140 in half. This estimated average delta multiplied by the $0.50 gain on the stock equals a $35 profit. The delta was zero after the adjustment made at $40.50, when 140 shares were sold. When the stock reached $41, another $35 was reaped from the average delta of 70 over the $0.50 move. This process was repeated every time the stock rose $0.50 and the delta was covered.

Day Four

Day four offers a pleasant surprise for Harry. That morning, the stock opens $4 lower. He promptly covers his short delta of 11.2 by buying 1,120 shares of the stock at $38 a share. The stock barely moves the rest of the day and closes at $38.

Bought 1,120 shares at $38
$$1,120 \times \$\ 4 \div 2 = \$2,240$$
$$-1\ \text{day theta} \times \$50 = \underline{(\$\ 50)}$$
$$\$2,190\ \text{profit}$$

An exponentially larger profit was made because there was $4 worth of gains on the growing delta when the stock gapped open. The whole position delta was covered $4 lower, so both the delta and the dollar amount gained on that delta had a chance to grow. Again, Harry can estimate the average delta over the $4 move to be half of 11.20. Multiplying that by the $4 stock advance gives him his gamma profit of $2,240. After accounting for theta, the net profit is $2,190.

Days Five and Six

Days five and six are the weekend; the market is closed.

$$-2 \text{ days theta} \times \$50 = \$100 \text{ loss}$$

Day Seven

This is a quiet day after the volatility of the past week. Today, the stock slowly drifts up $0.25 by the end of the day. Harry sells 70 shares of stock at $38.25 to cover long deltas.

$$
\begin{array}{rl}
\text{Sold 70 shares at } \$38.25 & \\
70 \times \$\ 0.25 \div 2 = & \$\ 9 \\
-1 \text{ day theta} \times \$50 \qquad = & (\$50) \\
\hline
& (\$41) \text{ loss}
\end{array}
$$

This day was a loser for Harry, as profits from gamma were not enough to cover his theta.

Art and Science

Although this was a very simplified example, it was typical of how a profitable week of gamma scalping plays out. This stock had a pretty volatile week, and overall the week was a winner: there were four losing days and three winners. The number of losing days includes the weekends. Weekends and holidays are big hurdles for long-gamma traders because of the theta loss. The biggest contribution to this being a winning week was made by the gap open on day four. Part of the reason was the sheer magnitude of the move, and part was the fact that the deltas weren't covered too soon, as they had been on day three.

In a perfect world, a long-gamma trader will always buy the low of the day and sell the high of the day when covering deltas. This, unfortunately, seldom happens. Long-gamma traders are very often wrong when trading stock to cover deltas.

Being wrong can be okay on occasion. In fact, it can even be rewarding. Day three was profitable despite the fact that 140 shares were sold at $40.50, $41, and $41.50. The stock closed at $42; the first three stock trades were losers. Harry sold stock at a lower price than the close. But the position still made money because of his positive gamma. To be sure, Harry would like to have sold all 560 shares at $42 at the end of the day. The day's profits would have been significantly higher.

The problem is that no one knows where the stock will move next. On day three, if the stock had topped out at $40.50 and Harry did not sell stock because he thought it would continue higher, he would have missed an opportunity. Gamma scalping is not an exact science. The art is to pick spots that capture the biggest moves possible without missing opportunities.

There are many methods traders have used to decide where to cover deltas when gamma scalping: the daily standard deviation, a fixed percentage of the stock price, a fixed nominal value, covering at a certain time of day, "market feel." No system appears to be absolutely better than another. This is where it gets personal. Finding what works for you, and what works for the individual stocks you trade, is the art of this science.

Gamma, Theta, and Volatility

Clearly, more volatile stocks are more profitable for gamma scalping, right? Well . . . maybe. Recall that the higher the implied volatility, the lower the gamma and the higher the theta of at-the-money (ATM) options. In many cases, the more volatile a stock, the higher the implied volatility (IV). That means that a volatile stock might have to move more for a trader to scalp enough stock to cover the higher theta.

Let's look at the gamma-theta relationship from another perspective. In this example, for 0.50 of theta, Harry could buy 2.80 gamma. This relationship is based on an assumed 25 percent implied volatility. If IV were 50 percent, theta for this 20 lot would be higher, and the gamma would be lower. At a volatility of 50, Harry could buy 1.40 gammas for 0.90 of theta. The gamma is more expensive from a theta perspective, but if the stock's statistical volatility is significantly higher, it may be worth it.

Gamma Hedging

Knowing that the gamma and theta figures of Exhibit 13.1 are derived from a 25 percent volatility assumption offers a benchmark with which to gauge the potential profitability of gamma trading the options. If the stock's standard deviation is below 25 percent, it will be difficult to make money being long gamma. If it is above 25 percent, the play becomes easier to trade.

EXHIBIT 13.2   Greeks for 20-lot delta-neutral short call.

Gamma vs. Theta

Short 20 40-strike calls Long 1,000 shares at $40	
Delta	0
Gamma	−2.80
Theta	+0.50
Vega	−1.15

There is more scalping opportunity, there are more opportunities for big moves, and there are more likely to be gaps in either direction. The 25 percent volatility input not only determines the option's theoretical value but also helps determine the ratio of gamma to theta.

A 25 percent or higher realized volatility in this case does not guarantee the trade's success or failure, however. Much of the success of the trade has to do with how well the trader scalps stock. Covering deltas too soon leads to reduced profitability. Covering too late can lead to missed opportunities.

Trading stock well is also important to gamma sellers with the opposite trade: sell calls and buy stock delta neutral. In this example, a trader will sell 20 ATM calls and buy stock on a delta-neutral ratio.

Sell 20 40-strike calls (50 delta) ---------- (short 1,000 deltas)
Buy 1,000 shares at $40 ------------------- (long 1,000 deltas)

This is a bearish position in realized volatility. It is the opposite of the trade in the last example. Consider again that 25 percent IV is the benchmark by which to gauge potential profitability. Here, if the stock's volatility is below 25, the chances of having a profitable trade are increased. Above 25 is a bit more challenging.

In this simplified example, a different trader, Mary, plays the role of gamma seller. Over the same seven-day period as before, instead of buying calls, Mary sold a 20 lot. Exhibit 13.2 shows the analytics for the trade. For the purposes of this example, we assume that gamma remains constant and the trader is content trading odd lots of stock.

Day One

This was one of the volatile days. The stock rallied from $40 to $42 early in the day and had fallen back down to $40 by the end of the day. Big moves like this are hard to trade as a short-gamma trader. As the stock rose to $42, the negative delta would have been increasing. That means losses were adding up at an increasing rate. The only way to have stopped the hemorrhaging of money as the stock continued to rise would have been to buy stock. Of course, if Mary buys stock and the stock then declines, she has a loser.

Let's assume the best-case scenario. When the stock reached $42 and she had a −560 delta, Mary correctly felt the market was overbought and would retrace. Sometimes, the best trades are the ones you don't make. On this day, Mary traded no stock. When the stock reached $40 a share at the end of the day, she was back to being delta neutral. Theta makes her a winner today.

$$\text{One-day theta} \times 50 = \$50 \text{ profit}$$

Because of the way Mary handled her trade, the volatility of day one was not necessarily an impediment to it being profitable. Again, the assumption is that Mary made the right call not to negative scalp the stock. Mary could have decided to hedge her negative gamma when the stock reach $42 and the position delta was at −$560 by buying stock and then selling it at $40.

There are a number of techniques for hedging deltas resulting from negative gamma. The objective of hedging deltas is to avoid losses from the stock trending in one direction and creating increasingly adverse deltas but not to overtrade stock and negative scalp.

Day Two

Recall that this day had a small dip and then recovered to close again at $40. It is more reasonable to assume that on this day there was no negative scalping. A $0.40 decline is a more typical move in a stock and nothing to be afraid of. The 112 delta created by negative gamma when the stock fell wouldn't be perceived as a major concern by most traders in most situations. It is reasonable to assume Mary would take no action. Today, again, was a winner thanks to theta.

$$\text{One-day theta} \times 50 = \$50 \text{ profit}$$

Day Three

Day three saw the stock price trending. It slowly drifted up $2. There would have been some judgment calls throughout this day. Again, delta-neutral trades are for active traders. Prepare to watch the market much of the day if implementing this kind of strategy.

When the stock was at $41 a share, Mary decided to guard against further advances in stock price and hedged her delta. At that point, the position would have had a −2.80 delta. She bought 280 shares at $41.

As the day progressed, the market proved Mary to be right. The stock rose to $42 giving the position a delta of −2.80 again. She covered her deltas at the end of the day by buying another 280 shares.

$$
\begin{aligned}
&\text{Bought 280 shares at \$41} \\
&\qquad -280 \times \$\ 1 \div 2 = (\$140) \\
&\text{Bought 280 shares at \$42} \\
&\qquad -280 \times \$\ 1 \div 2 = (\$140) \\
&\qquad\qquad\qquad\qquad\qquad\quad (\$280) \\
&\underline{\text{1 day theta} \times \$50 \qquad = \$\ 50} \\
&\qquad\qquad\qquad\qquad\qquad (\$230)\ \text{loss}
\end{aligned}
$$

Covering the negative deltas to get flat at $41 proved to be a smart move today. It curtailed an exponentially growing delta and let Mary take a smaller loss at $41 and get a fresh start. While the day was a loser, it would have been $280 worse if she had not purchased stock at $41 before the run-up to $42. This is evidenced by the fact that she made a $280 profit on the 280 shares of stock bought at $41, since the stock closed at $42.

Day Four

Day four offered a rather unpleasant surprise. This was the day that the stock gapped open $4 lower. This is the kind of day short-gamma traders dread. There is, of course, no right way to react to this situation. The stock can recover, heading higher; it can continue lower; or it can have a dead-cat bounce, remaining where it is after the fall.

Staring at a quite contrary delta of 11.20, Mary was forced to take action by selling stock. But how much stock was the responsible amount to sell for a pure short-gamma trader not interested in trading direction? Selling 1,120 shares would bring the position back to being delta neutral, but the only way the trade would stay delta neutral would be if the stock stayed right where it was.

Hedging is always a difficult call for short-gamma traders. Long-gamma traders are taking a profit on deltas with every stock trade that covers their deltas. Short-gamma traders are always taking a loss on delta. In this case,

Mary decided to cover half her deltas by selling 560 shares. The other 560 deltas represent a loss, too; it's just not locked in.

$$
\begin{aligned}
\text{Sold 560 shares at \$38} & \\
-560 \times \$\ 4 \div 2 &= (\$1,120) \\
\text{Long 560 deltas from negative gamma} & \\
-560 \times \$\ 4 \div 2 &= (\$1,120) \\
\underline{\text{1 day theta} \times \$50 \quad\quad} &= \$\quad 50 \\
&\ (\$2,190)\ \text{loss}
\end{aligned}
$$

Here, Mary made the conscious decision not to go home flat. On the one hand, she was accepting the risk of the stock continuing its decline. On the other hand, if she had covered the whole delta, she would have been accepting the risk of the stock moving in either direction. Mary felt the stock would regain some of its losses. She decided to lead the stock a little, going into the weekend with a positive delta bias.

Days Five and Six

Days five and six are the weekend.

$$2 \text{ days theta} \times \$50 = \$100 \text{ profit}$$

Day Seven

This was the quiet day of the week, and a welcome respite. On this day, the stock rose just $0.25. The rise in price helped a bit. Mary was still long 560 deltas from Friday. Negative gamma took only a small bite out of her profit.

The P&(L) can be broken down into the profit attributable to the starting delta of the trade, the estimated loss from gamma, and the gain from theta.

$$
\begin{aligned}
\text{Long 560 deltas} & \\
560 \times \$0.25 \quad\quad &= \$140 \\
-70 \text{ deltas created from gamma} & \\
70 \times \$0.25 \div 2 &= (\$\quad 9) \\
\underline{\text{1 day theta} \times \$50 \quad\quad} &= \$\quad 50 \\
& \$181 \text{ profit}
\end{aligned}
$$

Mary ends these seven days of trading worse off than she started. What went wrong? The bottom line is that she sold volatility on an asset that proved to be volatile. A $4 drop in price of a $42 dollar stock was a big move. This stock certainly moved at more than 25 percent volatility. Day four alone made this trade a losing proposition.

Could Mary have done anything better? Yes. In a perfect world, she would not have covered her negative deltas on day 3 by buying 280 shares at $41 and another 280 at $42. Had she not, this wouldn't have been such a bad week. With the stock ending at $38.25, she lost $1,050 on the 280 shares she bought at $42 ($3.75 times 280) and lost $770 on the 280 shares bought at $41 ($2.75 times 280). Then again, if the stock had continued higher, rising beyond $42, those would have been good buys.

Mary can't beat herself up too much for protecting herself in a way that made sense at the time. The stock's $2 rally is more to blame than the fact that she hedged her deltas. That's the risk of selling volatility: the stock may prove to be volatile. If the stock had not made such a move, she wouldn't have faced the dilemma of whether or not to hedge.

Conclusions

The same stock during the same week was used in both examples. These two traders started out with equal and opposite positions. They might as well have made the trade with each other. And although in this case the vol buyer (Harry) had a pretty good week and the vol seller (Mary) had a not-so-good week, it's important to notice that the dollar value of the vol buyer's profit was not the same as the dollar value of the vol seller's loss. Why? Because each trader hedged his or her position differently. Option trading is not a zero-sum game.

Option-selling delta-neutral strategies work well in low-volatility environments. Small moves are acceptable. It's the big moves that can blow you out of the water.

Like long-gamma traders, short-gamma traders have many techniques for covering deltas when the stock moves. It is common to cover partial deltas, as Mary did on day four of the last example. Conversely, if a stock is expected to continue along its trajectory up or down, traders will sometimes overhedge by buying more deltas (stock) than they are short or selling more than they are long, in anticipation of continued price rises. Daily standard deviation derived from implied volatility is a common measure used by short-gamma players to calculate price points at which to enter hedges. Market feel and other indicators are also used by experienced traders when deciding when and how to hedge. Each trader must find what works best for him or her.

Smileys and Frowns

The trade examples in this chapter have all involved just two components: calls and stock. We will explore delta-neutral strategies in other chapters that involve more moving parts. Regardless of the specific makeup of the position, the P&(L) of each individual leg is not of concern. It is the profitability of the position as a whole that matters. For example, after a volatile move in a stock occurs, a positive-gamma trader like Harry doesn't care whether the calls or the stock made the profit on the move. The trader would monitor the net delta that was produced—positive or negative—and cover accordingly. The process is the same for a negative-gamma trader. In either case, it is gamma and delta that need to be monitored closely.

Gamma can make or break a trade. P&(L) diagrams are helpful tools that offer a visual representation of the effect of gamma on a position. Many option-trading software applications offer P&(L) graphing applications to study the payoff of a position with the days to expiration as an adjustable variable to study the same trade over time.

P&(L) diagrams for these delta-neutral positions before the options' expiration generally take one of two shapes: a smiley or a frown. The shape of the graph depends on whether the position gamma is positive or negative. Exhibit 13.3 shows a typical positive-gamma trade.

EXHIBIT 13.3   P&(L) diagram for a positive-gamma delta-neutral position/l.

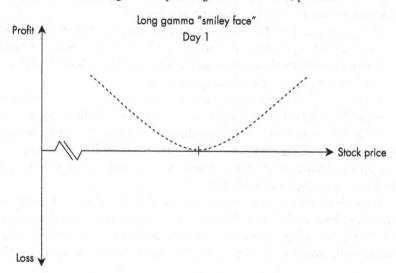

EXHIBIT 13.4 The effect of time on P&(L).

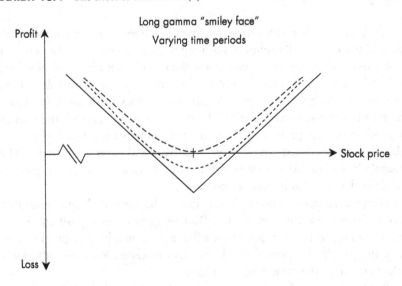

This diagram is representative of the P&L of a delta-neutral positive-gamma trade calculated using the prices at which the trade was executed. With this type of trade, it is intuitive that when the stock price rises or falls, profits increase because of favorably changing deltas. This is represented by the graph's smiley-face shape. The corners of the graph rise higher as the underlying moves away from the center of the graph.

The graph is a two-dimensional snapshot showing that the higher or lower the underlying moves, the greater the profit. But there are other dimensions that are not shown here, such as time and IV. Exhibit 13.4 shows the effects of time on a typical long-gamma trade.

As time passes, the reduction in profit is reflected by the center point of the graph dipping farther into negative territory. That is the effect of time decay. The long options will have lost value at that future date with the stock still at the same price (all other factors held constant). Still, a move in either direction can lead to a profitable position. Ultimately, at expiration, the payoff takes on a rigid kinked shape.

In the delta-neutral long call examples used in this chapter the position becomes net long stock if the calls are in-the-money at expiration or net short stock if they are out-of-the-money and only the short stock remains. Volatility, as well, would move the payoff line vertically. As IV increases, the

EXHIBIT 13.5 Short-gamma frown.

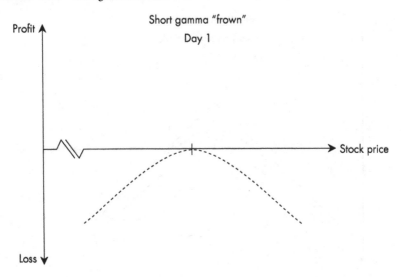

options become worth more at each stock price, and as IV falls, they are worth less, assuming all other factors are held constant.

A delta-neutral short-gamma play would have a P&(L) diagram quite the opposite of the smiley-faced long-gamma graph. Exhibit 13.5 shows what is called the short-gamma frown.

At first glance, this doesn't look like a very good proposition. The highest point on the graph coincides with a profit of zero, and it only gets worse as the price of the underlying rises or falls. This is enough to make any trader frown. But again, this snapshot does not show time or volatility. Exhibit 13.6 shows the payout diagram as time passes.

A decrease in value of the options from time decay causes an increase in profitability. This profit potential pinnacles at the center (strike) price at expiration. Rising IV will cause a decline in profitability at each stock price point. Declining IV will raise the payout on the Y axis as profitability increases at each price point.

Smileys and frowns are a mere graphical representation of the technique discussed in this chapter: buying and selling realized volatility. These P&(L) diagrams are limited, because they show the payout only of stock-price movement. The profitability of direction-indifferent and direction-neutral trading is also influenced by time and implied volatility. These actively traded strategies are best evaluated on a gamma-theta basis. Long-gamma

EXHIBIT 13.6 The effect of time on the short-gamma frown.

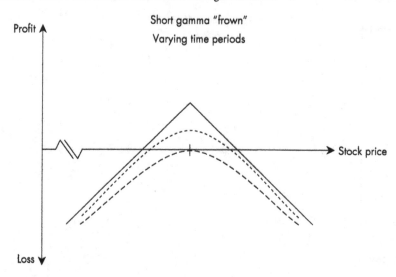

traders strive each day to scalp enough to cover the day's theta, while short-gamma traders hope to keep the loss due to adverse movement in the underlying lower than the daily profit from theta.

The strategies in this chapter are the same ones traded in Chapter 12. The only difference is the philosophy. Ultimately, both types of volatility are being traded using these and other option strategies. Implied and realized volatility go hand in hand.

CHAPTER 14

Studying Volatility Charts

Implied and realized volatility are both important to option traders. But equally important is to understand how the two interact. This relationship is best studied by means of a volatility chart. Volatility charts are invaluable tools for volatility traders (and all option traders for that matter) in many ways.

First, volatility charts show where implied volatility (IV) is now compared with where it's been in the past. This helps a trader gauge whether IV is relatively high or relatively low. Vol charts do the same for realized volatility. The realized volatility line on the chart answers three questions:

1. Have the past 30 days been more or less volatile for the stock than usual?
2. What is a typical range for the stock's volatility?
3. How much volatility did the underlying historically experience in the past around specific recurring events?

When IV lines and realized volatility lines are plotted on the same chart, the divergences and convergences of the two spell out the whole volatility story for those who know how to read it.

Nine Volatility Chart Patterns

Each individual stock and the options listed on it have their own unique realized and implied volatility characteristics. If we studied the vol charts of 1,000 stocks, we'd likely see around 1,000 different volatility patterns. The number of permutations of the relationship of realized to implied volatility is nearly infinite, but for the sake of discussion, we will categorize volatility charts into nine general patterns.[1]

1. Realized Volatility Rises, Implied Volatility Rises

The first volatility chart pattern is that in which both IV and realized volatility rise. In general, this kind of volatility chart can line up three ways: implied can rise more than realized volatility; realized can rise more than implied; or they can both rise by about the same amount. The chart below shows implied volatility rising at a faster rate than realized vol. The general theme in this case is that the stock's price movement has been getting more volatile, and the option prices imply even higher volatility in the future.

This specific type of volatility chart pattern is commonly seen in active stocks with a lot of news. Stocks du jour, like some Internet stocks during the tech bubble of the late 1990s, story stocks like Apple (AAPL) around the release of the iPhone in 2007, have rising volatilities, with the IV outpacing the realized volatility. Sometimes individual stocks and even broad market indexes and exchange-traded funds (ETFs) see this pattern, when the market is declining rapidly, like in the summer of 2011.

A delta-neutral long-volatility position bought at the beginning of May, according to Exhibit 14.1, would likely have produced a winner. IV took off, and there were sure to be plenty of opportunities to profit from gamma with realized volatility gaining strength through June and July.

Looking at the right side of the chart, in late July, with IV at around 50 percent and realized vol at around 35 percent, and without the benefit of knowing what the future will bring, it's harder to make a call on how to trade

EXHIBIT 14.1   Realized volatility rises, implied volatility rises.

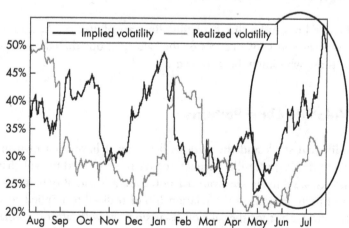

Source: Chart courtesy of iVolatility.com

the volatility. The IV signals that the market is pricing a higher future level of stock volatility into the options. If the market is right, gamma will be good to have. But is the price right? If realized volatility does indeed catch up to implied volatility—that is, if the lines converge at 50 or realized volatility rises above IV—a trader will have a good shot at covering theta. If it doesn't, gamma will be very expensive in terms of theta, meaning it will be hard to cover the daily theta by scalping gamma intraday.

The question is: why is IV so much higher than realized? If important news is expected to be released in the near future, it may be perfectly reasonable for the IV to be higher, even significantly higher, than the stock's realized volatility. One big move in the stock can produce a nice profit, as long as theta doesn't have time to work its mischief. But if there is no news in the pipeline, there may be some irrational exuberance—in the words of ex-Fed chairman Alan Greenspan—of option buyers rushing to acquire gamma that is overvalued in terms of theta.

In fact, a lack of expectation of news could indicate a potential bearish volatility play: sell volatility with the intent of profiting from daily theta and a decline in IV. This type of play, however, is not for the fainthearted. No one can predict the future. But one thing you can be sure of with this trade: you're in for a wild ride. The lines on this chart scream volatility. This means that negative-gamma traders had better be good and had better be right!

In this situation, hedgers and speculators in the market are buying option volatility of 50 percent, while the stock is moving at 35 percent volatility. Traders putting on a delta-neutral volatility-selling strategy are taking the stance that this stock will not continue increasing in volatility as indicated by option prices; specifically, it will move at less than 50 percent volatility—hopefully a lot less. They are taking the stance that the market's expectations are wrong.

Instead of realized and implied volatility both trending higher, sometimes there is a sharp jump in one or the other. When this happens, it could be an indication of a specific event that has occurred (realized volatility) or news suddenly released of an expected event yet to come (implied volatility). A sharp temporary increase in IV is called a spike, because of its pointy shape on the chart. A one-day surge in realized volatility, on the other hand, is not so much a volatility spike as it is a realized volatility mesa. Realized volatility mesas are shown in Exhibit 14.2.

The patterns formed by the gray line in the circled areas of the chart shown below are the result of typical one-day surges in realized volatility. Here, the 30-day realized volatility rose by nearly 20 percentage points, from about 20 percent to about 40 percent, in one day. It remained around

EXHIBIT 14.2 Volatility mesas.

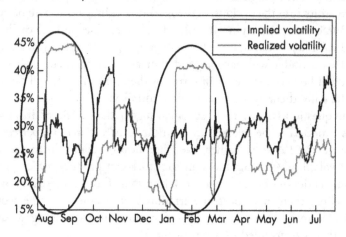

Source: Chart courtesy of iVolatility.com

the 40 percent level for 30 days and then declined 20 points just as fast as it rose.

Was this entire 30-day period unusually volatile? Not necessarily. Realized volatility is calculated by looking at price movements within a certain time frame, in this case, thirty business days. That means that a really big move on one day will remain in the calculation for the entire time. Thirty days after the unusually big move, the calculation for realized volatility will no longer contain that one-day price jump. Realized volatility can then drop significantly.

2. Realized Volatility Rises, Implied Volatility Remains Constant

This chart pattern can develop from a few different market conditions. One scenario is a one-time unanticipated move in the underlying that is not expected to affect future volatility. Once the news is priced into the stock, there is no point in hedgers' buying options for protection or speculators' buying options for a leveraged bet. What has happened has happened.

There are other conditions that can cause this type of pattern to materialize. In Exhibit 14.3, the IV was trading around 25 for several months, while the realized volatility was lagging. With hindsight, it makes perfect sense that something had to give—either IV needed to fall to meet realized, or realized would rise to meet market expectations. Here, indeed,

EXHIBIT 14.3 Realized volatility rises, implied volatility remains constant.

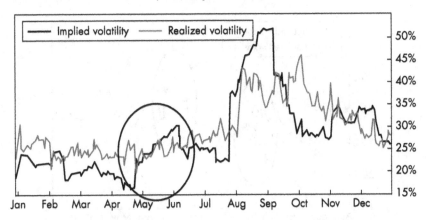

Source: Chart courtesy of iVolatility.com

the latter materialized as realized volatility had a steady rise to and through the 25 level in May. Implied, however remained constant.

Traders who were long volatility going into the May realized-vol rise probably reaped some gamma benefits. But those who got in "too early," buying in January or February, would have suffered too great of theta losses before gaining any significant profits from gamma. Time decay (theta) can inflict a slow, painful death on an option buyer. By studying this chart in hindsight, it is clear that options were priced too high for a gamma scalper to have a fighting chance of covering the daily theta before the rise in May.

This wasn't necessarily an easy vol-selling trade before the May realized-vol rise, either, depending on the trader's timing. In early February, realized did in fact rise above implied, making the short volatility trade much less attractive.

Traders who sold volatility just before the increase in realized volatility in May likely ended up losing on gamma and not enough theta profits to make up for it. There was no volatility crush like what is often seen following a one-day move leading to sharply higher realized volatility. IV simply remained pretty steady throughout the month of May and well into June.

3. Realized Volatility Rises, Implied Volatility Falls

This chart pattern can manifest itself in different ways. In this scenario, the stock is becoming more volatile, and options are becoming cheaper. This

EXHIBIT 14.4   Realized volatility rises, implied volatility falls.

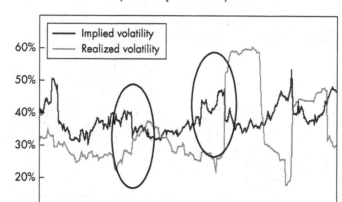

Source: Chart courtesy of iVolatility.com

may seem an unusual occurrence, but as we can see in Exhibit 14.4, volatility sometimes plays out this way. This chart shows two different examples of realized vol rising while IV falls.

The first example, toward the left-hand side of the chart, shows realized volatility trending higher while IV is trending lower. Although fundamentals can often provide logical reasons for these volatility changes, sometimes they just can't. Both implied and realized volatility are ultimately a function of the market. There is a normal oscillation to both of these figures. When there is no reason to be found for a volatility change, it might be an opportunity. The potential inefficiency of volatility pricing in the options market sometimes creates divergences such as this one that vol traders scour the market in search of.

In this first example, after at least three months of IV's trading marginally higher than realized volatility, the two lines converge and then cross. The point at which these lines meet is an indication that IV may be beginning to get cheap.

First, it's a potentially beneficial opportunity to buy a lower volatility than that at which the stock is actually moving. The gamma/theta ratio would be favorable to gamma scalpers in this case, because the lower cost of options compared with stock fluctuations could lead to gamma profits. Second, with IV at 35 at the first crossover on this chart, IV is dipping down into the lower part of its four-month range. One can make the case that it is getting cheaper from a historical IV standpoint. There is arguably an edge from the perspective of IV to realized volatility and IV to historical IV. This is an example of buying value in the context of volatility.

Furthermore, if the actual stock volatility is rising, it's reasonable to believe that IV may rise, too. In hindsight we see that this did indeed occur in Exhibit 14.4, despite the fact that realized volatility declined.

The example circled on the right-hand side of the chart shows IV declining sharply while realized volatility rises sharply. This is an example of the typical volatility crush as a result of an earnings report. This would probably have been a good trade for long volatility traders—even those buying at the top. A trader buying options delta neutral the day before earnings are announced in this example would likely lose about 10 points of vega but would have a good chance to more than make up for that loss on positive gamma. Realized volatility nearly doubled, from around 28 percent to about 53 percent, in a single day.

4. Realized Volatility Remains Constant, Implied Volatility Rises

Exhibit 14.5 shows that the stock is moving at about the same volatility from the beginning of June to the end of July. But during that time, option premiums are rising to higher levels. This is an atypical chart pattern. If this was a period leading up to an anticipated event, like earnings, one would anticipate realized volatility falling as the market entered a wait-and-see mode. But, instead, statistical volatility stays the same. This chart pattern

EXHIBIT 14.5 Realized volatility remains constant, implied volatility rises.

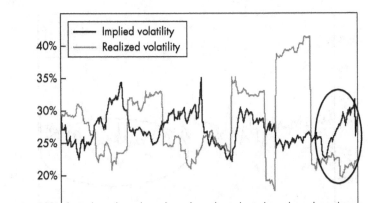

Source: Chart courtesy of iVolatility.com

may indicate a potential volatility-selling opportunity. If there is no news or reason for IV to have risen, it may simply be high tide in the normal ebb and flow of volatility.

In this example, the historical volatility oscillates between 20 and 24 for nearly two months (the beginning of June through the end of July) as IV rises from 24 to over 30. The stock price is less volatile than option prices indicate. If there is no news to be dug up on the stock to lead one to believe there is a valid reason for the IV's trading at such a level, this could be an opportunity to sell IV 5 to 10 points higher than the stock volatility. The goal here is to profit from theta or falling vega or both while not losing much on negative gamma. As time passes, if the stock continues to move at 20 to 23 vol, one would expect IV to fall and converge with realized volatility.

5. Realized Volatility Remains Constant, Implied Volatility Remains Constant

This volatility chart pattern shown in Exhibit 14.6 is typical of a boring, run-of-the-mill stock with nothing happening in the news. But in this case, no news might be good news.

Again, the gray is realized volatility and the black line is IV.

It's common for IV to trade slightly above or below realized volatility for extended periods of time in certain assets. In this example, the IV has traded in the high teens from late January to late July. During that same time, realized volatility has been in the low teens.

EXHIBIT 14.6 Realized volatility remains constant, implied volatility remains constant.

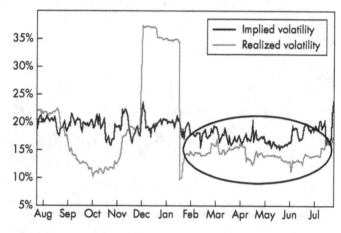

Source: Chart courtesy of iVolatility.com

This is a prime environment for option sellers. From a gamma/theta standpoint, the odds favor short-volatility traders. The gamma/theta ratio provides an edge, setting the stage for theta profits to outweigh negative-gamma scalping. Selling calls and buying stock delta neutral would be a trade to look at in this situation. But even more basic strategies, such as time spreads and iron condors, are appropriate to consider.

This vol-chart pattern, however, is no guarantee of success. When the stock oscillates, delta-neutral traders can negative scalp stock if they are not careful by buying high to cover short deltas and then selling low to cover long deltas. Time-spread and iron condor trades can fail if volatility increases and the increase results from the stock trending in one direction. The advantage of buying IV lower than realized, or selling it above, is statistical in nature. Traders should use a chart of the stock price in conjunction with the volatility chart to get a more complete picture of the stock's price action. This also helps traders make more informed decisions about when to hedge.

6. Realized Volatility Remains Constant, Implied Volatility Falls

Exhibit 14.7 shows two classic implied-realized convergences. From mid-September to early November, realized volatility stayed between 22 and 25. In mid-October the implied was around 33. Within the span of a few days, the implied vol collapsed to converge with the realized at about 22.

EXHIBIT 14.7 Realized volatility remains constant, implied volatility falls.

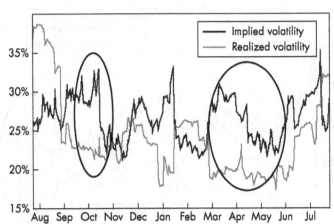

Source: Chart courtesy of iVolatility.com

There can be many catalysts for such a drop in IV, but there is truly only one reason: arbitrage. Although it is common for a small difference between implied and realized volatility—1 to 3 points—to exist even for extended periods, bigger disparities, like the 7- to 10-point difference here cannot exist for that long without good reason.

If, for example, IV always trades significantly above the realized volatility of a particular underlying, all rational market participants will sell options because they have a gamma/theta edge. This, in turn, forces options prices lower until volatility prices come into line and the arbitrage opportunity no longer exists.

In Exhibit 14.7, from mid-March to mid-May a similar convergence took place but over a longer period of time. These situations are often the result of a slow capitulation of market makers who are long volatility. The traders give up on the idea that they will be able to scalp enough gamma to cover theta and consequently lower their offers to advertise their lower prices.

7. Realized Volatility Falls, Implied Volatility Rises

This setup shown in Exhibit 14.8 should now be etched into the souls of anyone who has been reading up to this point. It is, of course, the picture of the classic IV rush that is often seen in stocks around earnings time. The more uncertain the earnings, the more pronounced this divergence can be.

EXHIBIT 14.8 Realized volatility falls, implied volatility rises.

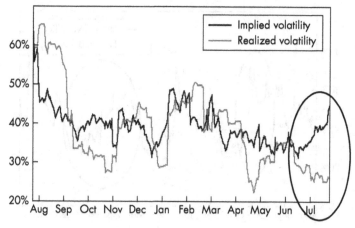

Source: Chart courtesy of iVolatility.com

Another classic vol divergence in which IV rises and realized vol falls occurs in a drug or biotech company when a Food and Drug Administration (FDA) decision on one of the company's new drugs is imminent. This is especially true of smaller firms without big portfolios of drugs. These divergences can produce a huge implied–realized disparity of, in some cases, literally hundreds of volatility points leading up to the announcement.

Although rising IV accompanied by falling realized volatility can be one of the most predictable patterns in trading, it is ironically one of the most difficult to trade. When the anticipated news breaks, the stock can and often will make a big directional move, and in that case, IV can and likely will get crushed. Vega and gamma work against each other in these situations, as IV and realized volatility converge. Vol traders will likely gain on one vol and lose on the other, but it's very difficult to predict which will have a more profound effect. Many traders simply avoid trading earnings events altogether in favor of less erratic opportunities. For most traders, there are easier ways to make money.

8. Realized Volatility Falls, Implied Volatility Remains Constant

This volatility shift can be marked by a volatility convergence, divergence, or crossover. Exhibit 14.9 shows the realized volatility falling from around 30 percent to about 23 percent while IV hovers around 25. The crossover here occurs around the middle of February.

EXHIBIT 14.9   Realized volatility falls, implied volatility remains constant.

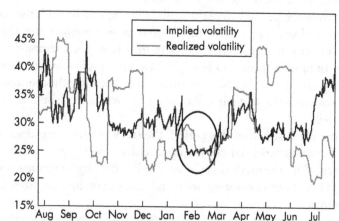

Source: Chart courtesy of iVolatility.com

The relative size of this volatility change makes the interpretation of the chart difficult. The last half of September saw around a 15 percent decline in realized volatility. The middle of October saw a one-day jump in realized of about 15 points. Historical volatility has had several dynamic moves that were larger and more abrupt than the seven-point decline over this six-week period. This smaller move in realized volatility is not necessarily an indication of a volatility event. It could reflect some complacency in the market. It could indicate a slow period with less trading, or it could simply be a natural contraction in the ebb and flow of volatility causing the calculation of recent stock-price fluctuations to wane.

What is important in this interpretation is how the options market is reacting to the change in the volatility of the stock—where the rubber hits the road. The market's apparent assessment of future volatility is unchanged during this period. When IV rises or falls, vol traders must look to the underlying stock for a reason. The options market reacts to stock volatility, not the other way around.

Finding fundamental or technical reasons for surges in volatility is easier than finding specific reasons for a decline in volatility. When volatility falls, it is usually the result of a lack of news, leading to less price action. In this example, probably nothing happened in the market. Consequently, the stock volatility drifted lower. But it fell below the lowest IV level seen for the six-month period leading up to the crossover. It was probably hard to take a confident stance in volatility immediately following the crossover. It is difficult to justify selling volatility when the implied is so cheap compared with its historic levels. And it can be hard to justify buying volatility when the options are priced above the stock volatility.

The two-week period before the realized line moved beneath the implied line deserves closer study. With the IV four or five points lower than the realized volatility in late January, traders may have been tempted to buy volatility. In hindsight, this trade might have been profitable, but there was surely no guarantee of this. Success would have been greatly contingent on how the traders managed their deltas, and how well they adapted as realized volatility fell.

During the first half of this period, the stock volatility remained above implied. For an experienced delta-neutral trader, scalping gamma was likely easy money. With the oscillations in stock price, the biggest gamma-scalping risk would have been to cover too soon and miss out on opportunities to take bigger profits.

Using the one-day standard deviation based on IV (described in Chapter 3) might have produced early covering for long-gamma traders.

Why? Because in late January, the standard deviation derived from IV was lower than the actual standard deviation of the stock being traded. In the latter half of the period being studied, the end of February on this chart, using the one-day standard deviation based on IV would have produced scalping that was too late. This would have led to many missed opportunities.

Traders entering hedges at regular nominal intervals—every $0.50, for example—would probably have needed to decrease the interval as volatility ebbed. For instance, if in late January they were entering orders every $0.50, by late February they might have had to trade every $0.40.

9. Realized Volatility Falls, Implied Volatility Falls

This final volatility-chart permutation incorporates a fall of both realized and IV. The chart in Exhibit 14.10 clearly represents the slow culmination of a highly volatile period. This setup often coincides with news of some scary event's being resolved—a law suit settled, unpopular upper management leaving, rumors found to be false, a happy ending to political issues domestically or abroad, for example. After a sharp sell-off in IV, from 75 to 55, in late October, marking the end of a period of great uncertainty, the stock volatility began a steady decline, from the low 50s to below 25. IV fell as well, although it remained a bit higher for several months.

EXHIBIT 14.10 Realized volatility falls, implied volatility falls.

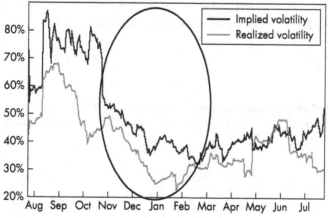

Source: Chart courtesy of iVolatility.com

In some situations where an extended period of extreme volatility appears to be coming to an end, there can be some predictability in how IV will react. To be sure, no one knows what the future holds, but when volatility starts to wane because a specific issue that was causing gyrations in the stock price is resolved, it is common, and intuitive, for IV to fall with the stock volatility. This is another type of example of reversion to the mean.

There is a potential problem if the high-volatility period lasted for an extended period of time. Sometimes, it's hard to get a feel for what the mean volatility should be. Or sometimes, because of the event, the stock is fundamentally different—in the case of a spin-off, merger, or other corporate action, for example. When it is difficult or impossible to look back at a stock's performance over the previous 6 to 12 months and appraise what the normal volatility should be, one can look to the volatility of other stocks in the same industry for some guidance.

Stocks that are substitutable for one another typically trade at similar volatilities. From a realized volatility perspective, this is rather intuitive. When one stock within an industry rises or falls, others within the same industry tend to follow. They trade similarly and therefore experience similar volatility patterns. If the stock volatility among names within one industry tends to be similar, it follows that the IV should be, too.

Regardless which of the nine patterns discussed here show up, or how the volatilities line up, there is one overriding observation that's representative of all volatility charts: vol charts are simply graphical representations of realized and implied volatility that help traders better understand the two volatilities' interaction. But the divergences and convergences in the examples in this chapter have profound meaning to the volatility trader. Combined with a comparison of current and past volatility (both realized and implied), they give traders insight into how cheap or expensive options are.

Note

1. The following examples use charts supplied by iVolatility.com. The gray line is the 30-day realized volatility, and the black line is the implied volatility.

PART IV

Advanced Option Trading

CHAPTER 15

Straddles and Strangles

Straddles and strangles are the quintessential volatility strategies. They are the purest ways to buy and sell realized and implied volatility. This chapter discusses straddles and strangles, how they work, when to use them, what to look out for, and the differences between the two.

Long Straddle

Definition: Buying one call and one put in the same option class, in the same expiration cycle, and with the same strike price.

Linearly, the long straddle is the best of both worlds—long a call and a put. If the stock rises, the call enjoys the unlimited potential for profit while the put's losses are decidedly limited. If the stock falls, the put's profit potential is bound only by the stock's falling to zero, while the call's potential loss is finite. Directionally, this can be a win-win situation—as long as the stock moves enough for one option's profit to cover the loss on the other. The risk, however, is that this may not happen. Holding two long options means a big penalty can be paid for stagnant stocks.

The Basic Long Straddle

The long straddle is an option strategy to use when a trader is looking for a big move in a stock but is uncertain which direction it will move. Technically, the Commodity Channel Index (CCI), Bollinger bands, or pennants are some examples of indicators which might signal the possibility of a breakout. Or fundamental data might call for a revaluation of the stock based on an impending catalyst. In either case, a long straddle, is a way for traders to position themselves for the expected move, without regard to direction. In this example, we'll study a hypothetical $70 stock poised for a breakout. We'll buy the one-month 70 straddle for 4.25.

> Buy one 1-month 70 call at 2.25
> Buy one 1-month 70 put at   2.00
>   Net Debit 4.25

Exhibit 15.1 shows the payout of the straddle at expiration.

At expiration, with the stock at $70, neither the call nor the put is in-the-money. The straddle expires worthless, leaving a loss of 4.25 in its wake from erosion. If, however, the stock is above or below $70, either the call or the put will have at least some value. The farther the stock price moves from the strike price in either direction, the higher the net value of the options.

Above $70, the call has value. If the underlying is at $74.25 at expiration, the put will expire worthless, but the call will be worth 4.25—the price initially paid for the straddle. Above this break-even price, the trade is a winner, and the higher, the better. Below $70, the put has value. If the underlying is at $65.75 at expiration, the call expires, and the put is worth 4.25. Below this breakeven, the straddle is a winner, and the lower, the better.

EXHIBIT 15.1 At-expiration diagram for a long straddle.

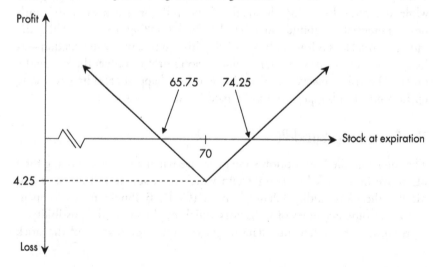

Why It Works

In this basic example, if the underlying is beyond either of the break-even points at expiration, the trade is a winner. The key to understanding this is the fact that at expiration, the loss on one option is limited—it can only fall to zero—but the profit potential on the other can be unlimited.

In practice, most active traders will not hold a straddle until expiration. Even if the trade is not held to term, however, movement is still beneficial—in fact, it is more beneficial, because time decay will not have depleted all the extrinsic value of the options. Movement benefits the long straddle because of positive gamma. But movement is a race against the clock—a race against theta. Theta is the cost of trading the long straddle. Only pay it for as long as necessary. When the stock's volatility appears poised to ebb, exit the trade.

Exhibit 15.2 shows the P&(L) of the straddle both at expiration and at the time the trade was made.

Because this is a short-term at-the-money (ATM) straddle, we will assume for simplicity that it has a delta of zero.[1] When the trade is consummated, movement can only help, as indicated by the dotted line on the exhibit. This is the classic graphic representation of positive gamma—the smiley face. When the stock moves higher, the call gains value at an increasing rate while the put loses value at a decreasing rate. When the stock

EXHIBIT 15.2 Long straddle P&(L) at initiation and expiration.

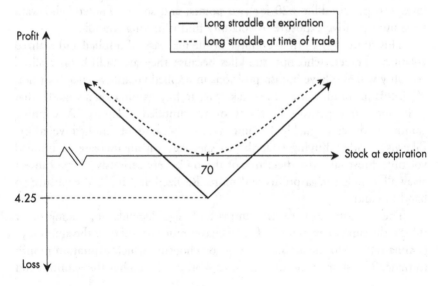

moves lower, the put gains at an increasing rate while the call loses at a decreasing rate. This is positive gamma.

This still may not be an entirely fair representation of how profits are earned. The underlying is not required to move continuously in one direction for traders to reap gamma profits. As described in Chapter 13, traders can scalp gamma by buying and selling stock to offset long or short deltas created by movement in the underlying. When traders scalp gamma, they lock in profits as the stock price oscillates.

The potential for gamma scalping is an important motivation for straddle buyers. Gamma scalping a straddle gives traders the chance to profit from a stock that has dynamic price swings. It should be second nature to volatility traders to understand that theta is the trade-off of gamma scalping.

The Big V

Gamma and theta are not alone in the straddle buyer's thoughts. Vega is a major consideration for a straddle buyer, as well. In a straddle, there are two long options of the same strike, which means double the vega risk of a single-leg trade at that strike. With no short options in this spread, the implied-volatility exposure is concentrated. For example, if the call has a vega of 0.05, the put's vega at that same strike will also be about 0.05. This means that buying one straddle gives the trader exposure of around 10 cents per implied volatility (IV) point. If IV rises by one point, the trader makes $10 per one-lot straddle, $20 for two points, and so on. If IV falls one point, the trader loses $10 per straddle, $20 for two points, and so on. Traders who want maximum positive exposure to volatility find it in long straddles.

This strategy is a prime example of the marriage of implied and realized volatility. Traders who buy straddles because they are bullish on realized volatility will also have bullish positions in implied volatility—like it or not. With this in mind, traders must take care to buy gamma via a straddle that it is not too expensive in terms of the implied volatility. A winning gamma trade can quickly become a loser because of implied volatility. Likewise, traders buying straddles to speculate on an increase in implied volatility must take the theta risk of the trade very seriously. Time can eat away all a trade's vega profits and more. Realized and implied exposure go hand in hand.

The relationship between gamma and vega depends on, among other things, the time to expiration. Traders have some control over the amount of gamma relative to the amount of vega by choosing which expiration month to trade. The shorter the time until expiration, the higher the gammas and the lower the vegas of ATM options. Gamma traders may be better served by buying short-term contracts that coincide with the period of perceived high stock volatility.

If the intent of the straddle is to profit from vega, the choice of the month to trade depends on which month's volatility is perceived to be too high or too low. If, for example, the front-month IV looks low compared with historical IV, current and historical realized volatility, and the expected future volatility, but the back months' IVs are higher and more in line with these other metrics, there would be no point in buying the back-month options. In this case, traders would need to buy the month that they think is cheap.

Trading the Long Straddle

Option trading is all about optimizing the statistical chances of success. A long-straddle trade makes the most sense if traders think they can make money on both implied volatility and gamma. Many traders make the mistake of buying a straddle just before earnings are announced because they anticipate a big move in the stock. Of course, stock-price action is only half the story. The option premium can be extraordinarily expensive just before earnings, because the stock move is priced into the options. This is buying after the rush and before the crush. Although some traders are successful specializing in trading earnings, this is a hard way to make money.

Ideally, the best time to buy volatility is before the move is priced in—that is, before everyone else does. This is conceptually the same as buying a stock in anticipation of bullish news. Once news comes out, the stock rallies, and it is often too late to participate in profits. The goal is to get in at the beginning of the trend, not the end—the same goal as in trading volatility.

As in analyzing a stock, fundamental and technical tools exist for analyzing volatility—namely, news and volatility charts. For fundamentals, buy the rumor, sell the news applies to the rush and crush of implied volatility. Previous chapters discussed fundamental events that affect volatility; be prepared to act fast when volatility-changing situations present themselves. With charts, the elementary concept of buy low, sell high is obvious, yet profound. Review Chapter 14 for guidance on reading volatility charts.

With all trading, getting in is easy. It's managing the position, deciding when to hedge and when to get out that is the tricky part. This is especially true with the long straddle. Straddles are intended to be actively managed. Instead of waiting for a big linear move to evolve over time, traders can take profits intermittently through gamma scalping. Furthermore, they hold the trade only as long as gamma scalping appears to be a promising opportunity.

Legging Out

There are many ways to exiting a straddle. In the right circumstances, legging out is the preferred method. Instead of buying and selling stock to lock in profits and maintain delta neutrality, traders can reduce their positions by selling off some of the calls or puts that are part of the straddle. In this technique, when the underlying rises, traders sell as many calls as needed to reduce the delta to zero. As the underlying falls, they sell enough puts to reduce their position to zero delta. As the stock oscillates, they whittle away at the position with each hedging transaction. This serves the dual purpose of taking profits and reducing risk.

A trader, Susan, has been studying Acme Brokerage Co. (ABC). Susan has noticed that brokerage stocks have been fairly volatile in recent past. Exhibit 15.3 shows an analysis of Acme's volatility over the past 30 days.

During this period, Acme stock ranged more than $11 in price. In this example, Acme's volatility is a function of interest rate concerns and other macroeconomic issues affecting the brokerage industry as a whole. As the stock price begins to level off in the latter half of the 30-day period, realized volatility begins to ebb. The front month's IV recedes toward recent lows as well. At this point, both realized and implied volatility converge at 36 percent. Although volatility is at its low for the past month, it is still relatively high for a brokerage stock under normal market conditions.

Susan does not believe that the volatility plaguing this stock is over. She believes that an upcoming scheduled Federal Reserve Board announcement will lead to more volatility. She perceives this to be a volatility-buying opportunity. Effectively, she wants to buy volatility on the dip. Susan pays 5.75 for 20 July 75-strike straddles.

Exhibit 15.4 shows the analytics of this trade with four weeks until expiration.

As with any trade, the risk is that the trader is wrong. The risk here is indicated by the −2.07 theta and the +3.35 vega. Susan has to scalp an average of at least $207 a day just to break even against the time decay. And

EXHIBIT 15.3 Acme Brokerage Co. volatility.

Stock Price	Realized Volatility	Front-Month Implied Volatility
30-day high $78.66	30-day high 47%	30-day high 55%
30-day low $66.94	30-day low 36%	30-day low 34%
Current px $74.80	Current vol 36%	Current vol 36%

EXHIBIT 15.4 Analytics for long 20 Acme Brokerage Co. 75-strike straddles.

Friday, four weeks before
expiration, stock at $74.80

Bought 20 75 calls	2.90
Bought 20 75 puts	2.85
Net Debit	5.75

Delta	+0.85
Gamma	+2.16
Theta	−2.07
Vega	+3.35

if IV continues to ebb down to a lower, more historically normal, level, she needs to scalp even more to make up for vega losses.

Effectively, Susan wants both realized and implied volatility to rise. She paid 36 volatility for the straddle. She wants to be able to sell the options at a higher vol than 36. In the interim, she needs to cover her decay just to break even. But in this case, she thinks the stock will be volatile enough to cover decay and then some. If Acme moves at a volatility greater than 36, her chances of scalping profitably are more favorable than if it moves at less than 36 vol. The following is one possible scenario of what might have happened over two weeks after the trade was made.

Week One

During the first week, the stock's volatility tapered off a bit more, but implied volatility stayed firm. After some oscillation, the realized volatility ended the week at 34 percent while IV remained at 36 percent. Susan was able to scalp stock reasonably well, although she still didn't cover her seven days of theta. Her stock buys and sells netted a gain of $1,100. By the end of week one, the straddle was 5.10 bid. If she had sold the straddle at the market, she would have ended up losing $200.

Profit from scalping stock: $1,100
Loss on straddle due to theta
$(5.10 − 5.75) \times 20 =$ ($1,300)
Net P&(L)   ($ 200)

Susan decided to hold her position. Toward the end of week two, there would be the Federal Open Market Committee (FOMC) meeting.

Week Two

The beginning of the week saw IV rise as the event drew near. By the close on Tuesday, implied volatility for the straddle was 40 percent. But realized volatility continued its decline, which meant Susan was not able to scalp to cover the theta of Saturday, Sunday, Monday, and Tuesday. But, the straddle was now 5.20 bid, 0.10 higher than it had been on previous Friday. The rising IV made up for most of the theta loss. At this point, Susan could have sold her straddle to scratch her trade. She would have lost $1,100 on the straddle [(5.20 − 5.75) × 20] but made $1,100 by scalping gamma in the first week. Susan decided to wait and see what the Fed chairman had to say.

By week's end, the trade had proved to be profitable. After the FOMC meeting, the stock shot up more than $4 and just as quickly fell. It continued to bounce around a bit for the rest of the week. Susan was able to lock in $5,200 from stock scalps. After much gyration over this two-week period, the price of Acme stock incidentally returned to around the same price it had been at when Susan bought her straddle: $74.50. As might have been expected after the announcement, implied volatility softened. By Friday, IV had fallen to 30. Realized volatility was sharply higher as a result of the big moves during the week that were factored into the 30-day calculation.

With seven more days of decay and a lower implied volatility, the straddle was 3.50 bid at midafternoon on Friday. Susan sold her 20-lot to close the position. Her profit for week two was $2,000.

$$
\begin{array}{rr}
\text{Profit from scalping stock:} & \$5,200 \\
\text{Loss on straddle due to theta and vega} & \\
(3.50 - 5.10) \times 20 = & (\$3,200) \\
\text{Net P\&(L)} & \$2,000 \\
\end{array}
$$

What went into Susan's decision to close her position? Susan had two objectives: to profit from a rise in implied volatility and to profit from a rise in realized volatility. The rise in IV did indeed occur, but not immediately. By Tuesday of the second week, vega profits were overshadowed by theta losses.

Gamma was the saving grace with this trade. The bulk of the gain occurred in week two when the Fed announcement was made. Once that event passed, the prospects for covering theta looked less attractive. They were further dimmed by the sharp drop in implied volatility from 40 to 30.

In this hypothetical scenario, the trade ended up profitable. This is not always the case. Here the profit was chiefly produced by one or two high-volatility days. Had the stock not been unusually volatile during this time, the trade would have been a certain loser. Even though implied volatility had risen four points by Tuesday of the second week, the trade did not yield a profit. The time decay of holding two options can make long straddles a tough strategy to trade.

Short Straddle

Definition: Selling one call and one put in the same option class, in the same expiration cycle, and with the same strike price.

Just as buying a straddle is a pure way to buy volatility, selling a straddle is a way to short it. When a trader's forecast calls for lower implied and realized volatility, a straddle generates the highest returns of all volatility-selling strategies. Of course, with high reward necessarily comes high risk. A short straddle is one of the riskiest positions to trade.

Let's look at a one-month 70-strike straddle sold at 4.25.

Sell one 1-month 70 call at 2.25
Sell one 1-month 70 put at 2.00
Net Credit 4.25

The risk is easily represented graphically by means of a P&(L) diagram. Exhibit 15.5 shows the risk and reward of this short straddle.

If the straddle is held until expiration and the underlying is trading below the strike price, the short put is in-the-money (ITM). The lower the stock, the greater the loss on the +1.00 delta from the put. The trade as a whole will be a loser if the underlying is below the lower of the two break-even points— in this case $65.75. This point is found by subtracting the premium received from the strike. Before expiration, negative gamma adversely affects profits as the underlying falls. The lower the underlying is trading below the strike price, the greater the drain on P&(L) due to the positive delta of the short put.

It is the same proposition if the underlying is above $70 at expiration. But in this case, it is the short call that would be in-the-money. The higher the underlying price, the more the −1.00 delta adversely impacts P&(L). If at expiration the underlying is above the higher breakeven, which in this case is $74.25 (the strike plus the premium), the trade is a loser. The higher the

EXHIBIT 15.5   Short straddle P&(L) at initiation and expiration.

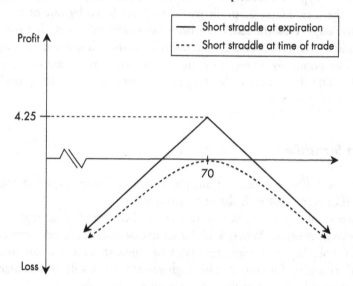

underlying, the worse off the trade. Before expiration, negative gamma creates negative deltas as the underlying climbs above the strike, eating away at the potential profit, which is the net premium received.

The best-case scenario is that the underlying is right at $70 at the closing bell on expiration Friday. In this situation, neither option is ITM, meaning that the 4.25 premium is all profit. In reaping the maximum profit, both time and price play roles. If the position is closed before expiration, implied volatility enters into the picture as well.

It's important to note that just because neither option is ITM if the underlying is right at $70 at expiration, it doesn't mean with certainty that neither option will be assigned. Sometimes options that are ATM or even out-of-the-money (OTM) get assigned. This can lead to a pleasant or unpleasant surprise the Monday morning following expiration. The risk of not knowing whether or not you will be assigned—that is, whether or not you have a position in the underlying security—is a risk to be avoided. It is the goal of every trader to remove unnecessary risk from the equation. Buying the call and the put for 0.05 or 0.10 to close the position is a small price to pay when one considers the possibility of waking up Monday morning to find a loss of hundreds of dollars per contract because a position you didn't even know you owned had moved against you. Most traders avoid this risk, referred to as pin risk, by closing short options before expiration.

The Risks with Short Straddles

Looking at an at-expiration diagram or even analyzing the gamma/theta relationship of a short straddle may sometimes lead to a false sense of comfort. Sometimes it looks as if short straddles need a pretty big move to lose a lot of money. So why are they definitely among the riskiest strategies to trade? That is a matter of perspective.

Option trading is about risk management. Dealing with a proverbial train wreck every once in a while is part of the game. But the big disasters can end one's trading career in an instant. Because of its potential—albeit sometimes small potential—for a colossal blowup, the short straddle is, indeed, one of the riskiest positions one can trade. That said, it has a place in the arsenal of option strategies for speculative traders.

Trading the Short Straddle

A short straddle is a trade for highly speculative traders who think a security will trade within a defined range and that implied volatility is too high. While a long straddle needs to be actively traded, a short straddle needs to be actively monitored to guard against negative gamma. As adverse deltas get bigger because of stock price movement, traders have to be on alert, ready to neutralize directional risk by offsetting the delta with stock or by legging out of the options. To be sure, with a short straddle, every stock trade locks in a loss with the intent of stemming future losses. The ideal situation is that the straddle is held until expiration and expires with the underlying right at $70 with no negative-gamma scalping.

Short-straddle traders must take a longer-term view of their positions than long-straddle traders. Often with short straddles, it is ultimately time that provides the payout. While long straddle traders would be inclined to watch gamma and theta very closely to see how much movement is required to cover each day's erosion, short straddlers are more inclined to focus on the at-expiration diagram so as not to lose sight of the end game.

There are some situations that are exceptions to this long-term focus. For example, when implied volatility gets to be extremely high for a particular option class relative to both the underlying stock's volatility and the historical implied volatility, one may want to sell a straddle to profit from a fall in IV. This can lead to leveraged short-term profits if implied volatility does, indeed, decline.

Because of the fact that there are two short options involved, these straddles administer a concentrated dose of negative vega. For those willing to bet big on a decline in implied volatility, a short straddle is an eager croupier. These trades are delta neutral and double the vega of a single-leg trade. But they're double the gamma, too. As with the long straddle, realized and implied volatility levels are both important to watch.

Short-Straddle Example

For this example, a trader, John, has been watching Federal XYZ Corp. (XYZ) for a year. During the 12 months that John has followed XYZ, its front-month implied volatility has typically traded at around 20 percent, and its realized volatility has fluctuated between 15 and 20 percent. The past 30 days, however, have been a bit more volatile. Exhibit 15.6 shows XYZ's recent volatility.

The stock volatility has begun to ease, trading now at a 22 volatility compared with the 30-day high of 26, but still not down to the usual 15-to-20 range. The stock, in this scenario, has traded in a channel. It currently lies in the lower half of its recent range. Although the current front-month implied volatility is in the lower half of its 30-day range, it's historically high compared with the 20 percent level that John has been used to seeing, and it's still four points above the realized volatility. John believes that the conditions that led to the recent surge in volatility are no longer present. His forecast is for the stock volatility to continue to ease and for implied volatility to continue its downtrend as well and revert to its long-term mean over the next week or two. John sells 10 September 105 straddles at 5.40.

Exhibit 15.7 shows the greeks for this trade.

The goal here is for implied volatility to fall to around 20. If it does, John makes $1,254 (6 vol points × 2.09 vega). He also thinks theta gains will outpace gamma losses. The following is a two-week examination of one possible outcome for John's trade.

Week One

The first week in this example was a profitable one, but it came with challenges. John paid for his winnings with a few sleepless nights. On the

EXHIBIT 15.6 XYZ volatility.

Stock Price	Realized Volatility	Front-Month Implied Volatility
30-day high $111.71	30-day high 26%	30-day high 30%
30-day low $102.05	30-day low 21%	30-day low 24%
Current px $104.75	Current vol 22%	Current vol 26%

EXHIBIT 15.7 Greeks for short XYZ straddle.

Friday, three weeks before
expiration, stock at $104.75

Sold 10 105 calls 2.70	
Sold 10 105 puts 2.70	
Net Debit 5.40	

Delta	+0.26
Gamma	−1.18
Theta	+1.20
Vega	−2.09

Monday following his entry into the trade, the stock rose to $106. While John collected a weekend's worth of time decay, the $1.25 jump in stock price ate into some of those profits and naturally made him uneasy about the future.

At this point, John was sitting on a profit, but his position delta began to grow negative, to around −1.22 [(−1.18 × 1.25) + 0.26]. For a $104.75 stock, a move of $1.25—or just over 1 percent—is not out of the ordinary, but it put John on his guard. He decided to wait and see what happened before hedging.

The following day, the rally continued. The stock was at $107.30 by noon. His delta was around −3. In the face of an increasingly negative delta, John weighed his alternatives: He could buy back some of his calls to offset his delta, which would have the added benefit of reducing his gamma as well. He could buy stock to flatten out. Lastly, he could simply do nothing and wait. John felt the stock was overbought and might retrace. He also still believed volatility would fall. He decided to be patient and enter a stop order to buy all of his deltas at $107.50 in case the stock continued trending up. The XYZ shares closed at $107.45 that day.

This time inaction proved to be the best action. The stock did retrace. Week one ended with Federal XYZ back down around $105.50. The IV of the straddle was at 23. The straddle finished up week one offered at $4.10.

Week Two

The future was looking bright at the start of week two until Wednesday. Wednesday morning saw XYZ gap open to $109. When you have a short straddle, a $3.50 gap move in the underlying tends to instantly give you a sinking feeling in the pit of your stomach. But the damage was truly not that bad. The offer in the straddle was 4.75, so the position was still a winner if John bought it back at this point.

Gamma/delta hurt. Theta helped. A characteristic that enters into this trade is volatility's changing as a result of movement in the stock price. Despite the fact that the stock gapped $3.50 higher, implied volatility fell by 1 percent, to 22. This volatility reaction to the underlying's rise in price is very common in many equity and index options. John decided to close the trade. Nobody ever went broke taking a profit.

The trade in this example was profitable. Of course, this will not always be the case. Sometimes short straddles will be losers—sometimes big ones. Big moves and rising implied volatility can be perilous to short straddles and their writers. If the XYZ stock in the previous example had gapped up to $115—which is not an unreasonable possibility—John's trade would have been ugly.

Synthetic Straddles

Straddles are the pet strategy of certain professional traders who specialize in trading volatility. In fact, in the mind of many of these traders, a straddle is all there is. Any single-legged trade can be turned into a straddle synthetically simply by adding stock.

Chapter 6 discussed put-call parity and showed that, for all intents and purposes, a put is a call and a call is a put. For the most part, the greeks of the options in the put-call pair are essentially the same. The delta is the only real difference. And, of course, that can be easily corrected. As a matter of perspective, one can make the case that buying two calls is essentially the same as buying a call and a put, once stock enters into the equation.

Take a non-dividend-paying stock trading at $40 a share. With 60 days until expiration, a 25 volatility, and a 4 percent interest rate, the greeks of the 40-strike calls and puts of the straddle are as follows:

Option	Delta	Gamma	Theta	Vega
Long one 40-strike call	0.55	0.096	−0.016	0.064
Long one 40-strike put	−0.46	0.099	−0.012	0.064
Long 40-straddle	0.09	0.195	−0.028	0.128

Essentially, the same position can be created by buying one leg of the spread synthetically. For example, in addition to buying one 40 call, another 40 call can be purchased along with shorting 100 shares of stock to create a 40 put synthetically.

	Option	Delta	Gamma	Theta	Vega
	Long one 40-strike call	0.55	0.096	−0.016	0.064
Synthetic put {	Long one 40-strike call	0.55	0.096	−0.016	0.064
	Short 100 shares	−1.00			
	Long synth 40-straddle	0.10	0.192	−0.032	0.128

Combined, the long call and the synthetic long put (long call plus short stock) creates a synthetic straddle. A long synthetic straddle could have similarly been constructed with a long put and a long synthetic call (long put plus long stock). Furthermore, a short synthetic straddle could be created by selling an option with its synthetic pair.

Notice the similarities between the greeks of the two positions. The synthetic straddle functions about the same as a conventional straddle. Because the delta and gamma are nearly the same, the up-and-down risk is nearly the same. Time and volatility likewise affect the two trades about the same. The only real difference is that the synthetic straddle might require a bit more cash up front, because it requires buying or shorting the stock. In practice, straddles will typically be traded in accounts with retail portfolio margining or professional margin requirements (which can be similar to retail portfolio margining). So the cost of the long stock or margin for short stock is comparatively small.

Long Strangle

Definition: Buying one call and one put in the same option class, in the same expiration cycle, but with different strike prices. Typical long strangles involve an OTM call and an OTM put. A strangle in which an ITM call and an ITM put are purchased is called a long guts strangle.

A long strangle is similar to a long straddle in many ways. They both require buying a call and a put on the same class in the same expiration month. They are both buying volatility. There are, however, some functional differences. These differences stem from the fact that the options have different strike prices.

Because there is distance between the strike prices, from an at-expiration perspective, the underlying must move more for the trade to show a profit.

Exhibit 15.8 illustrates the payout of options as part of a long strangle on a $70 stock. The graph is much like that of Exhibit 15.1, which shows the payout of a long straddle. But the net cost here is only 1.00, compared with 4.25 for the straddle with the same time and volatility inputs. The cost is lower because this trade consists of OTM options instead of ATM options. The breakdown is as follows:

Buy one 1-month 75 call at 0.60
Buy one 1-month 65 put at 0.40
Net Debit 1.00

The underlying has a bit farther to go by expiration for the trade to have value. If the underlying is above $75 at expiration, the call is ITM and has value. If the underlying is below $65 at expiration, the put is ITM and has value. If the underlying is between the two strike prices at expiration both options expire and the 1.00 premium is lost.

An important difference between a straddle and a strangle is that if a strangle is held until expiration, its break-even points are farther apart than those of a comparable straddle. The 70-strike straddle in Exhibit 15.1 had a

EXHIBIT 15.8 Long strangle at-expiration diagram.

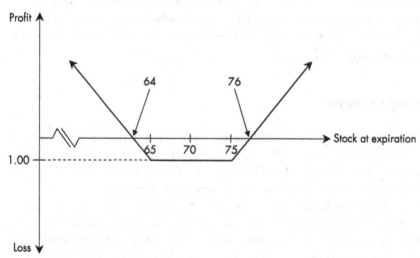

lower breakeven of $65.75 and an upper break-even of $74.25. The comparable strangle in this example has break-even prices of $64 and $76.

But what if the strangle is not held until expiration? Then the trade's greeks must be analyzed. Intuitively, two OTM options (or ITM ones, for that matter) will have lower gamma, theta, and vega than two comparable ATM options. This has a two-handed implication when comparing straddles and strangles.

On the one hand, from a realized volatility perspective, lower gamma means the underlying must move more than it would have to for a straddle to produce the same dollar gain per spread, even intraday. But on the other hand, lower theta means the underlying doesn't have to move as much to cover decay. A lower nominal profit but a higher percentage profit is generally reaped by strangles as compared with straddles.

A long strangle composed of two OTM options will also give positive exposure to implied volatility but, again, not as much as an ATM straddle would. Positive vega really kicks in when the underlying is close to one of the strike prices. This is important when anticipating changes in the stock price and in IV.

Say a trader expects implied volatility to rise as a result of higher stock volatility. As the stock rises or falls, the strangle will move toward the price point that offers the highest vega (the strike). With a straddle, the stock will be moving away from the point with the highest vega. If the stock doesn't move as anticipated, the lower theta and vega of the strangle compared with the ATM straddle have a less adverse effect on P&L.

Long-Strangle Example

Let's return to Susan, who earlier in this chapter bought a straddle on Acme Brokerage Co. (ABC). Acme currently trades at $74.80 a share with current realized volatility at 36 percent. The stock's volatility range for the past month was between 36 and 47. The implied volatility of the four-week options is 36 percent. The range over the past month for the IV of the front month has been between 34 and 55.

As in the long-straddle example earlier in this chapter, there is a great deal of uncertainty in brokerage stocks revolving around interest rates, credit-default problems, and other economic issues. An FOMC meeting is expected in about one week's time about whose possible actions analysts' estimates vary greatly, from a cut of 50 basis points to no cut at all. Add a pending earnings release to the docket, and Susan thinks Acme may move quite a bit.

EXHIBIT 15.9 Long straddle versus long strangle.

Friday, four weeks before
expiration, stock at $74.80

Long 20 ABC 75 Straddles   Long 20 ABC 70–80 Strangles

Bought 20 75 calls 2.90	Bought 20 80 calls 1.05
Bought 20 75 puts 2.85	Bought 20 70 puts 1.30
Net Debit 5.75	Net Debit 2.35

Delta	+0.85	Delta	+0.23
Gamma	+2.16	Gamma	+1.70
Theta	−2.07	Theta	−1.71
Vega	+3.35	Vega	+2.80

In this case, however, instead of buying the 75-strike straddle, Susan pays 2.35 for 20 one-month 70–80 strangles. Exhibit 15.9 compares the greeks of the long ATM straddle with those of the long strangle.

The cost of the strangle, at 2.35, is about 40 percent of the cost of the straddle. Of course, with two long options in each trade, both have positive gamma and vega and negative theta, but the exposure to each metric is less with the strangle. Assuming the same stock-price action, a strangle would enjoy profits from movement and losses from lack of movement that were similar to those of a straddle—just nominally less extreme.

For example, if Acme stock rallies $5, from $74.80 to $79.80, the gamma of the 75 straddle will grow the delta favorably, generating a gain of 1.50, or about 25 percent. The 70–80 strangle will make 1.15 from the curvature of the delta—almost a 50 percent gain.

With the straddle and especially the strangle, there is one more detail to factor in when considering potential P&L: IV changes due to stock price movement. IV is likely to fall as the stock rallies and rise as the stock declines. The profits of both the long straddle and the long strangle would likely be adversely affected by IV changes as the stock rose toward $79.80. And because the stock would be moving away from the straddle strike and toward one of the strangle strikes, the vegas would tend to become more similar for the two trades. The straddle in this example would have a vega of 2.66, while the strangle's vega would be 2.67 with the underlying at $79.80 per share.

Short Strangle

Definition: Selling one call and one put in the same option class, in the same expiration cycle, but with different strike prices. Typically, an OTM call and

EXHIBIT 15.10   Short strangle at-expiration diagram.

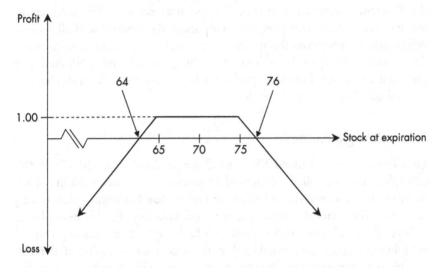

an OTM put are sold. A strangle in which an ITM call and an ITM put are sold is called a short guts strangle.

A short strangle is a volatility-selling strategy, like the short straddle. But with the short strangle, the strikes are farther apart, leaving more room for error. With these types of strategies, movement is the enemy. Wiggle room is the important difference between the short-strangle and short-straddle strategies. Of course, the trade-off for a higher chance of success is lower option premium.

Exhibit 15.10 shows the at-expiration diagram of a short strangle sold at 1.00, using the same options as in the diagram for the long strangle.

Note that if the underlying is between the two strike prices, the maximum gain of 1.00 is harvested. With the stock below $65 at expiration, the short put is ITM, with a +1.00 delta. If the stock price is below the lower breakeven of $64 (the put strike minus the premium), the trade is a loser. The lower the stock, the bigger the loss. If the underlying is above $75, the short call is ITM, with a −1.00 delta. If the stock is above the upper breakeven of $76 (the call strike plus the premium), the trade is a loser. The higher the stock, the bigger the loss.

Intuitively, the signs of the greeks of this strangle should be similar to those of a short straddle—negative gamma and vega, positive theta. That means that increased realized volatility hurts. Rising IV hurts. And time heals all wounds—unless, of course, the wounds caused by gamma are greater than the net premium received.

This brings us to an important philosophical perspective that emphasizes the differences between long straddles and strangles and their short counterparts. Losses from rising vega are temporary; the time value of all options will be zero at expiration. But gamma losses can be permanent and profound. These short strategies have limited profit potential and unlimited loss potential. Although short-term profits (or losses) can result from IV changes, the real goal here is to capture theta.

Short-Strangle Example

Let's revisit John, a Federal XYZ (XYZ) trader. XYZ is at $104.75 in this example, with an implied volatility of 26 percent and a stock volatility of 22. Both implied and realized volatility are higher than has been typical during the past twelve months. John wants to sell volatility. In this example, he believes the stock price will remain in a fairly tight range, causing realized volatility to revert to its normal level, in this case between 15 and 20 percent.

He does everything possible to ensure success. This includes scanning the news headlines on XYZ and its financials for a reason not to sell volatility. Playing devil's advocate with oneself can uncover unforeseen yet valid reasons to avoid making bad trades. John also notes the recent price range, which has been between $111.71 and $102.05 over the past month. Once John commits to an outlook on the stock, he wants to set himself up for maximum gain if he's right and, for that matter, to maximize his chances of being right. In this case, he decides to sell a strangle to give himself as much margin for error as possible. He sells 10 three-week 100–110 strangles at 1.80.

Exhibit 15.11 compares the greeks of this strangle with those of the 105 straddle.

As expected, the strangle's greeks are comparable to the straddle's but of less magnitude. If John's intention were to capture a drop in IV, he'd be better off selling the bigger vega of the straddle. Here, though, he wants to see the premium at zero at expiration, so the strangle serves his purposes better. What he is most concerned about are the breakevens—in this case, 98.20 and 111.8. The straddle has closer break-even points, of $99.60 and $110.40.

Despite the fact that in this case, John is not really trading the greeks or IV per se, they still play an important role in his trade. First, he can use theta to plan the best strangle to trade. In this case, he sells the three-week strangle because it has the highest theta of the available months. The second month strangle has a −0.71 theta, and the third month has a −0.58 theta. With strangles, because the options are OTM, this disparity in theta among the

EXHIBIT 15.11 Short straddle vs. short strangle.

Friday, three weeks before
expiration, stock at $104.75

Short 10 XYZ 105 Straddles   Short 10 XYZ 100–110 Strangles

Sold 10 105 calls 2.70	Sold 10 110 calls .95
Sold 10 105 puts 2.70	Sold 10 100 puts .85
Net Credit 5.40	Net Credit 1.80

Delta	+0.26	Delta	+0.13
Gamma	−1.18	Gamma	−0.91
Theta	+1.20	Theta	+0.92
Vega	−2.09	Vega	−1.61

tradable months may not always be the case. But for this trade, if he is still bearish on realized volatility after expiration, John can sell the next month when these options expire.

Certainly, he will monitor his risk by watching delta and gamma. These are his best measures of directional exposure. He will consider implied volatility in the decision-making process, too. An implied volatility significantly higher than the realized volatility can be a red flag that the market expects something to happen, but there's a bigger payoff if there is no significant volatility. An IV significantly lower than the realized can indicate the risk of selling options too cheaply: the premium received is not high enough, based on how much the stock has been moving. Ideally, the IV should be above the realized volatility by between 2 and 20 percent, perhaps more for highly speculative traders.

Limiting Risk

The trouble with short straddles and strangles is that every once in a while the stock unexpectedly reacts violently, moving by three or more standard deviations. This occurs when there is a takeover, an extreme political event, a legal action, or some other extraordinary incident. These events can be guarded against by buying farther OTM options for protection. Essentially, instead of selling a straddle or a strangle, one sells an iron butterfly or iron condor. Then, when disaster strikes, it's not a complete catastrophe.

How Cheap Is Too Cheap?

At some point, the absolute premium simply is not worth the risk of the trade. For example, it would be unwise to sell a two-month 45–55 strangle for 0.10 no matter what the realized volatility was. With the knowledge that there is always a chance for a big move, it's hard to justify risking dollars to make a dime.

Note

1. This depends on interest, dividends, and time to expiration. The delta will likely not be exactly zero.

CHAPTER 16

Ratio Spreads and Complex Spreads

The purpose of spreading is to reduce risk. Buying one contract and selling another can reduce some or all of a trade's risks, as measured by the greeks, compared with simply holding an outright option. But creative traders have the ability to exercise great control over their greeks risk. They can practically eliminate risk in some greeks, while retaining risks in just the desired greeks. To do so, traders may have to use more complex, and less conventional spreads. These spreads often involve buying or selling options in quantities other than one-to-one ratios.

Ratio Spreads

The simplest versions of these strategies used by retail traders, institutional traders, proprietary traders, and others are referred to as *ratio spreads*. In ratio spreads, options are bought and sold in quantities based on a ratio. For example, a 1:3 spread is when one option is bought (or sold) and three are sold (or bought)—a ratio of one to three. This kind of ratio spread would be called a "one-by-three."

However, some option positions can get a lot more complicated. Market makers and other professional traders manage a complex inventory of long and short options. These types of strategies go way beyond simple at-expiration diagrams. This chapter will discuss the two most common types of ratio spreads—backspreads and ratio vertical spreads—and also the delta-neutral position management of market makers and other professional traders.

Backspreads

Definition: An option strategy consisting of more long options than short options having the same expiration month. Typically, the trader is long calls (or puts) in one series of options and short a fewer number of calls (or puts) in another series with the same expiration month in the same option class. Some traders, such as market makers, refer generically to any delta-neutral long-gamma position as a backspread.

Shades of Gray

In its simplest form, trading a backspread is trading a one-by-two call or put spread and holding it until expiration in hopes that the underlying stock's price will make a big move, particularly in the more favorable direction. But holding a backspread to expiration as described has its challenges. Let's look at a hypothetical example of a backspread held to term and its at-expiration diagram.

With the stock at $71 and one month until March expiration:

> Sell 1 March 70 call at 3.20
> Buy 2 March 75 calls at <u>1.10</u> each
> Net Credit 1.00

In this example, there is a credit of 3.20 from the sale of the 70 call and a debit of 1.10 for each of the two 75 calls. This yields a total net credit of 1.00 (3.20 − 1.10 − 1.10). Let's consider how this trade performs if it is held until expiration.

If the stock falls below $70 at expiration, all the calls expire and the 1.00 credit is all profit. If the stock is between $70 and $75 at expiration, the 70 call is in-the-money (ITM) and the −1.00 delta starts racking up losses above the breakeven of $71 (the strike plus the credit). At $75 a share this trade suffers its maximum potential loss of $4. If the stock is above $75 at expiration, the 75 calls are ITM. The net delta of +1.00, resulting from the +2.00 deltas of the 75 calls along with the −1.00 delta of the 70 call, makes money as the stock rises. To the upside, the trade is profitable once the stock is at a high enough price for the gain on the two 75 calls to make up for the loss on the 70 call. In this case, the breakeven is $79 (the $4 maximum potential loss plus the strike price of 75).

While it's good to understand this at-expiration view of this trade, this diagram is a bit misleading. What does the trader of this spread want to have

EXHIBIT 16.1 Backspread at expiration.

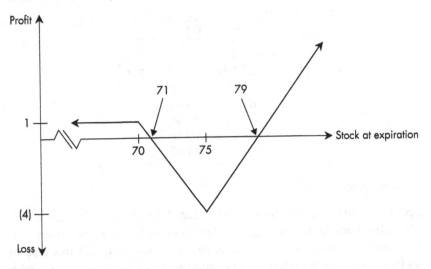

happen? If the trader is bearish, he could find a better way to trade his view than this, which limits his gains to 1.00—he could buy a put. If the trader believes the stock will make a volatile move in either direction, the back-spread offers a decidedly limited opportunity to the downside. A straddle or strangle might be a better choice. And if the trader is bullish, he would have to be very bullish for this trade to make sense. The underlying needs to rise above $79 just to break even. If instead he just bought 2 of the 75 calls for 1.10, the maximum risk would be 2.20 instead of 4, the breakeven would be $77.20 instead of $79, and profits at expiration would rack up twice as fast above the breakeven, since the trader is net long two calls instead of one. Why would a trader ever choose to trade a backspread?

The backspread is a complex spread that can be fully appreciated only when one has a thorough knowledge of options. Instead of waiting patiently until expiration, an experienced backspreader is more likely to gamma scalp intermittent opportunities. This requires trading a large enough position to make scalping worthwhile. It also requires appropriate margining (either professional-level margin requirements or retail portfolio margining). For example, this 1:2 contract backspread has a delta of −0.02 and a gamma of +0.05. Fewer than 10 deltas could be scalped if the stock moves up and down by one point. It becomes a more practical trade as the position size increases. Of course, more practical doesn't necessarily guarantee it will be more profitable. The market must cooperate!

EXHIBIT 16.2 Greeks for 20:40 backspread with the underlying at $71.

One month until expiration
stock at $71

Sold 20 70 calls	at 3.20	$\frac{IV}{32\%}$
Bought 40 75 calls	at 1.10	30%
Net Credit	1.00	

Delta	−0.46
Gamma	+1.06
Theta	−0.55
Vega	+1.07

Backspread Example

Let's say a 20:40 contract backspread is traded. (*Note:* In trader lingo this is still called a one-by-two; it is just traded 20 times.) The spread price is still 1.00 credit per contract; in this case, that's $2,000. But with this type of trade, the spread price is not the best measure of risk or reward, as it is with some other kinds of spreads. Risk and reward are best measured by delta, gamma, theta, and vega. Exhibit 16.2 shows this trade's greeks.

Backspreads are volatility plays. This spread has a +1.07 vega with the stock at $71. It is, therefore, a bullish implied volatility (IV) play. The IV of the long calls, the 75s, is 30 percent, and that of the 70s is 32 percent. Much as with any other volatility trade, traders would compare current implied volatility with realized volatility and the implied volatility of recent past and consider any catalysts that might affect stock volatility. The objective is to buy an IV that is lower than the expected future stock volatility, based on all available data. The focus of traders of this backspread is not the dollar credit earned. They are more interested in buying a 30 volatility—that's the focus.

But the 75 calls' IV is not the only volatility figure to consider. The short options, the 70s, have implied volatility of 32 percent. Because of their lower strike, the IV is naturally higher for the 70 calls. This is vertical skew and is described in Chapter 3. The phenomenon of lower strikes in the same option class and with the same expiration month having higher IV is very common, although it is not always the case.

Backspreads usually involve trading vertical skew. In this spread, traders are buying a 30 volatility and selling a 32 volatility. In trading the skew, the traders are capturing two volatility points of what some traders would call edge by buying the lower volatility and selling the higher.

Based on the greeks in Exhibit 16.2, the goal of this trade appears fairly straightforward: to profit from gamma scalping and rising IV. But, sadly,

EXHIBIT 16.3 70–75 backspread greeks at various stock prices.

	$62	$64	$66	$68	$70	$72	$74	$76	$78
	−1.46	−2.17	−2.63	−2.50	−1.38	+0.72	−3.65	+7.00	+10.3
Γ	−0.35	−0.32	−0.11	+0.29	+0.81	+1.29	+1.61	+1.70	+1.59
θ	+0.23	+0.24	+0.17	−0.04	−0.37	−0.73	−1.05	−1.22	−1.2
V	−0.36	−0.35	−0.16	+0.26	+0.86	+1.50	+2.01	+2.27	+2.24

what appears to be straightforward is not. Exhibit 16.3 shows the greeks of this trade at various underlying stock prices.

Notice how the greeks change with the stock price. As the stock price moves lower through the short strike, the 70 strike calls become the more relevant options, outweighing the influence of the 75s. Gamma and vega become negative, and theta becomes positive. If the stock price falls low enough, this backspread becomes a very different position than it was with the stock price at $71. Instead of profiting from higher implied and realized volatility, the spread needs a lower level of both to profit.

This has important implications. First, gamma traders must approach the backspread a little differently than they would most spreads. The backspread traders must keep in mind the dynamic greeks of the position. With a trade like a long straddle, in which there are no short options, traders scalping gamma simply buy to cover short deltas as the stock falls and sell to cover long deltas as the stock rises. The only risks are that the stock may not move enough to cover theta or that the traders may cover deltas too soon to maximize profits.

With the backspread, the changing gamma adds one more element of risk. In this example, buying stock to flatten out delta as the stock falls can sometimes be a premature move. Traders who buy stock may end up with more long deltas than they bargained for if the stock falls into negative-gamma territory.

Exhibit 16.3 shows that with the stock at $68, the delta for this trade is −2.50. If the traders buy 250 shares at $68, they will be delta neutral. If the stock subsequently falls to $62 a share, instead of being short 1.46 deltas, as the figure indicates, they will be long 1.04 because of the 250 shares they bought. These long deltas start to hurt as the stock continues lower. Backspreaders must therefore anticipate stock movements to avoid overhedging. The traders in this example may decide to lean short if the stock shows signs of weakness.

Leaning short means that if the delta is −2.50 at $68 a share, the traders may decide to underhedge by buying just 100 or 200 shares. If the stock continues to fall and negative gamma kicks in, this gives the traders some cushion to the downside. The short delta of the position moves closer to being flat as the stock falls. Because there is a long strike and a short strike in this delta-neutral position, trading ratio spreads is like trading a long and a short volatility position at the same time. Trading backspreads is not an exact science. The stock has just as good a chance of rising as it does of falling, and if it does rise and the traders have underhedged at $68, they will not participate in all the gains they would have if they had fully hedged by buying 250 shares of stock. If trading were easy, everyone would do it!

Backspreaders must also be conscious of the volatility of each leg of the spread. There is an inherent advantage in this example to buying the lower volatility of the 75 calls and selling the higher volatility of the 70 calls. But there is also implied risk. Equity prices and IV tend to have an inverse relationship. When stock prices fall—especially if the drop happens quickly—IV will often rise. When stock prices rise, IV often falls.

In this backspread example, as the stock price falls to or through the short strike, vega becomes negative in the face of a potentially rising IV. As the stock price rises into positive vega turf, there is the risk of IV's declining. A dynamic volatility forecast should be part of a backspread-trading plan. One of the volatility questions traders face in this example is whether the two-point volatility skew between the two strike prices is enough to compensate for the potential adverse vega move as the stock price changes.

Put backspreads have the opposite skew/volatility issues. Buying two lower-strike puts against one higher-strike put means the skew is the other direction—buying the higher IV and selling the lower. The put backspread would have long gamma/vega to the downside and short gamma/vega to the upside. But if the vega firms up as the stock falls into positive-vega territory, it would be in the trader's favor. As the stock rises, leading to negative vega, there is the potential for vega profits if IV indeed falls. There are a lot of things to consider when trading a backspread. A good trader needs to think about them all before putting on the trade.

Ratio Vertical Spreads

Definition: An option strategy consisting of more short options than long options having the same expiration month. Typically, the trader is short calls (or puts) in one series of options and long a fewer number of calls (or puts) in another series in the same expiration month on the same option class.

A ratio vertical spread, like a backspread, involves options struck at two different prices—one long strike and one short. That means that it is a volatility strategy that may be long or short gamma or vega depending on where the underlying price is at the time. The ratio vertical spread is effectively the opposite of a backspread. Let's study a ratio vertical using the same options as those used in the backspread example.

With the stock at $71 and one month until March expiration:

Buy 1 March 70 call at 3.20
Sell 2 March 75 calls at <u>1.10</u> each
Net Debit 1.00

In this case, we are buying one ITM call and selling two OTM calls. The relationship of the stock price to the strike price is not relevant to whether this spread is considered a ratio vertical spread. Certainly, all these options could be ITM or OTM at the time the trade is initiated. It is also not important whether the trade is done for a debit or a credit. If the stock price, time to expiration, volatility, or number of contracts in the ratio were different, this could just as easily been a credit ratio vertical.

Exhibit 16.4 illustrates the payout of this strategy if both legs of the 1:2 contract are still open at expiration.

This strategy is a mirror image of the backspread discussed previously in this chapter. With limited risk to the downside, the maximum loss to the

EXHIBIT 16.4 Short ratio spread at expiration.

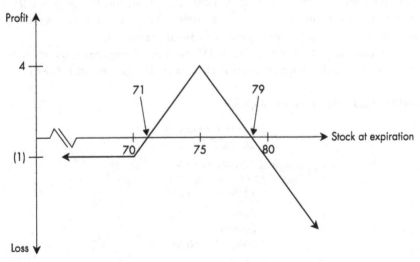

trade is the initial debit of 1 if the stock is below $70 at expiration and all the calls expire. There is a maximum profit potential of 4 if the stock is at the short strike at expiration. There is unlimited loss potential, since a short net delta is created on the upside, as one short 75 call is covered by the long 70 call, and one is naked. The breakevens are at $71 and $79.

Low Volatility

With the stock at $71, gamma and vega are both negative. Just as the backspread was a long volatility play at this underlying price, this ratio vertical is a short-vol play here. As in trading a short straddle, the name of the game is low volatility—meaning both implied and realized.

This strategy may require some gamma hedging. But as with other short volatility delta-neutral trades, the fewer the negative scalps, the greater the potential profit. Delta covering should be implemented in situations where it looks as if the stock will trend deep into negative-gamma territory. Murphy's Law of trading dictates that delta covering will likely be wrong at least as often as it is right.

Ratio Vertical Example

Let's examine a trade of 20 contracts by 40 contracts. Exhibit 16.5 shows the greeks for this ratio vertical.

Before we get down to the nitty-gritty of the mechanics and management of this trade—the how—let's first look at the motivations for putting the trade on—the why. For the cost of 1.00 per spread, this trader gets a leveraged position if the stock rises moderately. The profits max out with the stock at the short-strike target price—$75—at expiration.

Another possible profit engine is IV. Because of negative vega, there is the chance of taking a quick profit if IV falls in the interim. But short-term

EXHIBIT 16.5 Short ratio vertical spread greeks.

One month until expiration
stock at $71

Bought 20 70 calls	at 3.20	IV 32%
Sold 40 75 calls	at 1.10	30%
Net Debit	1.00	

Delta	+0.46
Gamma	−1.06
Theta	+0.55
Vega	−1.07

losses are possible, too. IV can rise, or negative gamma can hurt the trader. Ultimately, having naked calls makes this trade not very bullish. A big move north can really hurt.

Basically, this is a delta-neutral-type short-volatility play that wins the most if the stock is at $75 at expiration. One would think about making this trade if the mechanics fit the forecast. If this trader were a more bullish than indicated by the profit and loss diagram, a more-balanced bull call spread would be a better strategy, eliminating the unlimited upside risk. If upside risk were acceptable, this trader could get more aggressive by trading the spread one-by-three. That would result in a credit of 0.05 per spread. There would then be no ultimate risk below $70 but rather a 0.05 gain. With double the naked calls, however, there would be double punishment if the stock rallied strongly beyond the upside breakeven.

Ultimately, mastering options is not about mastering specific strategies. It's about having a thorough enough understanding of the instrument to be flexible enough to tailor a position around a forecast. It's about minimizing the unwanted risks and optimizing exposure to the intended risks. Still, there always exists a trade-off in that where there is the potential for profit, there is the possibility of loss—you can always be wrong.

Recalling the at-expiration diagram and examining the greeks, the best-case scenario is intuitive: the stock at $75 at expiration. The biggest theta would be right at that strike. But that strike price is also the center of the biggest negative gamma. It is important to guard against upward movement into negative delta territory, as well as movement lower where the position has a slightly positive delta. Exhibit 16.6 shows what happens to the greeks of this trade as the stock price moves.

As the stock begins to rise from $71 a share, negative deltas grow fast in the short term. Careful trend monitoring is necessary to guard against a rally. The key, however, is not in knowing what will happen but in skillfully hedging against the unknown. The talented option trader is a disciplined risk manager, not a clairvoyant.

EXHIBIT 16.6 Ratio vertical spread at various prices for the underlying.

	$62	$64	$66	$68	$70	$72	$74	$76	$78
Δ	+1.46	+2.17	+2.63	+2.50	+1.38	−0.72	−3.65	−7.00	−10.3
Γ	+0.35	+0.32	+0.11	−0.29	−0.81	−1.29	−1.61	−1.70	−1.59
θ	−0.23	−0.24	−0.17	+0.04	+0.37	+0.73	+1.05	+1.22	+1.2
V	+0.36	+0.35	+0.16	−0.26	−0.86	−1.50	−2.01	−2.27	−2.24

One of the risks that the trader willingly accepted when placing this trade was short gamma. But when the stock moves and deltas are created, decisions have to be made. Did the catalyst(s)—if any—that contributed to the rise in stock price change the outlook for volatility? If not, the decision is simply whether or not to hedge by buying stock. However, if it appears that volatility is on the rise, it is not just a delta decision. A trader may consider buying some of the short options back to reduce volatility exposure.

In this example, if the stock rises and it's feared that volatility may increase, a good choice may be to buy back some of the short 75-strike calls. This has the advantage of reducing delta (buy enough deltas to flatten out) and reducing gamma and vega. Of course, the downside to this strategy is that in purchasing the calls, a loss is likely to be locked in. Unless a lot of time has passed or implied volatility has dropped sharply, the calls will probably be bought at a higher price than they were sold.

If the stock makes a violent move upward, a loss will be incurred. Whether this loss is locked in by closing all or part of the position, the account will still be down in value. The decision to buy the calls back at a loss is based on looking forward. Nothing good can come of looking back.

How Market Makers Manage Delta-Neutral Positions

While market makers are not position traders per se, they are expert position managers. For the most part, market makers make their living by buying the bid and selling the offer. In general, they don't act; they react. Most of their trades are initiated by taking the other side of what other people want to do and then managing the risk of the positions they accumulate.

The business of a market maker is much like that of a casino. A casino takes the other side of people's bets and, in the long run, has a statistical (theoretical) edge. For market makers, because theoretical value resides in the middle of the bid and the ask, these accommodating trades lead to a theoretical profit—that is, the market maker buys below theoretical value and sells above. Actual profit—cold, hard cash you can take to the bank—is, however, dependent on sound management of the positions that are accumulated.

My career as a market maker was on the floor of the Chicago Board Options Exchange (CBOE) from 1998 to 2005. Because, over all, the trades I made had a theoretical edge, I hoped to trade as many contracts as possible on my markets without getting too long or too short in any option series or any of my greeks.

As a result of reacting to order flow, market makers can accumulate a large number of open option series for each class they trade, resulting in a single position. For example, Exhibit 16.7 shows a position I had in Ford Motor Co. (F) options as a market maker.

EXHIBIT 16.7 Market-maker position in Ford Motor Co. options.

140,700 shares of Ford Motor Co.			
		C	P
Jan-02	10	9	
Jan-02	12.5	−9	−192
Jan-02	15	−443	−563
Jan-02	17.5	109	330
Jan-02	20	−848	−23
Jan-02	22.5	74	
Jan-02	25	48	−567
Jan-02	27.5	19	−130
Jan-02	30	920	−8
Jan-02	35	114	−9
Jan-02	40	25	
Jan-02	45	−26	
Feb-02	12.5	−3	
Feb-02	15	−29	4
Feb-02	17.5	−29	10
Feb-02	20	2	23
Mar-02	10	−1	
Mar-02	12.5	2	−21
Mar-02	15	−81	−73
Mar-02	17.5	70	37
Mar-02	20	−88	46
Mar-02	22.5	−24	16

(*Continued*)

EXHIBIT 16.7 (Continued)

	140,700 shares of Ford Motor Co.		
		C	P
Mar-02	25	−8	3
Mar-02	27.5	−11	−1
Mar-02	30	−1	
Jun-02	10	−2	−3
Jun-02	12.5	−9	−1
Jun-02	15	−50	203
Jun-02	17.5	114	29
Jun-02	20	65	98
Jun-02	22.5	−12	28
Jun-02	25	2	27
Jan-03	10	−28	3
Jan-03	12.5	−5	−6
Jan-03	15	−138	81
Jan-03	17.5	−193	−120
Jan-03	20	402	1525
Jan-03	22.5	−41	86
Jan-03	25	−193	66
Jan-03	30	−251	26
Jan-03	35	−44	−35
Jan-04	10	−13	
Jan-04	15	−66	15
Jan-04	17.5	−33	
Jan-04	20	−15	6
Jan-04	25	6	24
Jan-04	30	−3	
Jan-04	35	6	
Units		−710	933

EXHIBIT 16.8 Analytics for market-maker position in Ford Motor Co. (stock at $15.72).

Delta	+1,075
Gamma	−10,191
Theta	+1,708
Vega	+7,171
Rho	−33,137

With all the open strikes, this position is seemingly complex. There is not a specific name for this type of "spread." The position was accumulated over a long period of time by initiating trades via other traders selling options to me at prices I wanted to buy them—my bid—and buying options from me at prices I wanted to sell them—my offer. Upon making an option trade, I needed to hedge directional risk immediately. I usually did so by offsetting my option trades by taking the opposite delta position in the stock—especially on big-delta trades. Through this process of providing liquidity to the market, I built up option-centric risk.

To manage this risk I needed to watch my other greeks. To be sure, trying to draw a P&L diagram of this position would be a fruitless endeavor. Exhibit 16.8 shows the risk of this trade in its most distilled form.

The +1,075 delta shows comparatively small directional risk relative to the −10,191 gamma. Much of the daily task of position management would be to carefully guard against movement by delta hedging when necessary to earn the $1,708 per day theta.

Much of the negative gamma/positive theta comes from the combined 1,006 short January 15 calls and puts. (Note that because this position is traded delta neutral, the net long or short options at each strike is what matters, not whether the options are calls or puts. Remember that in delta-neutral trading, a put is a call, and a call is a put.) The positive vega stems from the fact that the position is long 1,927 January 2003 20-strike options.

Although this position has a lot going on, it can be broken down many ways. Having long LEAPS options and short front-month options gives this position the feel of a time spread. One way to think of where most of the gamma risk is coming from is to bear in mind that the 15 strike is synthetically short 503 straddles (1,006 options ÷ two). But this position overall is not like a straddle. There are more strikes involved—a lot more. There is more short gamma to the downside if the price of Ford falls toward

$12.50. To the upside, the 17.50 strike is long a combined total of 439 options. Looking at just the 15 and 17.50 strikes, we can see something that looks more like a ratio spread: 1,006:439. If the stock were at $17.50, the gamma would be around +5,000.

With the stock at $15.72, there is realized volatility risk of F rallying, but with gamma changing from negative to positive as the stock rallies, the risk of movement decreases quickly. The 20 strike is short 871 options which brings the position back to negative-gamma territory. Having alternating long and short strikes, sometimes called a butterflied position, is a handy way for market makers to reduce risk. A position is perfectly butterflied if it has alternating long and short strikes with the same number of contracts.

Through Your Longs to Your Shorts

With market-maker-type positions consisting of many strikes, the greatest profit is gained if the underlying security moves through the longs to the shorts. This provides kind of a win-win scenario for greeks traders. In this situation, traders get the benefit of long gamma as the stock moves higher or lower through the long strike. They also reap the benefits of theta when the stock sits at the short strike.

Trading Flat

Most market makers like to trade flat—that is, profit from the bid-ask spread and strive to lower exposure to direction, time, volatility, and interest as much as possible. But market makers are at the mercy of customer orders, or paper, as it's known in the industry. If someone sells, say, the March 75 calls to a market maker at the bid, the best-case scenario is that moments later someone else buys the same number of the same calls—the March 75s, in this case—from that same market maker at the offer. This is locking in a profit.

Unfortunately, this scenario seldom plays out this way. In my seven years as a market maker, I can count on one hand the number of times the option gods smiled upon me in such a way as to allow me to immediately scalp an option. Sometimes, the same option will not trade again for a week or longer. Very low-volume options trade "by appointment only." A market maker trading illiquid options may hold the position until it expires, having no chance to get out at a reasonable price, often taking a loss on the trade.

More typically, if a market maker buys an option, he must sell a different option to lessen the overall position risk. The skills these traders master are to lower bids and offers on options when they are long gamma and/or vega and to raise bids and offers on options when they are short gamma and/or vega. This raising and lowering of markets is done to manage risk.

Effectively, this is your standard high school economics supply-and-demand curves in living color. When the market demands (buys) all the options that are supplied (offered) at a certain price, the price rises. When the market supplies (sells) all the options demanded (bid) at a price level, the price falls. The catalyst of supply and demand is the market maker and his risk tolerance. But instead of the supply and demand for individual options, it is supply and demand for gamma, theta, and vega. This is trading option greeks.

Hedging the Risk

Delta is the easiest risk for floor traders to eliminate quickly. It becomes second nature for veteran floor traders to immediately hedge nearly every trade with the underlying. Remember, these liquidity providers are in the business of buying option bids and selling option offers, not speculating on direction.

The next hurdle is to trade out of the option-centric risk. This means that if the market maker is long gamma, he needs to sell options; if he's short gamma, he needs to buy some. Same with theta and vega. Market makers move their bids and offers to avoid being saddled with too much gamma, theta, and vega risk. Experienced floor traders are good at managing option risk by not biting off more than they can chew. They strive to never buy or sell more options than they can spread off by selling or buying other options. This breed of trader specializes in trading the spread and managing risk, not in predicting the future. They're market makers, not market takers.

Trading Skew

There are some trading strategies for which market makers have a natural propensity that stems from their daily activity of maintaining their positions. While money managers who manage equity funds get to know the fundamentals of the stocks they trade very well, options market makers know the volatility of the option classes they trade. When they adjust their markets in reacting to order flow, it's, mechanically, implied volatility that they are raising or lowering to change theoretical values. They watch this figure very carefully and trade its subtle changes.

A characteristic of options that many market makers and some other active professional traders observe and trade is the volatility skew. Savvy traders watch the implied volatility of the strikes above the at-the-money (ATM)—referred to as *calls,* for simplicity—compared with the strikes below the ATM, referred to as *puts.* In most stocks, there typically exists a "normal" volatility skew inherent to options on that stock. When this skew gets out of line, there may be an opportunity.

Say for a particular option class, the call that is 10 percent OTM typically trades about four volatility points lower than the put that is 10 percent OTM. For example, for a $50 stock, the 55 calls are trading at a 21 IV and the 45 puts are trading at a 25 volatility. If the 45 puts become bid higher, say, nine points above where the calls are offered—for instance, the puts are bid at 32 volatility bid while the calls are offered at 23 vol—a trader can speculate on the skew reverting back to its normal relationship by selling the puts, buying the calls, and hedging the delta by selling the right amount of stock.

This position—long a call, short a put with a different strike, and short stock on a delta-neutral ratio—is called a risk reversal. The motive for risk reversals is to capture vega as the skew realigns itself. But there are many risk factors that require careful attention.

First, as in other positions consisting of both long and short strikes, the gamma, theta, and vega of the position will vary from positive to negative depending on the price of the underlying. Risk-reversal traders must be prepared to trade long gamma (and battle time decay) when the stock rallies closer to the long-call strike and trade short gamma (and assume the risk of possible increased realized volatility) when the stock moves closer to the short-put strike.

As for vega, being short implied volatility on the downside and long on the upside is inherently a potentially bad position whichever way the stock moves. Why? As equities decline in price, the implied volatility of their options tends to rise. But the downside is where the risk reversal has its short vega. Furthermore, as equities rally, their IV tends to fall. That means the long vega of the upside hurts as well.

When Delta Neutral Isn't Direction Indifferent

Many dynamic-volatility option positions, such as the risk reversal, have vega risk from potential IV changes resulting from the stock's moving. This is indirectly a directional risk. While having a delta-neutral position hedges against the rather straightforward directional risk of the position delta, this hidden risk of stock movement is left unhedged. In some circumstances, a delta-lean can help abate some of the vega risk of stock-price movement.

Say an option position has fairly flat greeks at the current stock price. Say that given the way this particular position is set up, if the stock rises, the position is still fairly flat, but if the stock falls, short lower-strike options will lead to negative gamma and vega. One way to partially hedge this position is to lean short deltas—that is, instead of maintaining a totally flat delta, have a slightly short delta. That way, if the stock falls, the trade profits some on the short stock to partially offset some of the anticipated vega losses. The trade-off of this hedge is that if the stock rises, the trade loses on the short delta.

Delta leans are more of an art than a science and should be used as a hedge only by experienced vol traders. They should be one part of a well-orchestrated plan to trade the delta, gamma, theta, and vega of a position. And, to be sure, a delta lean should be entered into a model for simulation purposes before executing the trade to study the up-and-down risk of the position. If the lean reduces the overall risk of the position, it should be implemented. But if it creates a situation where there is an anticipated loss if the stock moves in either direction and there is little hope of profiting from the other greeks, the lean is not the answer—closing the position is.

Managing Multiple-Class Risk

Most traders hold option positions in more than one option class. As an aside, I recommend doing so, capital and experience permitting. In my experience, having positions in multiple classes psychologically allows for a certain level of detachment from each individual position. Most traders can make better decisions if they don't have all their eggs in one basket.

But holding a portfolio of option positions requires one more layer of risk management. The trader is concerned about the delta, gamma, theta, vega, and rho not only of each individual option class but also of the portfolio as a whole. The trader's portfolio is actually one big position with a lot of moving parts. To keep it running like a well-oiled machine requires monitoring and maintaining each part to make sure they are working together. To have the individual trades work in harmony with one another, it is important to keep a well-balanced series of strategies.

Option trading requires diversification, just like conventional linear stock trading or investing. Diversification of the option portfolio is easily measured by studying the portfolio greeks. By looking at the net greeks of the portfolio, the trader can get some idea of exposure to overall risk in terms of delta, gamma, theta, vega, and rho.

CHAPTER 17

Putting the Greeks into Action

This book was intended to arm the reader with the knowledge of the greeks needed to make better trading decisions. As the preface stated, this book is not so much a how-to guide as a how-come tutorial. It is step one in a three-step learning process:

Step One: Study. First, aspiring option traders must learn as much as possible from books such as this one and from other sources, such as articles, both in print and online, and from classes both in person and online. After completing this book, the reader should have a solid base of knowledge of the greeks.

Step Two: Paper Trade. A truly deep understanding requires practice, practice, and more practice! Fortunately, much of this practice can be done without having real money on the line. Paper trading—or simulated trading—in which one trades real markets but with fake money is step two in the learning process. I highly recommend paper trading to kick the tires on various types of strategies and to see how they might work differently in reality than you thought they would in theory.

Step Three: Showtime! Even the most comprehensive academic study or windfall success with paper profits doesn't give one a true feel for how options work in the real world. There are some lessons that must be learned from the black and the blue. When there's real money on the line, you will trade differently—at least in the beginning. It's human nature to be cautious with wealth. This is not a bad thing. But emotions should not override sound judgment. Start small—one or two lots per trade—until you can make rational decisions based on what you have learned, keeping emotions in check.

This simple three-step process can take years of diligent work to get it right. But relax. Getting rich quick is truly a poor motivation for trading options. Option trading is a beautiful thing! It's about winning. It's about beating the market. It's about being smart. Don't get me wrong—wealth can be a nice by-product. I've seen many people who have made a lot of money trading options, but it takes hard work. For every successful option trader I've met, I've met many more who weren't willing to put in the effort, who brashly thought this is easy, and failed miserably.

Trading Option Greeks

Traders must take into account all their collective knowledge and experience with each and every trade. Now that you're armed with knowledge of the greeks, use it! The greeks come in handy in many ways.

Choosing between Strategies

A very important use of the greeks is found in selecting the best strategy for a given situation. Consider a simple bullish thesis on a stock. There are plenty of bullish option strategies. But given a bullish forecast, which option strategy should a trader choose? The answer is specific to each unique opportunity. Trading is situational.

Example 1

Imagine a trader, Arlo, is studying the following chart of Agilent Technologies Inc. (A). See Exhibit 17.1.

The stock has been in an uptrend for six weeks or so. Close-to-close volatility hasn't increased much. But intraday volatility has increased greatly as indicated by the larger candles over the past 10 or so trading sessions. Earnings is coming up in a week in this example, however implied volatility

EXHIBIT 17.1   Agilent Technologies Inc. daily candles.

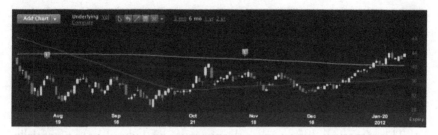

Source: Chart courtesy of Livevol® Pro (www.livevol.com)

has not risen much. It is still "cheap" relative to historical volatility and past implied volatility. Arlo is bullish. But how does he play it? He needs to use what he knows about the greeks to guide his decision.

Arlo doesn't want to hold the trade through earnings, so it will be a short-term trade. Thus, theta is not much of a concern. The low-priced volatility guides his strategy selection in terms of vega. Arlo certainly wouldn't want a short-vega trade. Not with the prospect of implied volatility potential rising going into earnings. In fact, he'd actually want a big positive vega position. That rules out a naked/cash-secured put, put credit spread and the likes.

He can probably rule out vertical spreads all together. He doesn't need to spread off theta. He doesn't want to spread off vega. Positive gamma is attractive for this sort of trade. He wouldn't want to spread that off either. Plus, the inherent time component of spreads won't work well here. As discussed in Chapter 9, the bulk of vertical spreads profits (or losses) take time to come to fruition. The deltas of a call spread are smaller than an outright call. Profits would come from both delta and theta, if the stock rises to the short strike and positive theta kicks in.

The best way for Arlo to play this opportunity is by buying a call. It gives him all the greeks attributes he wants (comparatively big positive delta, gamma and vega) and the detriment (negative theta) is not a major issue.

He'd then select among in-the-money (ITM), at-the-money (ATM), and out-of-the-money (OTM) calls and the various available expiration cycles. In this case, because positive gamma is attractive and theta is not an issue, he'd lean toward a front month (in this case, three week) option. The front month also benefits him in terms of vega. Though the vegas are smaller for short-term options, if there is a rise in implied volatility leading up to earnings, the front month will likely rise much more than the rest. Thus, the trader has a possibility for profits from vega.

Example 2

A trader, Luke, is studying the following chart for United States Steel Corp. (X). See Exhibit 17.2.

This stock is in a steady uptrend, which Luke thinks will continue. Earnings are out and there are no other expected volatility events on the horizon. Luke thinks that over the next few weeks, United States Steel can go from its current price of around $31 a share to about $34. Volatility is midpriced in this example—not cheap, not expensive.

This scenario is different than the previous one. Luke plans to potentially hold this trade for a few weeks. So, for Luke, theta is an important concern. He cares somewhat about volatility, too. He doesn't necessarily want to be long it in case it falls; he doesn't want to be short it in case it rises. He'd like to spread it off; the lower the vega, the better (positive or negative). Luke really just wants delta play that he can hold for a few weeks without all the other greeks getting in the way.

For this trade, Luke would likely want to trade a debit call spread with the long call somewhat ITM and the short call at the $34 strike. This way, Luke can start off with nearly no theta or vega. He'll retain some delta, which will enable the spread to profit if United States Steel rises and as it approaches the 34 strike, positive theta will kick in.

This spread is superior to a pure long call because of its optimized greeks. It's superior to an OTM bull put spread in its vega position and will likely produce a higher profit with the strikes structured as such too, as it would have a bigger delta.

Integrating greeks into the process of selecting an option strategy must come natural to a trader. For any given scenario, there is one position that best exploits the opportunity. In any option position, traders need to find the optimal greeks position.

EXHIBIT 17.2   United States Steel Corp. daily candles.

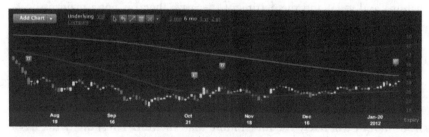

Source: Chart courtesy of Livevol® Pro (www.livevol.com)

Managing Trades

Once the trade is on, the greeks come in handy for trade management. The most important rule of trading is *Know Thy Risk*. Knowing your risk means knowing the influences that expose your position to profit or peril in both absolute and incremental terms. At-expiration diagrams reveal, in no uncertain terms, what the bottom-line risk points are when the option expires. These tools are especially helpful with simple short-option strategies and some long-option strategies. Then traders need the greeks. After all, that's what greeks are: measurements of option risk. The greeks give insight into a trade's exposure to the other pricing factors. Traders must know the greeks of every trade they make. And they must always know the net-portfolio greeks at all times. These pricing factors ultimately determine the success or failure of each trade, each portfolio, and eventually each trader.

Furthermore, always—and I do mean always—traders must know their up and down risk, that is, the directional risk of the market moving up or down certain benchmark intervals. By definition, moves of three standard deviations or more are very infrequent. But they happen. In this business anything can happen. Take the "flash crash of 2010 in which the Dow Jones Industrial Average plunged more than 1,000 points in "a flash." In my trading career, I've seen some surprises. Traders have to plan for the worst.

It's not too hard to tell your significant other, "Sorry I'm late, but I hit unexpected traffic. I just couldn't plan for it." But to say, "Sorry, I lost our life savings, and the kids' college fund, and our house because the market made an unexpected move. I couldn't plan for it," won't go over so well. The fact is, you *can* plan for it. And as an option trader, you have to. The bottom line is, expect the unexpected because the unexpected will sometimes happen. Traders must use the greeks and up and down risk, instead of relying on other common indicators, such as the HAPI.

The HAPI: The Hope and Pray Index

So you bought a call spread. At the opening bell the next morning, you find that the market for the underlying has moved lower—a lot lower. You have a loss on your hands. What do you do? Keep a positive attitude? Wear your lucky shirt? Pray to the options gods? When traders finds themselves hoping and praying—I swear I'll never do that again if I can just get out of this position!—it is probably time for them to take their losses and move on to the next trade. The Hope and Pray Index is a contraindicator. Typically, the higher it is, the worse the trade.

There are two numbers a trader can control: the entry price and the exit price. All of the other flashing green and red numbers on the screen are out of the trader's control. Savvy traders observe what the market does and make decisions on whether and when to enter a position and when to exit. Traders who think about their positions in terms of probability make better decisions at both of these critical moments.

In entering a trade, traders must consider their forecast, their assessment of the statistical likelihood of success, the potential payout and loss, and their own tolerance for risk. Having considered these criteria helps the traders stay the course and avoid knee-jerk reactions when the market moves in the wrong direction. Trading is easy when positions make money. It is how traders deal with adverse positions that separates good traders from bad.

Good traders are good at losing money. They take losses quickly and let profits run. Accepting, before entering the trade, the statistical nature of trading can help traders trade their positions with less emotion. It then becomes a matter of competent management of those positions based on their knowledge of the factors affecting option values: the greeks. Learning to think in terms of probability is among the most difficult challenges for a new options trader.

Chapter 5 discussed my Would I Do It Now? Rule, in which a trader asks himself: if I didn't currently have this position, would I put it on now at current market prices? This rule is a handy technique to help traders filter out the noise in their heads that clouds judgment and to help them to make rational decisions on whether to hold a position, close it out or adjust it.

Adjusting

Sometimes the position a trader starts off with is not the position he or she should have at present. Sometimes positions need to be changed, or adjusted, to reflect current market conditions. Adjusting is very important to option traders. To be good at adjusting, traders need to use the greeks.

Imagine a trader makes the following trade in Halliburton Company (HAL) when the stock is trading $36.85.

Sell 10 February 35—36—38—39 iron condors at 0.45

February has 10 days until expiration in this example. The greeks for this trade are as follows:

Delta: −6.80
Gamma: −119.20
Theta: +21.90
Vega: −12.82

The trader has a neutral outlook, which can be inferred by the near-flat delta. But what if the underlying stock begins to rise? Gamma starts kicking in. The trader can end up with a short-biased delta that loses exponentially if the stock continues to climb. If Halliburton rises (or falls for that matter) the trader needs to recalibrate his outlook. Surely, if the trader becomes bullish based on recent market activity, he'd want to close the trade. If the trader is bearish, he'd probably let the negative delta go in hopes of making back what was lost from negative gamma. But what if the trader is still neutral?

A neutral trader needs a position that has greeks which reflect that outlook. The trader would want to get delta back towards zero. Further, depending on how much the stock rises, theta could start to lose its benefit. If Halliburton approaches one of the long strikes, theta could move toward zero, negating the benefit of this sort of trade all together. If after the stock rises, the trader is still neutral at the new underlying price level, he'd likely adjust to get delta and theta back to desired territory.

A common adjustment in this scenario is to roll the call-credit-spread legs of the iron condor up to higher strikes. The trader would buy ten 38 calls and sell ten 39 calls to close the credit spread. Then the trader would buy 10 of the 39 calls as sell 10 of the 40 calls to establish an adjusted position that is short a 10 lot of the February 35−36−39−40 iron condor.

This, of course, is just one possible adjustment a trader can make. But the common theme among all adjustments is that the trader's greeks must reflect the trader's outlook. The position greeks best describe what the position is—that is, how it profits or loses. When the market changes it affects the dynamic greeks of a position. If the market changes enough to make a trader's position greeks no longer represent his outlook, the trader must adjust the position (adjust the greeks) to put it back in line with expectations.

In option trading there are an infinite number of uses for the greeks. From finding trades, to planning execution, to managing and adjusting them, to planning exits; the greeks are truly a trader's best resource. They help traders see potential and actual position risk. They help traders project potential and actual trade profitability too. Without the greeks, a trader is at a disadvantage in every aspect of option trading. Use the greeks on each and every trade, and exploit trades to their greatest potential.

I wish you good luck!

For me, trading option greeks has been a labor of love through the good trades and the bad. To succeed in the long run at greeks trading—or any endeavor, for that matter—requires enjoying the process. Trading option greeks can be both challenging and rewarding. And remember, although option trading is highly statistical and intellectual in nature, a little luck never hurt! That said, good luck trading!

About the Author

DAN PASSARELLI is an author, trader, and former member of the Chicago Board Options Exchange (CBOE) and CME Group. Dan has written two books on options trading—*Trading Option Greeks* and *The Market Taker's Edge*. He is also the founder and CEO of Market Taker Mentoring, a leading options education firm that provides personalized, one-on-one mentoring for option traders and online classes. The company web site is *www.markettaker.com*.

Dan began his trading career on the floor of the CBOE as an equity options market maker. He also traded agricultural options and futures on the floor of the Chicago Board of Trade (now part of CME Group).

In 2005, Dan joined CBOE's Options Institute and began teaching both basic and advanced trading concepts to retail traders, brokers, institutional traders, financial planners and advisers, money managers, and market makers. In addition to his work with the CBOE, he has taught options strategies at the Options Industry Council (OIC), the International Securities Exchange (ISE), CME Group, the Philadelphia Stock Exchange, and many leading options-based brokerage firms. Dan has been seen on FOX Business News and other business television programs. Dan also contributes to financial publications such as TheStreet.com, SFO.com, and the CBOE blog.

Dan can be reached at his web site, MarketTaker.com, or by e-mail: *dan@markettaker.com*. He can be followed on Twitter at *twitter.com/Dan_Passarelli*.

Index